"All regular readers of the Bible [...] to sex and violence in the Bible, [...] there are or how explicit the re[...] ~~book serves the useful~~ purpose of showing us exactly how much sex and violence there is in the Bible, as well as the precise nature of the references to the human body. It is a work of painstaking research and scholarship. If the concentration of examples makes for uncomfortable reading, it is nonetheless important that we confront the subject. We need to know what kind of book the Bible is, and additionally we can assume that the references to sex and violence in the Bible tell us something that God wants us to know."

—**Leland Ryken**, Professor of English, Wheaton College

"At last, a book that deals soberly with the fact that the Bible addresses the earthy aspects of life and that does so in a way that honors not just the Bible's content but also the Bible's intentional modes of expression. This is a needed adult antidote to the crudity of the schoolboy culture that sadly seems to have gained the upper hand in church circles in recent years."

—**Carl R. Trueman**, Paul Woolley Professor of Church History, Westminster Theological Seminary

"Brutally blunt, delicately discreet, strongly scriptural. An excellent resource for the Christian who wants to understand the Bible's revelation of the baser aspects of human nature and sinful reality. Smith thoroughly catalogues and examines biblical passages about sex and violence with an evenhanded fairness and respect for the Bible and his readers. This book should challenge Christian prudes and religious libertines alike."

—**Brian Godawa**, Author, *Hollywood Worldviews*, *Chronicles of the Nephilim*; Screenwriter, *To End All Wars*

"The Bible is not for the squeamish. It is full of bodies, and with bodies come fluids and emissions, sex and seductions, battles and blood. Joseph W. Smith's *Sex and Violence in the Bible* is an unexpurgated reminder to us that nothing human is alien to God's Word. If you are a Victorian prude, read this book at your peril."

—**Peter J. Leithart**, Senior Fellow, Theology and Literature, Dean of Graduate Studies, New Saint Andrews College, Moscow, Idaho

"Some people have a rather rosy picture of the Bible, both Old and New Testaments. They may think the Bible is a collection of sayings that include only encouragements, promises, and high-sounding sentiments. But readers can come to that conclusion only if they haven't actually read the Bible or have done so selectively. Joseph W. Smith wants us to come to terms with the Bible as it is—filled with stories and images of sex and violence. His purpose is to shock us, but not gratuitously. He wants to shock us into reckoning with the real Bible and the real God to which it points."

> —**Tremper Longman III**, Robert H. Gundry Professor of Biblical Studies, Westmont College

"At first, looking only at the title, I was worried that this book would be mainly of prurient interest. To be sure, it is not for the faint of heart. But what the author manages to show convincingly is how very frank and honest the Bible is about subjects that are often avoided or handled gingerly by today's Christians. In a word, he convinces us that the Bible is not a prudish book. Smith's study provides a great resource on these two subjects, which indeed pervade the Scriptures. The take-home from this exhaustive examination of the relevant texts is that we would be well advised to share the Bible's realism, if we wish to share its message of truth."

> —**William Edgar**, Professor of Apologetics, Westminster Theological Seminary

SEX AND VIOLENCE IN THE BIBLE

A Survey of Explicit Content in the Holy Book

JOSEPH W. SMITH III

P U B L I S H I N G

P.O. BOX 817 • PHILLIPSBURG • NEW JERSEY 08865-0817

Unless otherwise indicated, all Scripture quotations are from The Holy Bible, English Standard Version, copyright © 2001 by Crossway, a publishing ministry of Good News Publishers. Used by permission. All rights reserved.

Material quoted from the footnotes, introductions, and other study aids in the *ESV Study Bible* is taken from the *ESV® Student Study Bible* (*The Holy Bible, English Standard Version®*), copyright © 2008 by Crossway Bibles, a publishing ministry of Good News Publishers. Used by permission. All rights reserved.

Scripture quotations marked (CEV) are from the Contemporary English Version. Copyright © 1991, 1992, 1995 by American Bible Society. Used by permission.

Scripture quotations marked *The Message* are taken from *The Message*. Copyright © 1993, 1994, 1995, 1996, 2000, 2001, 2002. Used by permission of NavPress Publishing Group.

Scripture quotations marked (NASB) are taken from the New American Standard Bible®. Copyright © 1960, 1962, 1963, 1968, 1971, 1972, 1973, 1975, 1977, 1995 by The Lockman Foundation. Used by permission.

Scripture quotations marked (NIV) are taken from the Holy Bible, New International Version®, NIV®. Copyright © 1973, 1978, 1984 by Biblica, Inc.™ Used by permission of Zondervan. All rights reserved worldwide.

Scripture quotations marked (NKJV) are taken from the Holy Bible, New King James Version. Copyright © 1979, 1980, 1982, Thomas Nelson, Inc. Used by permission. All rights reserved.

Scripture quotations marked (NLT) are taken from the Holy Bible, New Living Translation, copyright © 1996, 2004, 2007 by Tyndale House Foundation. Used by permission of Tyndale House Publishers, Inc., Carol Stream, Illinois 60188. All rights reserved.

Italics within Scripture quotations indicate emphasis added.

ISBN: 978-1-59638-835-2 (pbk)
ISBN: 978-1-59638-836-9 (ePub)
ISBN: 978-1-59638-837-6 (Mobi)

Printed in the United States of America

Library of Congress Control Number: 2013919299

For my wife

"You have made my heart beat faster, my sister, my bride."

"All Scripture is breathed out by God and profitable for teaching, for reproof, for correction, and for training in righteousness, that the man of God may be competent, equipped for every good work."
2 Timothy 3:16–17

Contents

Acknowledgments   ix

Introduction: "I Was Very Eager to Write to You"   xi

PART 1: "UNCOVERING NAKEDNESS"—*SEX*

1. "Please Give Me Some": A Few Aphrodisiacs   3

2. "Covering His Feet": The Man's Body   7

3. "I Will Lay Hold of Its Fruit": The Woman's Body   17

4. "Your Shame Will Be Seen": Disrobing and Nudity   27

5. "If They Cannot Exercise Self-Control": Premarital Sex   33

6. "Be Drunk with Love!": Intercourse and Marriage   43

7. "Your Lewd Whorings": Adultery   55

8. "The Wages of a Dog": Prostitution   69

9. "You Shall Not": Bestiality, Voyeurism, Incest, and Homosexuality   77

PART 2: "THE BLOOD GUSHED OUT"—*VIOLENCE*

10. "I Will Drench the Land": Blood and Gore   95

11. "Weeping and Gnashing of Teeth": Beatings, Attacks, and Tortures   103

12. "He Violated Her": Rape   113

13. "Wallowing in His Blood": Dismemberment and Other Disgusting Deaths   123

14. "The Smoke of a Furnace": Death by Fire   143

15. "And Sons Shall Eat Their Fathers": Cannibalism   149

16. "This Abomination": Murdering Children   155

17. "120,000 in One Day": Mass Killings and Assassinations   163

PART 3: "ANY UNCLEAN THING"— OTHER BLUNT OR UNSAVORY MATERIAL

18. "Unclean until the Evening": Menstruation, Semen, and Other "Discharges"   181

19. "Wasting Disease and Fever": Bowels, Boils, Tumors, and Leprosy   191

20. "Their Flesh Will Rot": Vomit, Corpses, and Other Gross-Outs   199

21. "And the Dung Came Out": Feces and Urine   207

Conclusion: "Think about These Things"   215

Select Bibliography   221

Index of Scripture   227

Index of Subjects and Names   233

Acknowledgments

I WOULD LIKE TO THANK Brian Godawa not only for providing me with the initial inspiration for this project, but also for his enthusiastic response to my first draft. I am also grateful to Rev. Roth Reason and Rev. Paul Browne for loaning me piles and piles of Bible commentaries during the research process—and to Paul especially for his comments and encouragement on the manuscript.

I would also like to thank the many scholars on whose work I have relied so heavily in this text—particularly Daniel I. Block, Robert L. Thomas, the various contributors to the excellent *ESV Study Bible*, and Bernard Katz's Internet article "Biblical Euphemisms" (http://freethoughtperspective.net/?p=3028). In addition, I made regular use of the excellent Bible Gateway website, which carries dozens of Bible versions and is invaluable when comparing English translations of individual texts (see www.biblegateway.com).

Unless otherwise noted, discussion of the actual meanings of ancient Greek and Hebrew terms relies on Thomas's *New American Standard Exhaustive Concordance of the Whole Bible* (Holman, 1981); I also use the English spelling of these words provided in Thomas's helpful book.

A special thanks to my lovely and supportive wife, who not only gave me my copy of Thomas's volume many years ago, but also served as sole breadwinner in our home for several months so that I could finish this project. I'm likewise grateful for her careful proofreading of the final draft, which saved me from a number of embarrassing errors.

And finally, a word about two decisions I made to cut down on visual clutter in my text. First, while I made extensive use of notes in the *ESV Study Bible*, I have provided footnoted citations for this material only when the location is not immediately apparent. In other words, readers wishing to locate this cited matter in the original source can often do so without a citation or page number—because virtually all ESV commentary occurs at the chapter and verse under discussion. And second, in Scripture quotations that use only the first part of a sentence, I often left out the three ellipsis points that normally belong at the end (. . .)—when my omission did not seem to affect the meaning of the quoted material.

Introduction

"I Was Very Eager to Write to You"

SEVERAL MONTHS AGO, I hosted a church-sponsored showing of the award-winning 2012 film *The Artist*. Afterward, a few attenders expressed concern over my choice, calling the film "dark," "disturbing," and not appropriate for a church setting.

While I apologized for inaccurately promoting the film as "family friendly"—after all, it does have drinking, attempted suicide, and what is politely known as a "crude gesture"—I was nonetheless baffled by this response. Is a film like *The Artist*—with lots of laughter, dancing, self-sacrifice, lovely black-and-white photography, and a joyous ending—really darker and more disturbing than, for example, the gory and dismal Old Testament book of Judges? Is it less appropriate in a church than the vivid sexual imagery from Song of Solomon 5–7? Is it more disturbing than Ezekiel 16 and 23, which use the word "whore" nearly 40 times, along with other unsavory talk about breasts, nipples, and the private parts of donkeys? Have these movie-going friends—whose opinions I respect and whose complaints I took seriously—fully grappled with the vast amount of explicit material in the Holy Bible?

In his commentary on Ezekiel, Iain M. Duguid asks a similar question: "If the sermons preached in our churches were movies, what rating would the distributors give them? In many churches, every sermon would rate a 'G' ('General Audiences'). There is nothing in them to offend anyone, young or old, seeker or convert alike." While the great British preacher C. H. Spurgeon said of Ezekiel 16, "A minister can scarcely read it in public," Duguid wonders "if contemporary Christians need to be as shielded from unpleasant realities as we tend to think": "Fire and brimstone sermons that focus alone on hell and God's wrath may be a serious misrepresentation of the true God, but so also are a continuous diet of polite decorous sermons that only mention heaven and God's love. Sin is ugly, offensive, and depraved, and people need to hear that side of the Christian message too." Pointing out that R-rated content may be necessary to portray the full horror of Nazi concentration camps in a film like *Schindler's List*, Duguid observes, "Sometimes only an 'R' rated sermon does justice to the outrage of sin."[1]

But of course, Ezekiel is not the only biblical book that provokes revulsion in its readers. As writer and filmmaker Brian Godawa puts it, the Scriptures contain "detailed accounts and descriptions of every immoral act known to humanity. A cursory perusal of these depictions of vice is enough to make any concerned reader blush. But it only proves that sex and violence are not always literary taboo in Holy Writ. In fact, the acknowledgement of evil is treated as the necessary prerequisite of redemption." Later, Godawa adds, "Shocking metaphor and explicit drama are common means by which God communicates to people when they have become thick-skulled, dull of hearing or wicked of heart. . . . We must face the fact that the Scriptures depict sinful acts that are revolting to our sensibilities. The portrayal of good and the portrayal of evil are two sides of God's revelation to us of his one good and holy truth."[2]

With passages like this, Godawa provided the initial inspiration for this project; his thoughtful 2002 volume *Hollywood Worldviews* has a dandy little appendix whose title I appropriated for the book you are holding. In a few attention-grabbing pages, Godawa frankly catalogs the principal graphic material in the Old and New Testaments—and I thought to myself, "Why not go whole hog and cover it all?" So I began compiling a list of passages to deal with—Eglon's ghastly murder in Judges 3; Onan's *coitus interruptus* in Genesis 38; Paul's vicious insult in Galatians 5:12—thinking that I might amass 40 or 50 texts.

Yeah, right.

After an entire summer of work and study, I had collected not a few dozen but rather several hundred such passages—giving me plenty

1. Iain M. Duguid, *Ezekiel*, The NIV Application Commentary (Grand Rapids: Zondervan, 1999), 215–18.
2. Brian Godawa, *Hollywood Worldviews: Watching Films with Wisdom and Discernment* (Downers Grove, IL: InterVarsity, 2002), 188, 199–200.

of work to do and also yielding a basic thesis: there's a lot of sex and violence in the Bible.

My purpose has been simply to show this, in a rather focused and concentrated form, and thus to demonstrate that Christians needn't be terribly squeamish about explicit content. In conjunction with this, I planned to unpack, clarify, and explain some of these graphic passages, many of which have been obscured by idiom, figurative language, and overly genteel English translations—not to mention the vast geographical and chronological distance between the culture in which the Bible was originally written and that of our own time. I wanted to show, in other words, exactly what the Bible says and means in each case.

Yet as I worked my way through the texts, another equally vital goal emerged. Perhaps there was a reason for so much indirect material, for the Bible's frequent brevity, vagueness, and lack of detail regarding sex and violence—and for the euphemisms found so often even in the original Greek and Hebrew terminology. In our sex-and-violence-obsessed culture, perhaps the Bible is useful as an aesthetic guide not only in what it does say and show, but also in what it *doesn't*. For this reason, my treatment of various passages here sometimes involves much more explanation and detail than the actual text provides—both so we can understand what is actually happening, and so we can see what the Bible writers are choosing *not* to describe.

Because of the scope and nature of my task, I have tried to refrain from excessive editorializing about the texts. That is, I want to explain what they say and what they mean, and thus to show which Bible passages are or are not blunt and graphic. However, I have little desire to speculate about the writers' motives for candor or restraint. It would be presumptuous and foolish to concoct some overarching criteria—probably artificial, possibly dangerous—showing "when it's OK" to be explicit and when it isn't. Neither the Bible writers nor the Holy Spirit feel compelled to defend their bluntness or their moderation, and I won't attempt to do so, either.

In the same way, it is not my purpose here to justify God's commands and intentions as expressed in Holy Scripture. The Bible's attitudes toward premarital sex, gender roles, homosexuality, and mass killings are highly controversial in today's culture, and while I feel strongly that God has full prerogative to tell us what is truly right and wrong, it would radically alter the size and shape of this project if I waded into these controversies instead of focusing on my key topic: the vast number and precise meaning of explicit passages in the Bible. I have made some comments along these lines where appropriate, but defense of God's ways has not been my principal focus here.

I realize that in sticking strictly to the texts at hand, and keeping my own opinions to a minimum, I run the risk of presenting what is essentially a list—and a very long list at that. I have worked hard to maintain a smooth flow and a style that is reasonably casual while also maintaining proper reverence and respect.

A few other notes regarding my methodology are necessary. In order to maintain a reasonable length and pace, I have not dealt with every single Bible passage referencing sex, bloodshed, disease, or other uncomfortable topics. Yet at the same time, in those passages I did choose, I have bolstered my explanations with frequent notes and references to commentaries and other scholarly works. While some readers might prefer fewer of these, I have deliberately "shown my work" in order to demonstrate that my readings of these texts are neither far-fetched nor irresponsible—that I am not, as it were, a loose cannon seeking unsavory implications in all kinds of perfectly innocuous passages.

Along the same lines, I have tried to limit my sources to strictly evangelical scholars who believe that the Bible is God's inerrant Word— which has not generally been the case with other studies like mine. Indeed, several books on "sex in the Bible" already exist, but, as it happens, none of them view Scripture as infallible. Let's not allow those who play fast-and-loose with Holy Writ to have the last word on such important subjects.

And while I am writing for an audience that also believes in the truth of God's Word, I have nonetheless tried not to presume a broad and detailed knowledge of Scripture on the part of every reader. Background on characters, families, locations, and ancient customs—as well as Hebrew and Greek words and expressions—is provided wherever possible.

And finally, my topical arrangement has created yet another sticky issue, namely, the same passage being discussed in several different places. As an example, the shockingly blunt descriptions of Israel's spiritual "whoredom" in Ezekiel 16 and 23 are discussed in numerous chapters, because they include material on the male and female body as well as prostitution, rape, and adultery. This has necessitated several cross-references (e.g., "see pages 27–28"), not only to avoid repetition but also because I do not assume that every reader will read every chapter in the exact order I have used.

Indeed, for some, *Sex and Violence in the Bible* may serve as a sort of reference book: rather than read the volume cover to cover—which may, after all, get somewhat tiresome—some readers may wish to look at one or two chapters; others may be considering one certain passage and wondering, "Does it *really* say that?" This is why I have also provided an index of Scripture passages covered in the book.

You will no doubt notice that I have quoted an extraordinary number of such verses and passages. It has been my desire to focus on the language, the text, and the details presented in God's Word—to listen, and give it our fullest attention. Just as the Bible can defend itself to an unbelieving world, so also in matters of sex and violence, the Bible clearly speaks for itself.

Let's hear what it has to say.

PART I

"Uncovering Nakedness"—Sex

"Please Give Me Some"

A Few Aphrodisiacs

WHAT BETTER PLACE to start than with those sometimes-obscure substances that are supposed to "put one in the mood"?

Merriam-Webster's Collegiate Dictionary defines "aphrodisiac" as a food or drug "that arouses or is held to arouse sexual desire."[1]

Probably the best-known Bible passage featuring these substances is Genesis 30, in which Rachel and Leah, the two wives of the Old Testament patriarch Jacob, squabble over some mandrakes found by Leah's oldest son, Reuben. Rachel, still upset that her husband's other wife had already borne four sons when she herself had none, urged Leah to "please give me some of your son's mandrakes." Meeting resistance from her marital rival, Rachel then arranged a trade, offering one more night with Jacob in exchange for the plants—a transaction that resulted in yet another son for Leah (Gen. 30:14–17).

In his commentary on this passage, Gordon J. Wenham tells us that "in ancient times, mandrakes were famed for arousing sexual desire . . . and for helping barren women to conceive."[2] The alleged link between these plants and sexual fertility may have been heightened by the fact that the mandrake's roots "were thought to resemble

---

1. "Aphrodisiac," in *Merriam-Webster's Collegiate Dictionary*, 11th ed. (Springfield, MA: Merriam-Webster, 2004).

2. Gordon J. Wenham, *Genesis 16–50*, Word Biblical Commentary, vol. 2 (Dallas: Word, 1994), 246.

male and female genitalia"[3] and by the way the ancient Hebrew word for "mandrakes" (duda'im) bears some resemblance to one form of "love" (dodim).

Indeed, in Hebrew, "mandrake" also sounds a bit like the phrase "my beloved" (dodi),[4] which appears fairly often in Song of Solomon; and as it happens, Solomon's Song is the only other book in Scripture where mandrakes make an appearance (Song 7:13). That's not surprising, since Solomon's famous love poem is a cornucopia of fruits and spices that were thought to stimulate love and desire.

Nard, for example—mentioned in Song of Solomon 1:12—was "much in demand as a love-potion." Pomegranates (Song 4:3) were likewise used in some Mesopotamian love potions, and all the spices in 4:14—nard, saffron, calamus, cinnamon, frankincense, myrrh, and aloes—have erotic overtones in much ancient Middle Eastern love poetry. Indeed, three of these—myrrh, aloes, and cinnamon—also show up in Proverbs 7:17, where a scheming adulteress boasts of their use as she seduces a wayward young man.[5]

In his comments on Proverbs 7, Bruce K. Waltke points out that myrrh was sometimes "pulverized into a fine power and placed in a sachet worn between a woman's breasts,"[6] which appears to be the case in Song of Solomon 1:13: "My beloved is to me a pouch of myrrh which lies all night between my breasts" (NASB).

Similarly, the raisin cakes requested by the lovesick woman in Song 2 may have been regarded as possessing aphrodisiac qualities. She also mentions apples, which are associated with love and fertility in 8:5; and so the young woman in 2:5 may be asking for "food that, while strengthening her, will also heighten her experience of love."[7]

Raisin cakes reappear in Hosea 3:1, where they seem to be used by Hosea's adulterous wife as "part of her harlot's hire, and perhaps a sexual

3. Marvin H. Pope, *Song of Songs: A New Translation with Introduction and Commentary*, The Anchor Bible, vol. 7C (Garden City, NY: Doubleday, 1977), 648.

4. Chana Bloch and Ariel Bloch, eds., *The Song of Songs: The World's First Great Love Poem* (New York: Modern Library, 2006), 208.

5. G. Lloyd Carr, *The Song of Solomon: An Introduction and Commentary*, Tyndale Old Testament Commentaries (Leicester, UK: Inter-Varsity, 1984), 85, 117, 126.

6. Bruce K. Waltke, *The Book of Proverbs, Chapters 1–15*, New International Commentary on the Old Testament (Grand Rapids: Eerdmans, 2004), 379.

7. Iain Provan, *Ecclesiastes, Song of Songs*, The NIV Application Commentary (Grand Rapids: Zondervan, 2001), 286.

stimulant."[8] They also show up in Jeremiah 44:19, where it becomes clearer that their use in Solomon and Hosea does indeed carry strong sexual overtones. G. Lloyd Carr tells us that in the Jeremiah passage—where the cakes are offered in pagan worship to a female deity, "the queen of heaven"—these delicacies were almost certainly "made either in the shape of a nude female with exaggerated sexual organs, or frequently in triangular shape representing the female genitalia."[9]

As an object intended to evoke the private parts, this particular aphrodisiac points directly to our next topic.

8. David Allan Hubbard, *Hosea: An Introduction and Commentary*, Tyndale Old Testament Commentaries (Leicester, UK: Inter-Varsity, 1989), 91.
9. Carr, *Song of Solomon*, 92.

2

"Covering His Feet"

The Man's Body

IN THE LAST CHAPTER, we saw that the raisin cakes mentioned in Hosea and Song of Solomon were probably designed to resemble female genitalia—but of course, the Bible writers do not come right out and say so. Either the reader is expected to know this already, or—perhaps more likely—the authors prefer not to get too detailed in their references to sexuality.

Indeed, this sort of reticence characterizes most Bible descriptions of the private parts. Perhaps the politest of these—so polite in fact, that some readers may not recognize the sexual reference—occurs in Paul's first letter to the Corinthians. Discussing divisions in the local church—which arose largely because some members considered themselves superior to others—the great apostle invokes a metaphor of the church-as-human-body, with some bodily members that are "weaker" or apparently inferior. Nonetheless, "on those parts of the body that we think less honorable we bestow the greater honor, and our unpresentable parts are treated with greater modesty, which our more presentable parts do not require" (1 Cor. 12:22–24). Both Gordon D. Fee and David E. Garland agree that in this text Paul is referring euphemistically to the genitalia—the point being that we honor these organs by paying particular attention to them in terms of clothing and protection. Indeed, our special care for these vitals, despite their apparent weakness or "unpresentable" nature, actually reflects their crucial necessity to the body as a whole. After all, "a body can survive without eyes, ears, hands, and feet, but it cannot survive without the function of these unpresentable parts."[1]

In the Old Testament, the male's nether parts are nearly always described with similarly indirect euphemisms, such as "feet," "thigh," and "hand." Many Bible veterans, for example, know about Judges 3:24 and 1 Samuel 24:3, where a man is said to "relieve himself" (NASB, ESV, NIV). This phrase, itself an English euphemism, helps clarify the Hebrew idiom that is actually used in these passages to describe defecation: literally, "cover his feet." (Of course, the Hebrew phrase is somewhat literal, as a man's robe would likely be down around his feet during this activity.)

Some readers, however, may be less familiar with numerous other uses of "feet" that probably refer to the male or female genitalia.

The clearest of these is found in 2 Samuel, where Israel's King David learned that Bathsheba was pregnant. Since he had slept with her while her husband was off at war, David sought to hide his sin; so he called Uriah back from the battlefield and urged him, "Go down to your house and wash your feet." Surely David didn't care about the condition of Uriah's feet! Obviously, he was hoping instead that the man would sleep with his wife to account for the incriminating pregnancy. Uriah himself indicated that he understood the real meaning of "wash your feet" when he refused to enter his house, explaining that, with his comrades at war and the ark of the Lord in peril, he couldn't bring himself "to eat and to drink and to lie with my wife" (2 Sam. 11:6–11).

Other passages where "feet" are associated with private parts: Jeremiah 13:22, "Your skirts have been removed, and your heels have been exposed" (NASB); Deuteronomy 28:57, "the afterbirth that comes out from between her feet"; and Ezekiel 16:25, "You spread your legs to every passer-by" (NASB). In this final passage, "legs" is actually *regel*, the same Hebrew word translated as "feet" in 2 Samuel 11 and many other passages.

This same term is used in Isaiah 6:2, where the seraphim before God's throne have wings that cover their feet. Several writers include this passage with the other euphemistic uses of "feet," as though the angels were covering their privates; but commentator Alec Motyer wisely

1. David E. Garland, *1 Corinthians*, Baker Exegetical Commentary on the New Testament (Grand Rapids: Baker, 2003), 595–96. See also Gordon D. Fee, *The First Epistle to the Corinthians*, New International Commentary on the New Testament (Grand Rapids: Eerdmans, 1987), 613–14.

asserts that "attribution of sexuality to heavenly beings would be inappropriate." Edward J. Young agrees, suggesting instead that the feet here merely indicate "a less noble part of the body."[2]

On the other hand, in Exodus, Moses' wife "cut off her son's foreskin and touched Moses' feet with it"; here, she is probably not touching Moses' actual feet but rather symbolically transferring the circumcision to her husband's private parts (Ex. 4:24–26; more on this later in the chapter). Likewise, Isaiah 7:20 contains an evocative phrase in which the Lord promises judgment on Israel in the form of a metaphorical "razor" that will "shave . . . the head and the hair of the feet." Since men's feet are not traditionally hairy enough to warrant a shave that would result in public humiliation, Motyer is sure the final word here is indeed another euphemism for the private parts, and that the contrast between "the visible and hidden body hair expresses totality. . . . No part of the person will escape the hand of the enemy."[3]

Moving farther up the body, the word "thigh" has a similarly euphemistic meaning in several Old Testament passages. In Genesis 46:26, Exodus 1:5, and Judges 8:30, the Hebrew *yarek*—meaning "loin," "thigh," or "side"—is translated in a phrase indicating direct descent (as in, "came from the loins of Jacob," Ex. 1:5, NASB). This usage provides some context for the episode in Genesis 24 in which Abraham sent a servant back to his homeland to seek a suitable wife for Isaac. In verses 2 and 9, the patriarch put this unnamed messenger under oath by having the servant place his hand under his master's thigh, thereby securing a pledge "at the source of life," as Jacob later does with Joseph in Genesis 47:29.[4] In his commentary on Genesis, Gordon J. Wenham writes, "By putting his hand under Abraham's thigh, the servant was touching his genitalia and thus giving the oath a special solemnity. In the ancient Orient, oaths could be taken holding some sacred object in one's hands. . . . An oath by the seat of procreation is particularly apt in this instance, when it concerns the finding of a wife for Isaac."[5] Some scholars have claimed

2. Alec Motyer, *Isaiah: An Introduction and Commentary*, Tyndale Old Testament Commentaries (Leicester, UK: Inter-Varsity, 1999), 70; Edward J. Young, *The Book of Isaiah: The English Text, with Introduction, Exposition, and Notes*, vol. 2, *Chapters 19–39* (Grand Rapids: Eerdmans, 1969), 241.

3. Motyer, *Isaiah*, 80.

4. Bruce K. Waltke and Cathi J. Fredricks, *Genesis: A Commentary* (Grand Rapids: Zondervan, 2001), 327.

5. Gordon J. Wenham, *Genesis 16–50*, Word Biblical Commentary, vol. 2 (Dallas: Word, 1994), 141.

that this custom of "swearing by the testes" has given us such words as "testify" and "testament"—but this etymology is, shall we say, unattested.

The usage of *yarek* in Genesis 24 and 47, however, probably does explain the word's reappearance in Numbers 5:21–22, which details the curse for a woman who has committed adultery: her womb (or "belly") will swell and her "thigh fall away," a recompense that makes most sense not in reference to the upper leg, but rather as a figure for her loins, as in the passages above. "In adultery, the woman sinned in her 'thigh' and conceived in her 'belly.' Therefore it is fitting that these organs should be the scene of her punishment."[6]

And continuing on to the upper limbs, "It is now established beyond serious doubt that *yad* is occasionally used as a euphemism for the male copulative organ." *Yad* is the standard Hebrew term for "hand," and commentator G. Lloyd Carr is here referring to its use in Song of Solomon 5:4, where the phrase "My beloved put his hand to the latch" almost certainly describes, in politely metaphorical terms, the husband making sexual overtures to his wife. As Carr points out, double entendres are by nature delicate and thus often doubtful, but "this appears to be one text where the erotic meaning is present."[7] (For a more in-depth look at this passage, see chap. 3, pp. 22–23.) Less ambiguous is Isaiah 57:8, where the Lord rebukes Israel's spiritual adultery; that is, Israel has been patronizing other "lovers" besides her covenant Lord: "You have loved their bed, you have looked on nakedness." Rendered "manhood" in the NASB, the actual Hebrew word at the end of this verse is *yad*, or "hand."

Combining references to both hand and thigh, 1 Kings relates the story of Israel's King Rehoboam and his accession to the throne following the death of his father, Solomon. When Rehoboam's subjects asked him to "lighten the hard service of your father and his heavy yoke on us," the foolish new king responded by insisting that he would be even more severe than the previous ruler: "My little finger is thicker than my father's thighs" (1 Kings 12:4–10). The opening noun-phrase here is more accurately translated as "my little one" or "my little thing"; according to the *ESV Study Bible*, it is "most likely a reference to his sexual organ

---

6. Gordon J. Wenham, *Numbers: An Introduction and Commentary*, Tyndale Old Testament Commentaries (Leicester, UK: Inter-Varsity, 1981), 84. See also Iain M. Duguid, *Numbers: God's Presence in the Wilderness*, Preaching the Word (Wheaton, IL: Crossway, 2006), 74.

7. G. Lloyd Carr, *The Song of Solomon: An Introduction and Commentary*, Tyndale Old Testament Commentaries (Leicester, UK: Inter-Varsity, 1984), 134–35.

rather than a literal finger." Peter J. Leithart agrees, adding that the comparison with "loins" or "thigh" suggests "a phallic reference. . . . If Israel feels 'raped' by Solomon, Rehoboam plans to give them more of the same"; and Brian Godawa sees it as "a double entendre with the pinkie and the penis—a common male insult of powerlessness since the beginning of time."[8]

Probably the vaguest euphemism for male private parts is simply "body," as found in the ceremonial regulations about any man who "has a discharge from his body" (Lev. 15:2). Chapter 18 discusses these discharges in much more detail, but for now let us note that "body" here translates the common Hebrew term *basar*, usually rendered "flesh"; its euphemistic use here for the penis is clear from the passage as a whole, which deals with both male and female genital emissions such as semen and menstrual blood. In particular, Leviticus 15:3 clarifies the sexual sense of "body" with the addendum, "whether his body runs with his discharge, or his body is blocked up by his discharge."

Brian Godawa also sees a reference to the penis in Song of Solomon 5:14. Here, a young wife describes her lover thus: "His body is polished ivory, bedecked with sapphires." Godawa quotes the *Dictionary of Biblical Imagery*: "Once again the English translations are reticent and here intentionally obscure the more explicit Hebrew text. It is not his body that is like a slab of ivory, but rather his sexual organ, which is like a tusk of ivory."[9] The Hebrew word rendered here as "body" (*meeh*) literally means "internal organs, inward parts, belly"; it is translated "heart" earlier in the chapter (v. 4) and refers to the "middle" of the body in Daniel 2:32. Tremper Longman's commentary on the Song claims that the ivory, with its concomitant image of a tusk, "is at least suggestive of, if not explicitly referring to, the man's member"; yet even Longman admits that this reading is "adventurous"[10]—and we must also consider the context of the passage. In this portion of the Song, the woman is responding to an earlier request—probably from the "daughters of Jerusalem"—to

8. Peter J. Leithart, *1 and 2 Kings*, Brazos Theological Commentary on the Bible (Grand Rapids: Brazos, 2006), 92; Brian Godawa, *Hollywood Worldviews: Watching Films with Wisdom and Discernment* (Downers Grove, IL: InterVarsity, 2002), 193.

9. Leland Ryken, James C. Wilhoit, and Tremper Longman III, *Dictionary of Biblical Imagery* (Leicester, UK: Inter-Varsity, 1998), quoted in Godawa, *Hollywood Worldviews*, 192

10. Tremper Longman III, *Song of Songs*, New International Commentary on the Old Testament (Grand Rapids: Eerdmans, 2001), 173.

provide information about her beloved (Song 5:9). Can anyone imagine a newlywed bride in ancient Israel answering this request with a public description of her husband's penis?

In any case, the difficulties with this passage remind us again of the Bible's delicacy in sexual matters; oftentimes, we can't be certain what is being described because the language simply isn't explicit enough.

While a sexual interpretation of Song of Solomon 5:14 seems fairly questionable, that cannot be said of Ezekiel 23:20, a strong candidate for the grossest verse in the Bible. Ezekiel 16 and 23 are similar chapters that depict metaphorically the nations of Israel and Judah as young women, with God as a symbolic husband who has loved, raised, and nurtured them from birth. In both passages, the women are excoriated for having abandoned this figurative marriage to the Lord and spread their favors adulterously to other nations and gods. Much of this material will be covered more thoroughly in our later chapter on adultery, but for now let us observe that the verses here on male private parts have been made surprisingly tame in many English versions.

In Ezekiel 16:26, which describes one unfaithful woman's lovers, the ESV, NIV, and NASB say they are "lustful"—but the literal Hebrew phrase is "great of body," once again using *basar*. (The KJV has "great of flesh.") Thus, Bible commentator Daniel I. Block tells us that here "the prophet describes this lover in obscenely graphic terms: *your neighbors . . . with the huge organs.* In a later verse (23:20) he becomes even more specific, comparing the penis of Judah's paramours to the phallus of a donkey and their seminal fluid to that of a horse."[11]

Most modern translations render Ezekiel 23:20 as the ESV does: The woman's lovers had "members" that were "like those of donkeys" and "issue . . . like that of horses." This is hardly the clearest reading of what the text actually says. In the first phrase, "member" is again *basar*, or "flesh."—a word used for male genitalia in Leviticus 15. And "issue"— which clarifies the exact meaning of "member"—derives from a root meaning "to gush forth" or "a flood of rain, downpour."[12] Thus, the NIV is among the few English versions that nail this unseemly accusation:

---

11. Daniel I. Block, *The Book of Ezekiel, Chapters 1–24*, New International Commentary on the Old Testament (Grand Rapids: Eerdmans, 1997), 495.

12. Ibid., 742; see also Robert L. Thomas, ed., *The New American Standard Exhaustive Concordance of the Whole Bible* (Nashville: Holman, 1981), 1515.

"She lusted after her lovers, whose genitals were like those of donkeys and whose emission was like that of horses."

A few other Old Testament passages are similarly specific in discussing injuries to the male privates. Deuteronomy 25:11–12, for example, prescribes severe punishment for a wife who finds her husband fighting and tries to help by "seizing" his opponent's "private parts." And Deuteronomy 23:1 insists that "no one whose testicles are crushed or whose male organ is cut off shall enter the assembly of the LORD." (The King James Version renders this somewhat quaintly, referring to "he that is wounded in the stones, or hath his privy member cut off.")

These two obscure verses bring us at long last to the only Old Testament words that appear to be direct, specific, noneuphemistic references to male private parts: The first passage has *mabush*, or "genitals," and the second *shophkah*—here translated "male organ." Each remains somewhat indirect, for *mabush* derives from a word meaning "to be ashamed," and *shophkah* from a common term meaning "to pour out." And each passage represents the Bible's one and only use of the word in question.

As for the phrase in Deuteronomy 23 about injured testicles, it actually translates two words, both having to do with wounds or crushing; neither refers specifically to the testes. A distinct, non-idiomatic reference to that part of the male anatomy is reserved for Leviticus 21, another little-known verse that forbids priestly service to men with various deformities, one of which is "crushed testicles" (v. 20). Once again, this is an obscure Hebrew term used only here in the entire Old Testament.

These somewhat painful verses naturally point to our final topic in this chapter: circumcision, which is often discussed in the Old and New Testaments, but, as usual, not in much detail. Widely practiced in both ancient and modern times, circumcision is a minor surgical procedure in which the foreskin of the penis is removed, exposing the glans, which is otherwise concealed except during erection. Bible writers seem to assume that even this much information was well known to their audience, as the actual process is never described—except that Exodus 4:25 and Joshua 5:2 specify the use of flint knives. And of course, circumcision was usually performed on male children eight days after birth, as indicated at the rite's inception in Genesis 17. Here, as an outward sign of the covenant God was making with Abraham, the procedure was mandated for all male descendants of the great patriarch. Thereafter, we do not hear much more about its use on children—with the notable exception of one cryptic passage in Exodus.

Here Moses, having earlier fled from his childhood home in Egypt, was now returning to see about the Israelite kinsmen he had left behind. "At a lodging place on the way the Lord met him and sought to put him to death. Then Zipporah [Moses' wife] took a flint and cut off her son's foreskin and touched Moses' feet with it and said, 'Surely you are a bridegroom of blood to me!' So he him let alone" (Ex. 4:24–26).

The writer doesn't explain why God sought Moses' death, but probably this was due either to Moses' failure to circumcise his son, Gershom, or to Moses' own lack of circumcision. After all, Moses had been raised by Egyptians, who—like some other ancient societies that practiced this rite—performed circumcision only on adults, and then only partially. Commentators Peter Enns and John I. Durham are both sure that "feet" here is again a euphemism for genitalia; thus, Zipporah may be attempting to solve both problems by symbolically applying young Gershom's circumcision to Moses—possibly because performing this surgery on Moses himself would have incapacitated the man in the midst of a crucial journey.[13] But whatever the explanation, we are once again faced with an extraordinarily terse account of what must surely have been a bloody and uncomfortable exchange.

Speaking of discomfort, three other Old Testament narratives recount episodes of circumcision performed on adults—as it happens, numerous adults in all three cases.

The first is Genesis 34, in which a non-Israelite named Shechem falls for Jacob's daughter Dinah, rapes her, and then requests her hand in marriage. Dinah's father and brothers, angry because they know what has happened, insist that Shechem cannot marry Dinah unless he becomes "as we are by every male among you being circumcised" (Gen. 34:15). Surprisingly, Shechem's people agree to this stipulation; and after carrying out their commitment, they are all slain with swords by two of Dinah's brothers "on the third day, when they were sore" (v. 25). This heartless act is probably what later caused Jacob to reprove Simeon and Levi for their "violence" (Gen. 49:5).

13. John I. Durham, *Exodus*, Word Biblical Commentary, vol. 3 (Waco, TX: Word, 1987), 53, 58. See also Peter Enns, *Exodus*, The NIV Application Commentary (Grand Rapids: Zondervan, 2000), 133.

Later, in Joshua, the nation of Israel is about to enter the Promised Land after four decades of wandering in the wilderness; however, the younger generation born during this forty-year period had not been circumcised. And so, in a substantial act of faith at the beginning of a full-scale military campaign, every male is circumcised and instructed to remain "in their places in the camp until they were healed"—a ceremony of such massive proportions that this locale became known as "Gibeath-haaraloth," or "the hill of the foreskins" (Josh. 5:3, 8). Here again the use of flint knives is specified, even though iron tools were in use by this time. "The smooth and sharp surface of this sort of knife enjoyed popularity for ritual and non-ritual purposes long after the development of metal knives."[14]

And in 1 Samuel 18:20–27, the young Jewish soldier David has fallen in love with Michal, daughter of Israel's first king, Saul. In the words of Ralph W. Klein, David was "a poor man, presumably unable to pay the bride-price due for a princess," and so King Saul requested that David bring him one hundred foreskins taken from the bodies of Philistines, Israel's archenemies at that time. Because he viewed David as something of a rival, the crafty Saul hoped to get rid of him with this absurd request; but the valiant young warrior complied, bringing back twice as many foreskins as requested—possibly to save Saul from the unimaginable task of having to count his way through this disgusting bounty. Though the incident "strikes the modern reader as altogether gross," it reflects "ethnic humor, stirred by long antagonism."[15]

In the New Testament, baptism replaces circumcision as an outward sign of membership in God's family (Col. 2:11–12). In that era, as countless uncircumcised Gentiles were coming to Christ, the church was under frequent pressure from Jews to have these new converts circumcised. No one fought harder against this legalistic movement than the apostle Paul, and nowhere did he condemn it more vehemently than in Galatians, where he says of these so-called Judaizers, "I wish those who unsettle you would emasculate themselves!" (Gal. 5:12). Literally translated, the concluding phrase here is "cut themselves off." Paul deliberately uses the same verb that appears in Deuteronomy 23:1 in the then-widespread

14. Richard S. Hess, *Joshua: An Introduction and Commentary*, Tyndale Old Testament Commentaries (Leicester, UK: Inter-Varsity, 1996), 119.
15. Ralph W. Klein, *1 Samuel*, Word Biblical Commentary, vol. 10 (Waco, TX: Word, 1983), 190.

Greek translation of the Old Testament (known as the Septuagint); that verse, discussed above, refers to a man with his "male organ cut off." The NASB has "mutilate themselves," which Brian Godawa calls a "nice English translation of saying, 'I wish they would just go all the way and cut off their penises.'" Understandably, Richard N. Longenecker calls this "the crudest and rudest of all Paul's statements."[16] As we saw in Ezekiel 23:20, when stressing a point of the utmost seriousness—and often to people who seem spiritually deaf—the Bible writers do sometimes resort to rather explicit and graphic imagery.

Fortunately, scriptural material on the female body is considerably more pleasant—as we shall see shortly.

16. Godawa, *Hollywood Worldviews*, 194; Richard N. Longenecker, *Galatians*, Word Biblical Commentary, vol. 41 (Nashville: Nelson, 1990), 234.

3

"I Will Lay Hold of Its Fruit"

The Woman's Body

IN THE MILDLY AMUSING 1985 comedy *Summer Rental*, John Candy's character is accosted by a young woman who wants to show off her surgically augmented breasts. As she bares them for him (but not for the film's viewers), the happily married man fumbles for a diplomatic response, finally declaring: "Those are fun for the whole family."

While I don't plan to quote John Candy too often in my book, this little sentence seems to reflect the Bible's attitude pretty well.

In such verses as Genesis 49:25, Isaiah 60:16, and Luke 11:27, the breasts as a source of nourishment are described in the most glowing terms. For example: "Rejoice with Jerusalem, and be glad for her, . . . that you may nurse and be satisfied from her consoling breast; that you may drink deeply with delight from her glorious abundance" (Isa. 66:10–11).

More often, praise for the bosom is expressed without reference to nursing or babies, but simply as a source of frank excitement to a blessed husband. Most of these references occur in Song of Solomon, so let's work our way through that book one passage at a time.

In Song of Solomon 1:13, the young wife compares her lover to a sachet of spices resting between her breasts. The Hebrew verb used here means "to lodge, pass the night or abide"—and so, as Iain Provan puts it, the man "takes up residence in this place."[1] Thus the NASB has

---

1. Iain Provan, *Ecclesiastes, Song of Songs*, The NIV Application Commentary (Grand Rapids: Zondervan, 2001), 270.

an excellent translation of this verse: "My beloved is to me a pouch of myrrh which lies all night between my breasts."

Song of Solomon 2:17 takes this a step farther with a little wordplay in which the wife urges her lover to "be like a gazelle or a young stag on cleft mountains." The Hebrew noun translated "cleft mountains" is a rare one—*bether*—used nowhere else in Scripture; it could represent a geographic locale, but ancient Hebrew has no capital letters to help indicate this, and no such location is known. *Bether* comes from a root meaning "to cut in two" (used for the division of animals in Gen. 15:10); thus, the phrase in Song of Solomon 2:17 indicates "hills cut by a deep valley" and is "most naturally understood in the context as referring to the beloved's breasts."[2] So while the previous passage has the husband reposing himself at length upon his wife's bosom, here she urges him to climb around on it like an agile young creature on a mountain or hillside—though of course, it's expressed in playfully vague terminology. Provan sees an extension of this idea in Song of Solomon 4:6: "'Until the day breathes and the shadows flee,' says the man, 'I will go away to the mountain of myrrh and the hill of frankincense.'" Since the preceding verse describes the woman's breasts, verse 6 seems to imply that the excited young groom "will spend long hours" on these "two scented mountains."[3]

Indeed, in Song of Solomon 4:5 as well as 7:3, the husband confirms his delight in the bosom with a fetching simile well suited to the ancient rural setting in which the young woman was apparently raised: "Your two breasts are like two fawns, twins of a gazelle, that graze among the lilies." Here, "the perfect symmetry of the breasts" is amply conveyed by the parallel nouns, the term "twins" and the doubled use of "two"; meanwhile, the fawns' age indicates the youth, freshness, and petite size of these breasts—the latter quality being "the Arab ideal."[4]

Even more overt language occurs later, jibing nicely with the sense of aggressive playfulness in the *bether* passage from chapter 2: "Your stature is like a palm tree, and your breasts are like its clusters. I say I will climb the palm tree and lay hold of its fruit. Oh may your breasts

2. Ibid., 289.
3. Ibid., 317.
4. Marvin H. Pope, *Song of Songs: A New Translation with Introduction and Commentary*, The Anchor Bible 7C (Garden City, NY: Doubleday, 1977), 470.

be like clusters of the vine" (Song 7:7–8). G. Lloyd Carr tells us that the emphasis here is on the sweetness provided by "the heavy, dark fruit," and Marvin Pope adds that the Hebrew verb for "lay hold" implies "a certain vivacity or violence."[5]

In its final chapter, this little gem of a book concludes with an exchange between the woman and her brothers—perhaps a recollection of earlier times. They begin by saying, "We have a little sister, and she has no breasts," and therefore if she makes herself too available ("if she is a door"), they will protectively "enclose her with boards of cedar." The woman promptly responds by insisting that she is not a door but "a wall," and that her breasts are "like towers"—as if to say, "I am old enough to defend my own honor—and stop insulting the size of my breasts!" (Song 8:8–10). She then adds that to her husband she is like "one who finds peace." Because the verb here can be rendered "brings out," some readers feel that she and her body are calling forth a sense of "contentment," of "well-being and peaceful satisfaction" for her husband.[6]

If so, this comports well with the key Bible passage on breasts as a blessing, Proverbs 5:18–19: "Rejoice in the wife of your youth. . . . Let her breasts fill you at all times with delight; be intoxicated always in her love." According to Bruce K. Waltke, the Hebrew phrase for "breasts" here "originated in infant's babble; its cognate in Arabic means 'nipples' . . . ; it is associated with erotica in its only other uses (Ezek. 23:3, 8, 21). The source of the richest and most satisfying drink is the wife's erogenous members, represented by the breasts."[7] In her book on Christian womanhood, Nancy Wilson stresses the "at all times" aspect of this command, reminding the female reader not to be standoffish with her body because her husband is forbidden to desire any breasts but hers: "The question is, how are they to let their wives' breasts satisfy them *at all times* if they can never get near them? . . . Your breasts are his to enjoy. Let him! Enjoy his enjoyment of them and do not withhold from him what God has commanded him to be satisfied with."[8]

5. G. Lloyd Carr, *The Song of Solomon: An Introduction and Commentary,* Tyndale Old Testament Commentaries (Leicester, UK: Inter-Varsity, 1984), 162; Pope, *Song of Songs,* 636.

6. Provan, *Ecclesiastes,* 370.

7. Bruce K. Waltke, *The Book of Proverbs, Chapters 1–15,* New International Commentary on the Old Testament (Grand Rapids: Eerdmans, 2004), 321.

8. Nancy Wilson, *The Fruit of Her Hands: Respect and the Christian Woman* (Moscow, ID: Canon, 1997), 92.

As for the three verses in Ezekiel which Waltke cites when discussing Proverbs 5, they constitute the only major passage in Scripture where breasts are discussed in a negative context. There is one short reference in Hosea that speaks of adultery "between her breasts" (Hos. 2:2), but Ezekiel is much more graphic. Comparing the nations of Israel and Judah to a pair of whorish sisters who spread their favors to other lovers besides the Lord, Ezekiel writes that "the Egyptians handled your bosom and pressed your young breasts" (Ezek. 23:21; see also vv. 3 and 8). Commentator Daniel I. Block insists that "breasts" should be rendered "nipples" in all three verses, adding that "the description of the sisters' conduct leaves nothing to the imagination: they offered their breasts and nipples to the men of Egypt."[9]

It is worth noting that virtually all of these passages employ perfectly forthright language in dealing with this portion of the woman's body. However, when considering the female genitalia, we encounter a maze of euphemism, indirection, and figurative language; there isn't a single passage where we can say with unequivocal certainty that the female privates are definitely in view.

In chapter 2, we saw that the Hebrew word "feet" (*regel*) is often used as a euphemism for the male genitalia—and that it can also refer to the woman's genitalia in such passages as Deuteronomy 28:57 and Ezekiel 16:25 (see pp. 8-9). Bruce K. Waltke feels that Proverbs may be playing on this idiomatic use of "feet" when it describes a seductive adulteress, asserting that "her feet go down to death" (Prov. 5:5) and "her feet do not stay at home" (Prov. 7:11). Waltke takes this a step further in his examination of Proverbs 5:3, which tells us that "the lips of a forbidden woman drip honey, and her speech is smoother than oil." The Hebrew word for "speech" here is literally "palate," and Waltke suggests that both body parts serve as double entendres, particularly "lips," which refers "doubly to her lips with which she speaks and to her pudenda."[10]

While these readings seem tenuous, Ezekiel 16 is clearer in its metaphorical description of Jerusalem as a young woman under God's care who is now at "the age for love": "You grew up and became tall and

9. Daniel I. Block, *The Book of Ezekiel, Chapters 1-24*, New International Commentary on the Old Testament (Grand Rapids: Eerdmans, 1997), 734.

10. Waltke, *Proverbs 1-15*, 308-9.

arrived at full adornment. Your breasts were formed, and your hair had grown" (Ezek. 16:7–8). Both Iain M. Duguid and Daniel I. Block agree that the "hair" described here is undoubtedly in the genital region, since puberty is being described, and her regular hair would long since have made its appearance.[11]

As in Ezekiel 23 (discussed above), this young woman is later condemned because her "lust was poured out" on other lovers besides her Lord (Ezek. 16:36). Block informs us that "poured out" is a "difficult expression" which is clarified by a related Arabic cognate meaning "abnormal female genital discharge." Ezekiel, however, "has changed a pathological expression into an erotic image, referring to the female genital distillation produced at sexual arousal." While Block himself also translates the phrase euphemistically ("your passion was poured out"), he nonetheless avers that the prophet is again using the "explicit, almost pornographic" style he employs in 23:20–21 and elsewhere.[12]

Not surprisingly, the other biblical passages on female privates all occur in Song of Solomon, where imagery and metaphor tend to cloak the erotic discussion in deliberately vague terminology.

The verses at the center of the book, for example—Song of Solomon 4:16 and 5:1—are almost universally agreed to represent marital consummation: "Let my beloved come to his garden, and eat its choicest fruits," says the bride; and the groom responds by declaring, "I came to my garden." G. Lloyd Carr asserts that in this passage, "the 'garden' is used as a euphemism for the female sex organs," and thus the preceding material about the woman being "a garden locked" and "a fountain sealed" (Song 4:12) refers to her virginity before marriage.[13]

Indeed, in Song of Solomon 4:12–13, the original Hebrew for "garden" is literally "mound of stones," which "could itself be intended to speak of the vaginal area, in advance of the evident sexual consummation in 5:1."[14] In this same passage, the man somewhat enigmatically describes the woman's "shoots," a rare word which can be rendered "conduit" or "groove," and which one etymologist links with an Arabic

---

11. Iain M. Duguid, *Ezekiel*, The NIV Application Commentary (Grand Rapids: Zondervan, 1999), 210; Block, *Ezekiel 1–24*, 482.

12. Block, *Ezekiel 1–24*, 500.

13. Carr, *Song of Solomon*, 123.

14. Provan, *Ecclesiastes*, 319.

term for vagina. Though the dense figures of speech here leave all of this somewhat indefinite, Carr insists that the context "has obvious sexual overtones."[15]

Such overtones are much more apparent in Song of Solomon 5:2–6, a somewhat tricky passage in which the woman describes what is generally viewed as a late-night sexual overture from her husband—an overture she at first rejected:

> I slept, but my heart was awake.
> A sound! My beloved is knocking.
> "Open to me, my sister, my love,
>   my dove, my perfect one,
> for my head is wet with dew,
>   my locks with the drops of the night."
> I had put off my garment;
>   how could I put it on?
> I had bathed my feet;
>   how could I soil them?
> My beloved put his hand to the latch,
>   and my heart was thrilled within me.
> I arose to open to my beloved,
>   and my hands dripped with myrrh,
> my fingers with liquid myrrh,
>   on the handles of the bolt.
> I opened to my beloved,
>   but my beloved had turned and gone.

We have already noted more than once that "feet" and "hand" are frequent euphemisms for the sex organs (see pp. 8-11), and thus in verse 3 the young lady seems to be protesting that she has cleaned her privates and doesn't want to "soil them" again. And "given the attested use of 'hand' as a surrogate for the phallus, there can be no question that, whatever the context, the statement 'my love thrust his "hand" into the hole' would be suggestive of coital intromission"—or, the beginning of intercourse.[16] Of course, the ESV has "latch" instead of "hole," but the Hebrew word literally means "hole" (as in the KJV; the NASB has "opening");

15. Carr, *Song of Solomon*, 124; see also Pope, *Song of Songs*, 490.
16. Pope, *Song of Songs*, 519.

it is used elsewhere in Scripture to describe a cave (1 Sam. 14:11), an eye socket (Zech. 14:12), and a hole in a wall or a box (2 Kings 12:9; Ezek. 8:7). Further affirmation of Pope's reading is provided by Carr, who indicates that a better translation for "put his hand to" would be "thrust his hand into," because "the words demand the meaning of inserting something into a hole of some sort."[17]

If there remains any question about the sexual overtones in this passage, we can put it to rest by examining the woman's response: "my heart was thrilled within me" (v. 4). The Hebrew word used here for "heart"—*meeh*, discussed in chapter 2—literally means "internal organs, inward parts, belly." Sometimes rendered "body," it is translated as "womb" in Ruth 1:11 and is directly associated with procreation in Genesis 15:4; 25:23; 2 Samuel 7:12; and Isaiah 49:1. In other words, says Carr, "the focus of the thrill is specifically sexual."[18] Citing liquid imagery on the man's part ("my head is wet") and on the woman's too ("my hands dripped"), Provan posits that "her wetness responds to his."[19]

All this leads the *Dictionary of Biblical Imagery* to render verse 4 as follows: "My lover thrust his hand through the hole, and my vagina was inflamed."[20] Of course this sort of bluntness is precisely what the writer of the passage is tactfully avoiding, and I dare say most love poets would prefer to speak with a good deal more delicacy.

Indeed, it is just such delicacy that poses substantial difficulties in a later passage—Song of Solomon 7:1–6, where the man once again describes his bride's physique in richly detailed imagery. But while his previous description begins with her eyes and moves down the body (4:1–7), here he starts at the bottom and proceeds upward, describing her feet, thighs, navel, belly, breasts, neck, eyes, and hair. The key word for our discussion here is "navel," which he describes as "a rounded bowl that never lacks mixed wine" (Song 7:2). Several modern-day commentators see this as a veiled reference to the vulva—though that reading remains inconclusive.

17. Carr, *Song of Solomon*, 134.

18. Ibid., 135.

19. Provan, *Ecclesiastes*, 335.

20. Leland Ryken, James C. Wilhoit, and Tremper Longman III, *Dictionary of Biblical Imagery* (Leicester, UK: Inter-Varsity, 1998), quoted in Brian Godawa, *Hollywood Worldviews: Watching Films with Wisdom and Discernment* (Downers Grove, IL: InterVarsity, 2002), 191.

The Hebrew word for "navel" here—*shor*—appears only two other times in Scripture: Proverbs 3:7–8 is not helpful, but in Ezekiel 16:4 it means umbilical cord, which favors "navel" but does, after all, emerge from the vulva.

Carr suggests that the word is related to the Arabic *sirr*, meaning "secret parts," and to a root meaning "valley or place to be farmed," linking it to the sexualized garden imagery discussed above. Marvin Pope says *sirr* can mean "pudenda," "coition," and "fornication," but like others, he points out that there is a similar Arabic cognate, *surr*, which simply means "navel."[21]

Supporting a sexual reading of the word is the nature and order of the body parts described in verses 1–3: thighs, *shor*, belly, breasts. In the first place, all of these can be linked to sexuality. As we noted in chapter 2, "thigh" refers to genitalia in such passages as Genesis 24:2; 46:26; 47:29; Exodus 1:5; and Judges 8:30; it is used specifically for female privates in Numbers 5:21–22 (see pp. 9-10). And the Hebrew word used here for "belly" is translated "womb" in numerous other Scripture passages.

Carr tells us that "belly" refers to "the lower abdomen, below the navel"[22]—and so, with the motif of upward movement in this text, *shor* precedes "belly" because it is located well below the belly button. Thus, it makes sense to place *shor* in a lower and different part of the body than "belly," especially since "belly" is already named in the passage, whereas every other bodily area here gets mentioned only once.

Iain Provan bluntly asserts that the young groom is "astonished by that most intimate place between her legs, which reminds him of a bowl or cup filled with wine." Indeed, in a lengthy exegesis supporting "vulva" over "navel," Provan notes that the former is more naturally associated with liquid—the "mixed wine" of verse 2.[23] Both Tremper Longman and Marvin Pope agree, with Longman adding that "wine" also implies the man's desire to drink from this "sensual bowl."[24]

And he sees a similar suggestion in 4:16, where the woman invites her new husband into her garden to "eat its choicest fruits": "It is prob-

21. Carr, *Song of Solomon*, 157; Pope, *Song of Songs*, 617.
22. Carr, *Song of Solomon*, 158.
23. Provan, *Ecclesiastes*, 353.
24. Pope, *Song of Songs*, 617–18; Tremper Longman III, *Song of Songs*, New International Commentary on the Old Testament (Grand Rapids: Eerdmans, 2001), 194–95.

lematic to know how literally to take the verb *eat*, but there is no doubt about the fact that she invites him to sexual union of the most intimate type."[25] This idea may also be in view at 5:1, where the young husband describes marital consummation with the phrase "I ate my honeycomb with my honey." Carr points out that the Hebrew word used here for "honeycomb"—*yaar*—is nearly always translated as "forest" or "thicket," and that "ancient Near Eastern love poetry frequently uses both the image of honey and of the 'thicket' as euphemisms for the female genitalia."[26] It is possible, then, that these three verses—4:16; 5:1; and 7:2—constitute the Bible's only discussion of oral sex—and in rather positive terms, too.

In opposition to "vulva," however, the online resource *NET Bible* points out that the use of moisture in the verse provides no clearer guide to what is meant than the "heap of wheat" that is later used to describe her belly: neither image is intended literally. *NET Bible* also observes that the Mishnah—a series of ancient rabbinic writings on the Old Testament—translates *shor* as "navel."[27]

More generally, as Robert Alter writes, "The poetic decorum of the Song precludes the direct naming of sexual organs, though the poet may well intimate *correspondences* between navel, or mouth, or door latch, and the woman's hidden parts."[28] In their acclaimed 1995 translation of the Song, Chana and Ariel Bloch likewise insist that "vulva" would be "out of place in the delicately allusive language of the Song."[29] Indeed, having now spent roughly five hundred words unpacking a single term ("navel"), we might well conclude that the poet's simple tact is much more romantic and appropriate than the prosaic bluntness of trying to find a precise referent.

Concerning the Song of Solomon's indirect and allusive nature in such passages, the Blochs comment as follows:

> The language of the Song is at once voluptuous and reticent. "Let my lover come into his garden / and taste its delicious fruit" (4:16) is characteristic both in what it boldly asserts and in what it chooses to leave

25. Longman, *Song of Songs*, 158.

26. Carr, *Song of Solomon*, 129.

27. "The Song of Songs 7:2," *NET Bible*, 1996, http://classic.net.bible.org/verse.php?book=Sos&chapter=7&verse=2.

28. Robert Alter, "Afterword" to *The Song of Songs: The World's First Great Love Poem*, trans. Chana Bloch and Ariel Bloch (1995; repr., New York: Modern Library, 2006), 127.

29. Bloch and Bloch, *Song of Songs*, 41, 201.

unexpressed. We can appreciate its restraint by comparing this verse with, say, the invitation of Inanna, the goddess of love and fertility, to Dumuzi in the sacred marriage rite of Sumer: "Plow my vulva, my sweetheart." In the Song, sexuality is evoked primarily by metaphors. The use of metaphor that both reveals and conceals has the effect of enhancing the Song's eroticism, while the suggestive play of double entendre suffuses the whole landscape with eros.[30]

30. Ibid., 14.

4

"Your Shame Will Be Seen"

Disrobing and Nudity

THERE'S AN AWFUL LOT of nudity in the Bible.

The words "naked" or "nakedness" occur roughly one hundred times in the Old and New Testaments, with several other passages where clothes are stripped off—though many of these don't involve complete nudity.

The only one of these many verses to portray nakedness in a strictly positive light is Genesis 2:25, where the state of paradise before the fall is exemplified by the fact that "the man and his wife were both naked and were not ashamed."

After that, it's all downhill.

In Genesis 9:20–25, Noah, having safely endured the flood, planted a vineyard and made wine, "drank of the wine and became drunk and lay uncovered in his tent." One of his sons, Ham, "saw the nakedness of his father and told his two brothers outside," resulting in a curse on Ham's descendants. (More on this passage in chap. 9.)

Perhaps there is a mildly positive spin to the resistance put up by Jacob's son Joseph when vigorously pursued by the wife of his Egyptian employer, Potiphar, in Genesis 39. So great was her desire for this man who was "handsome in form and appearance," and so determined was Joseph's resistance, that one day, when they were alone, "she caught him by his garment, saying, 'Lie with me.' But he left his garment in her hand and fled"—a show of virtue that got Joseph jailed when Potiphar's wife later claimed he had tried to attack her (Gen. 39:6–18).

Considerably less honorable was the young disciple in Mark who fled when the soldiers arrived to arrest Jesus: "And a young man followed him, with nothing but a linen cloth about his body. And they seized him, but he left the linen cloth and ran away naked" (Mark 14:51–52). The Greek word for "naked" here can mean "poorly clothed" or stripped of outer garments—as in, respectively, James 2:15 and John 21:7. It may also have that less literal meaning in Acts 19:16, where several victims flee "naked and wounded" after being attacked by a man with an evil spirit. But in Mark 14:51–52, the word "naked" appears in both sentences, so that he literally wore "nothing but a linen sheet over his naked body" (NASB).

Since this incident is recorded only in Mark's Gospel, many scholars suspect that this fearful youth was the author himself, "but that out of modesty he did not include his own name."[1] Either way, it is possible Mark was thinking of the prophetic verse in Amos about God's future judgments: "He who is stout of heart among the mighty shall flee away naked in that day" (Amos 2:16). In any case, shortly after this young man's bare-bottomed flight, Christ himself was led off to be crucified—a form of punishment for which, according to most sources, the subject was nearly always stripped naked. Two gospel writers specify that Jesus' clothing was confiscated by Roman soldiers overseeing the execution (Mark 15:24; John 19:23–24), which may explain why the many women present were "looking on from a distance" (Matt. 27:55). But if Christ was indeed crucified fully nude, the detailed accounts of his death in all four Gospels never say so clearly, a tasteful reticence that, as we shall see in chapter 13, characterizes their entire description of this horrific event.

Many instances of the word "nakedness" occur in Old Testament regulations against illicit sex, particularly Leviticus 18, where the phrase "uncover nakedness" is almost certainly a Hebrew idiom for sexual intercourse (see pp. 45–46). However, at least one such set of regulations is indeed concerned with nudity; specifically, these laws work to ensure proper clothing and modesty among the priests ministering at the Lord's tabernacle. In Exodus 20:26, God insists that his priests "not go up by steps to my altar, that your nakedness not be exposed on it," and later they are told to wear "linen undergarments to cover their naked flesh," garments that must "reach from the hips to the thighs" (Ex. 28:42–43). These ordinances probably stem from the fact that many contemporary

1. *ESV Study Bible* (Wheaton, IL: Crossway, 2008), 1929.

28

pagan rites included nudity and ritual sex, while the Lord by contrast "wanted to be sure that his priests were always properly attired and that no exposure of the genitals would be possible as it was with the pagan priests."[2]

Another interesting passage on "exposure" can be found in 2 Samuel 6:14–20, where Israel's King David is "leaping and dancing" in joy as he accompanies the beloved ark of the Lord on its long-awaited return to Jerusalem. David's wife, Michal, reacts unfavorably to this display, lambasting her husband for "uncovering himself today before the eyes of his servants' female servants, as one of the vulgar fellows shamelessly uncovers himself!" Many commentators feel that Michal objected principally to David making a spectacle of himself, or to the fact that he was not wearing his kingly garb, but rather a simple priest's robe (the "linen ephod" of verse 14). Normally, as prescribed in Exodus 28 above, this ephod would have provided sufficient coverage; but it is possible that David "may have lost his loincloth during the ecstatic dancing."[3] In any case, the Hebrew word for "uncover" in this passage is the same one used for illicit sex in Leviticus 18 and 20, and David's dance was clearly a vigorous one, with several writers pointing out that "whirling" is a more accurate translation than "leaping."[4] For these reasons, some readers are convinced that David literally exposed himself here, particularly given the vividness of Michal's remarks about "vulgar fellows" and "shamelessness."

The most common biblical word for "naked" is the Hebrew *arom*, found in such places as Job 1:21 ("Naked I came from my mother's womb, and naked shall I return") and Ecclesiastes 5:15 ("As he came from his mother's womb he shall go again, naked as he came"). However, Barry G. Webb observes that in such passages as Isaiah 58:7 and Job 24:7–10—which describe the insufficient clothing of the poor—this term "does not necessarily indicate total nudity."[5] That may very well apply to several passages where *arom* is used of men who are prophesying; in some cases,

2. Ben Edward Akerley, *The X-Rated Bible: An Irreverent Survey of Sex in the Scriptures* (Los Angeles: Feral House, 1998), 71.

3. A. A. Anderson, *2 Samuel*, Word Biblical Commentary, vol. 11 (Waco, TX: Word, 1989), 107.

4. See, for example, Joyce G. Baldwin, *1 and 2 Samuel: An Introduction and Commentary*, Tyndale Old Testament Commentaries (Leicester, UK: Inter-Varsity, 1988), 209; and *ESV Study Bible*, 553.

5. Barry G. Webb, *The Message of Isaiah: On Eagles' Wings*, The Bible Speaks Today (Leicester, UK: Inter-Varsity, 1996), 97.

God has apparently instructed them to go naked. These would include 1 Samuel 19:24, where Israel's King Saul, gripped by the Spirit, "stripped off his clothes" and prophesied before Samuel while remaining "naked all that day and all that night," as well as Micah 1:8, where the prophet Micah declares, "I will go stripped and naked."

Probably the best known of these passages is Isaiah 20:2, in which God tells the great prophet (a contemporary of Micah), "Go, and loose the sackcloth from your waist and take off your sandals from your feet," with the result that "he did so, walking naked and barefoot." Edward J. Young is among the commentators who are sure that Isaiah was wearing an undergarment; Webb points out that if this wording implicitly meant total nudity, there would be no need to add "and barefoot." However, Webb does concede that the prophet's buttocks were almost certainly exposed, since God intended to use Isaiah as an object lesson predicting Israel's shame, which includes "buttocks uncovered" in verse 4. Webb adds, "It is highly improbable that he remained stripped round the clock," just as Ezekiel would hardly have lain on his side around the clock for 390 days in Ezekiel 4. Concerning Isaiah, Webb finds it "likely he appeared this way in public at least once each day over a three-year period."[6]

The future "nakedness" of Israel herein depicted so graphically by Isaiah clearly represents a divine curse—and indeed, that is the context behind much of the nudity that appears in Scripture, particularly among the Old Testament prophets. Occasionally this unequivocal sign of divine displeasure is visited upon pagan nations such as Nineveh (Nah. 3:4–6) and Babylon: "Strip off your robe, uncover your legs. . . . Your nakedness shall be uncovered, and your disgrace shall be seen" (Isa. 47:2–3). Habakkuk 2:16 sarcastically commands Babylon to "show your uncircumcision!"

More commonly, the curse is pronounced on God's people, with nakedness serving as a symbol of their shame, guilt, and exposure to punishment. Passages in this vein include Micah 1:11, Lamentations 1:8, and especially Jeremiah 13: "It is for the greatness of your iniquity that your skirts are lifted up and you suffer violence. . . . I myself will lift up your skirts over your face, and your shame will be seen" (Jer. 13:22, 26). "There may be an allusion here to the practice of stripping an adulterous woman of her garments. . . . Judah is a prostitute because of her idolatrous

6. Ibid., 97–98. See also Edward J. Young, *The Book of Isaiah: The English Text, with Introduction, Exposition, and Notes*, vol. 2, *Chapters 19–39* (Grand Rapids: Eerdmans, 1969), 55.

practices and as such will be exposed nude."[7] As indicated here by the phrase "suffer violence" in verse 22, the curse of exposure sometimes hints at sexual violation as well. In the words of R. K. Harrison, for example, Lamentations 1:8 depicts Judah as "a beautiful woman who has been ravished"[8]—and as mentioned above, the "nakedness uncovered" phraseology in Isaiah 47:3 usually implies illicit sexual relations.

In other places, nakedness and the threat of violation come as recompense for spiritual harlotry in which God's people are punished with the very thing they have pursued so eagerly—adulterous intercourse with pagan nations. Take Ezekiel 23, for instance, where God promises that the nation of Babylon will assault Judah, leaving her "naked and bare, and the nakedness of your whoring shall be uncovered. Your lewdness and your whoring have brought this upon you, because you played the whore with the nations and defiled yourself with their idols" (Ezek. 23:29–30).

In Nahum 3:4–5, by contrast, this recompense is applied to the Assyrian city of Nineveh because she too has acted sluttishly: given the "countless whorings of the prostitute," God declares, "I am against you, . . . and will lift up your skirts over your face; and I will make nations look at your nakedness." As David W. Baker puts it, "Because she, like a prostitute, had eagerly exposed her nakedness as part of her trade, so too it will be exposed to her shame before the surrounding nations." Tremper Longman adds, "From the context it is obvious that it is not the skirt that is uncovered but what is under it," pointing out that the fourth-century Latin translation of the Scriptures (known as the Vulgate) renders "skirt" as "*pudenda tua*": "your pud." But "instead of explicitly saying 'I will expose your vagina,'" Nahum substitutes a more tasteful euphemism.[9]

Commentator Douglas Stuart sees a similar idea in Hosea 2:10: "I will uncover her lewdness"; here, the final word is often translated "her genitals" and may serve as a euphemism for "parts of the female body normally covered out of propriety." This passage in Hosea describes

7. J. A. Thompson, *The Book of Jeremiah*, New International Commentary on the Old Testament (Grand Rapids: Eerdmans, 1980), 374.

8. R. K. Harrison, *Jeremiah and Lamentations: An Introduction and Commentary*, Tyndale Old Testament Commentaries (Leicester, UK: Inter-Varsity, 1973), 209.

9. David W. Baker, *Nahum, Habakkuk, Zephaniah: An Introduction and Commentary*, Tyndale Old Testament Commentaries (Leicester, UK: Inter-Varsity, 1988), 37; Tremper Longman III, *Nahum*, in *The Minor Prophets: An Exegetical and Expository Commentary*, vol. 2, *Obadiah, Jonah, Micah, Nahum, and Habakkuk*, ed. Thomas Edward McComiskey (Grand Rapids: Baker, 1993), 816.

the prophet's wife, Gomer, an adulteress who serves as an embodiment of Israel's unfaithfulness. Hubbard points out that "lewdness" here is the Hebrew *nabluth*, whose root (*nbl*) can mean "folly" (as in the name Nabal in 1 Samuel 25); he also observes that "uncover" literally means "reveal, lay bare, totally disclose"—implying a "maximum exposure of her shame." Stuart adds that the similar threat to "strip her naked" in Hosea 2:3 "recalls the curse language of a number of ancient Near Eastern treaties, wherein to be stripped naked like a prostitute is one metaphor of the punishment for breaking a treaty covenant."[10]

And with this idea of illicit sex—that is, sexuality condemned in the Scriptures—we have now arrived at our next topic.

10. Douglas Stuart, *Hosea–Jonah*, Word Biblical Commentary, vol. 31 (Waco, TX: Word, 1987), 44; David Allan Hubbard, *Hosea: An Introduction and Commentary*, Tyndale Old Testament Commentaries (Leicester, UK: Inter-Varsity, 1989), 78.

5

"If They Cannot Exercise Self-Control"

Premarital Sex

THE WELL-KNOWN commandments against adultery in Exodus 20:14 and Deuteronomy 5:18 have traditionally been taken to forbid not merely cheating on a spouse, but also a variety of other sins that might be subsumed under the heading "any sexual activity other than that between a man and woman married to each other."

As an example, the Westminster Larger Catechism—a seventeenth-century document that has guided Reformed Protestants for more than 350 years—claims that the seventh commandment forbids "adultery, fornication, rape, incest, sodomy, and all unnatural lusts," as well as pornography, indecent thoughts, and immodest apparel, among other things.[1]

There are several reasons for this broad understanding of a commandment that, on the surface, seems focused on married people. A principal consideration is the many other sexual injunctions subsequently codified in Israel's law, particularly in Leviticus and Deuteronomy. Many of these regulations will come up later in this book regarding such sins as incest and bestiality. For the purposes of this chapter, let us observe that the proscription against adultery almost certainly includes premarital sex. Applying cold logic to the issue, couples who engage in this activity

1. *The Confession of Faith and Catechisms: The Westminster Confession of Faith and Catechisms as Adopted by the Orthodox Presbyterian Church, with Proof Texts* (Willow Grove, PA: OPC Christian Education Committee, 2005), 280–82.

33

often wind up marrying someone else—in which case they have indeed had sex with someone other than their spouse.

More to the point, a ban on premarital sex underlies many other passages in Scripture, notably Exodus 22:16–17: "If a man seduces a virgin who is not betrothed and lies with her, he shall give the bride-price for her and make her his wife." The primary focus of this ordinance is financial—ensuring that the woman's family not lose the "bride-price" (normally paid by the groom to his bride's family) by suddenly finding their daughter compromised and thus unmarriageable. Nonetheless, the standard bride-price at that time was "equivalent to several years' wages," and thus this rule carried "the threat of huge damages in the case of premarital intercourse."[2] A similar verse is Deuteronomy 22:28–29, which involves not mere seduction but outright rape of the unmarried woman ("he has violated her"); here, the price due to her father is 50 shekels, with the added codicil that the man not only must marry the woman but also may not thereafter divorce her. These laws are designed "to protect the woman who is less likely to be married because she has been violated."[3]

Along the same lines, Deuteronomy 22:13–21 makes it unequivocally clear that women were expected to remain virgins until married. In this passage it is stated that if a husband claims his wife was not a virgin when they wed, he can challenge her parents to produce evidence of her virginity—perhaps "a garment stained with menstrual blood (v. 17), which demonstrates that she is not pregnant, or a stain of hymenal blood, showing that the girl's first intercourse took place on her wedding night."[4] Preserving the wedding-night linens stained with the bride's blood "was presumably a matter of wedding ritual, the initial placing of it, its presentation and entrustment to the parents all being part of the festivities, certifying that her parents had fulfilled their part of the bargain."[5] While upholding chastity and virginity, this is clearly a text—and a society—that is not squeamish about the mechanics of sexual activity.

A presumption of no-sex-before-marriage was apparently still in place among Jews living in the New Testament era. Early in the Gospel

---

2. *ESV Study Bible* (Wheaton, IL: Crossway, 2008), 180.
3. Ibid., 363.
4. Ibid.
5. J. G. McConville, *Deuteronomy*, Apollos Old Testament Commentaries (Nottingham, UK: Apollos-InterVarsity, 2002), 339.

accounts, for instance, we find the story of Jesus' father, Joseph, who learned that his betrothed was pregnant, but "resolved to divorce her quietly" rather than "put her to shame" with public exposure of what was clearly regarded as a sin (Matt. 1:19). The shame brought on by sex outside marriage is also hinted at in John, when Jesus arrests the attention of a Samaritan woman by observing, "The one you now have is not your husband" (John 4:18). And the idea of marriage as the only suitable place for sex is clear from 1 Corinthians 7:9, where Paul insists that if people "cannot exercise self-control, they should marry. For it is better to marry than to burn with passion."

As these passages indicate, the New Testament is often more vague than the Old in addressing sexual sins, and nowhere is there a verse that flatly states, "You cannot have sex before you're married." However, that is certainly what is implied by New Testament writers in their frequent use of the Greek word group that includes *porneia, porneuo, porne*, and *pornos*—the source of our word "pornography." This set of words can indicate general irreligious conduct, as in the condemnation of Esau for selling his birthright in Hebrews 12:16; yet even in this apparently nonsexual context, the ESV translates *pornos* as "sexually immoral"—the same sense this word group carries in nearly every other New Testament use. Our understanding of this terminology is governed by several issues, including its use to translate the Hebrew term *zanah* in the Septuagint, an ancient Greek version of the Old Testament that was widely known and used in the first-century church era; as we shall see in chapter 7, *zanah* usually means "whore" or "whoredom" (see pp. 59–61).

We can also determine the sense of these New Testament terms by examining the context in which they appear. In its various forms, the *porneuo* word group is used for incest in 1 Corinthians 5:1; homosexuality in Jude 7; sex with prostitutes in 1 Corinthians 6:18; sex that demonstrates "impurity" in 1 Thessalonians 4:2–7; and sex outside marriage in 1 Corinthians 7:2, Hebrews 13:4, and especially Matthew 5:32 and 19:9. Thus, various Bible dictionaries tell us that the set of words as a whole refers to "illicit sexual activities in general," to "any kind of illegitimate sexual intercourse,"[6] to "various extra-marital sexual modes of behavior insofar as they deviate from accepted social and religious norms (e.g.,

---

6. Robert J. Wyatt, "Immoral," in *The International Standard Bible Encyclopedia*, vol. 2, ed. Geoffrey W. Bromiley (Grand Rapids: Eerdmans, 1982), 808.

homosexuality, promiscuity, paedophilia, and especially prostitution)."[7] Literally, *porneia* means "fornication"—which *Merriam-Webster* defines as "consensual sexual intercourse between two persons not married to each other."[8]

One final reason for presuming that God's Word forbids premarital sex: the scriptural narratives involving this sin nearly always turn out badly for those who do it. Representative examples might include the Hivite prince Shechem, who raped Jacob's daughter, Dinah, and wound up getting slain while recovering from adult circumcision (Genesis 34). Or the Israelite in Numbers who brought a Midianite woman into his "chamber," whereupon the zealous Phinehas—responding to God's command to kill all those who had "whored" with the local people and their gods—slew them both, apparently while they were having sex (Num. 25:1–8; see pp. 125–26). Or Judges 16, where Samson fell for Delilah and was seduced into revealing the source of his great strength, after which "the Philistines seized him and gouged out his eyes and brought him down to Gaza and bound him with bronze shackles" (Judg. 16:4–21). And let's not forget Hophni and Phinehas, the sons of high priest Eli in the late days of the judges. Though their father reproved them because, among other things, "they lay with the women who were serving at the entrance to the tent of meeting," nonetheless "they would not listen to the voice of their father"; they were later killed by Philistines in a battle that also resulted in the loss of the ark of the covenant and eventually the death of Eli himself (1 Sam. 2:22–25; 4:17–18).

I noted above that the Bible's accounts of premarital or extramarital sex "nearly always" turn out badly. This phrase was intended to leave room for two books in which premarital sex is a bit more problematic— Ruth and Esther.

As her place in the canon indicates, Ruth was a young woman living in the Old Testament era of the judges; she was a native of Moab, a pagan nation located southeast of Israel. Ruth married a Jewish man whose family had come to Moab to escape famine in Israel. When Ruth's husband died and her widowed mother-in-law, Naomi, decided to return to Israel, Ruth insisted on going with her. In order to sustain both herself and

7. Horst Reisser, "*Porneuo,*" in *The New International Dictionary of New Testament Theology,* vol. 1, ed. Colin Brown (Grand Rapids: Regency-Zondervan, 1986), 497.

8. "Fornication," *Merriam-Webster's Collegiate Dictionary,* 11th ed. (Springfield, MA: Merriam-Webster, 2004).

Naomi in her new homeland, Ruth was given permission to gather left-over crops in the fields of Boaz, a godly man who was related to Naomi's deceased husband. In chapter 3, seeing that Boaz might make a good husband for her daughter-in-law, Naomi gave Ruth these instructions:

> "Is Boaz not our relative . . . ? See, he is winnowing barley tonight at the threshing floor. Wash therefore and anoint yourself, and put on your cloak and go down to the threshing floor, but do not make yourself known to the man until he has finished eating and drinking. But when he lies down, observe the place where he lies. Then go and uncover his feet and lie down, and he will tell you what to do." . . .
>
> And when Boaz had eaten and drunk, and his heart was merry, he went to lie down at the end of the heap of grain. Then she came softly and uncovered his feet and lay down. At midnight the man was startled and turned over, and behold, a woman lay at his feet! (Ruth 3:2–4, 7–8)

All this worked out rather well for Ruth: not only did Boaz later marry her, but also, through their great-grandson David, she thereby entered the lineage of Jesus Christ, being mentioned by name in Matthew 1:5. Nonetheless, a few commentators wonder whether there was something overtly sexual about her overtures to Boaz on the threshing floor—specifically, whether she uncovered something more than just his "feet."

Several aspects of this passage seem to support a sexual reading of Ruth's actions. The preliminary bathing of verse 2, for example, is a "normal first step in preparation for a sexual encounter and/or marriage," as may be the case with the young woman claimed by God in Ezekiel 16:9. Indeed, both Ezekiel 16 and Ruth 3 "contain the sequence of bathing, applying perfume, and putting on garments in preparation for an encounter with a male."[9]

Furthermore, "in the Ancient Near East immoral practices at harvest-time were by no means uncommon, and, indeed, appear to have been encouraged by the fertility rites practiced in some religions."[10] As hinted at in Hosea 9:1, "At winnowing time the threshing floor often became a place of illicit sexual behavior. Realizing that the men would

---

9. Daniel I. Block, *Judges, Ruth*, The New American Commentary (Nashville: Broadman, 1999), 683.

10. Arthur E. Cundall and Leon Morris, *Judges and Ruth: An Introduction and Commentary*, Tyndale Old Testament Commentaries (Leicester, UK: Inter-Varsity, 1968), 287.

spend the night in the fields next to the piles of grain, prostitutes would go out to them and offer their services."[11]

More to the point, the two sentences describing Ruth's actions (Ruth 3:4, 7) each contain three words that have strong sexual overtones in other parts of Scripture. "Uncover" is the same word used in the many laws against "uncovering the nakedness" of one's relatives in Leviticus 18 and 20; the term is a euphemism for sexual intercourse in these passages and others, such as Deuteronomy 22:30 and 27:20, and Ezekiel 22:10. Much of this will be discussed further in chapter 6, where we shall see that "lie" and "lay" (used six times in the Ruth passage above) are likewise common Old Testament idioms for coitus; again, they are often found in Leviticus 18 and 20, along with many other passages as well (Gen. 19:32–35; 39:7–12; Ex. 22:16–19; Deut. 27:20–23; 1 Sam. 2:22; 2 Sam. 13:14). And finally, as we noted in chapter 2, "feet" is yet another ancient Hebrew euphemism—in this case, one that is related to the male privates in such passages as Exodus 4:25, Judges 3:24, and 1 Samuel 24:3 (see pp. 8–9).

In view of all this, one writer has Ruth uncovering Boaz's "waist" in verse 7,[12] and scholar Daniel I. Block asserts that "under ordinary circumstances these look like the actions of a prostitute." But ultimately Block—a commentator and Wheaton College professor who, as we have seen elsewhere in this book, is not squeamish about explicit material—rejects the sexual reading of Ruth's actions, preferring to interpret the passage literally: she really did uncover Boaz's feet and lie down. Here are Block's rather persuasive reasons:

First, the word used for "feet" in this passage is not exactly the same one used in the others cited above, but is merely derived from that other more common term; it occurs elsewhere in Scripture only in Daniel 10:6, where it means "lower limbs," including feet, legs, and thighs. Second, the sexual interpretation ignores "the restraint and care with which Naomi chooses her words . . . and runs roughshod over the narrator's characterization of both her and Ruth in the story." Indeed, Naomi is portrayed in this little book as "consistently virtuous"—and the same can be said of Ruth too. And finally, if Ruth had been so brazen,

11. Block, *Judges, Ruth*, 685.
12. James Moffatt, *The Book of Judges and Ruth* (Hodder & Stoughton, 1906), cited in Cundall and Morris, *Judges and Ruth*, 286.

then Boaz—also quite virtuous throughout the tale—could hardly extol her as he does in Ruth 3:10–11: wishing that she may be "blessed by the LORD," he calls her "my daughter," praises her "kindness" and sexual virtue ("you have not gone after young men"), and sums up with the term "worthy"—the same Hebrew word used to describe an "excellent wife" in Proverbs 12:4 and 31:10.[13] The *ESV Study Bible* agrees with Block, asserting that "there is no evidence" for a sexual reading, and "it would be out of place in the story."[14]

Nonetheless, Naomi seems to be "taking a huge gamble" with her instructions to Ruth: "Obviously when Boaz awakes and discovers his feet uncovered and a woman lying nearby, the nonverbal communication is sufficiently ambiguous to be interpreted in any one of several ways." Given the context, Boaz could "willingly accept Ruth's overtures, in his grogginess interpreting her actions to be those of a common prostitute. After all, the events described occur in the dark days of the judges."[15]

Sinclair Ferguson agrees: The passage raises "serious questions, unsettling questions, about the risk to which Naomi is prepared to expose Boaz. Perfume, night-time, good food and wine, the warm physical closeness of an attractive woman . . . what man could miss the apparent message? . . . Would a man not find himself tempted, and is that not the central part of the plan?" Is this just a straightforward request for help, "or is there a hint of more—an invitation to physical, sexual intimacy? The tension of the story lies in the fact that the words are open to more than one interpretation. The word translated 'feet' . . . is translated 'legs' in Daniel 10:6. We are uncertain exactly what is happening here!"[16]

Again, the Bible's oft-noted narrative restraint leaves room for questions; but in the long run, Block's case against premarital sex in Ruth seems fairly ironclad.

There is, however, a good deal more uncertainty with Esther, a young Jewish woman in the book that bears her name. She lived in the fifth century B.C., when vast numbers of Jews had been exiled from Israel and lived in the north, under a succession of foreign powers including Assyria,

---

13. Block, *Judges, Ruth*, 686.
14. *ESV Study Bible*, 481.
15. Block, *Judges, Ruth*, 687.
16. Sinclair B. Ferguson, *Faithful God: An Exposition of the Book of Ruth* (n.p.: Bryntirion, 2005), 96–97.

Babylon, and Persia. Esther lived in Persia with her uncle, Mordecai, during the reign of King Ahasuerus, also known as Xerxes 1.

This king had a tiff with his wife, Vashti, that resulted in her permanent banishment from his presence—after which the king's attendants urged him to find a replacement: "Let the king appoint officers in all the provinces of his kingdom to gather all the beautiful young virgins to the harem in Susa the citadel. . . . And let the young woman who pleases the king be queen instead of Vashti" (Est. 2:3–4). After a twelve-month preparation period for beautification with various cosmetics, oils, and spices, each of the many women brought to Susa was then called to the king one at a time: "In the evening she would go in, and in the morning she would return to the second harem in the custody of Shaashgaz, the king's eunuch, who was in charge of the concubines. She would not go in to the king again, unless the king delighted in her and she was summoned by name" (Est. 2:14). Young Esther, who "had a beautiful figure and was lovely to look at," was "taken" as one of the young virgins in this mass queen-hunt; she then proceeded to win "favor in the eyes of all who saw her," including Hegai, "who had charge of the women"; finally, even the king himself "loved Esther more than all the women" and made her his queen (Est 2:15–17).

As the *ESV Study Bible* points out, the word "taken" leaves it somewhat unclear whether she went willingly or unwillingly. Given the phrase "the king's order and his edict" in Esther 2:8, "she presumably had no choice in the matter. Once there, she appears to have been fully compliant." Michael V. Fox cannot find "any hint that Esther in particular was forced into anything." He even suspects Mordecai of assuming that her promotion to queen would be "something desirable"[17]—an assertion supported by Mordecai's statement later in the book, when Esther's fellow Jews are threatened and she is in a position to intercede for them: "Who knows whether you have not come to the kingdom for such a time as this?" (Est. 4:14).

By contrast, Karen Jobes cites another commentator's insistence that Mordecai should have allowed himself to be killed rather than per-

---

17. Michael V. Fox, *Character and Ideology in the Book of Esther* (Grand Rapids: Eerdmans, 2001), 34.

mit his niece to have "intercourse with an uncircumcised heathen."[18] The shock of such a deed is exacerbated by the many existing scriptural commands forbidding Jews to intermarry with the pagan peoples around them (Ex. 34:12–16; Deut. 7:3; Josh. 23:12; etc.). Not to mention the clear implication of premarital sex.

Some have tried to read this passage in a light that allows Esther to "go in to the king" without necessarily having sex with him, as in the recent movie *One Night with the King* (2006); but this is tough to justify in light of the passage as a whole. Note, for instance, the word "harem" in Esther 2:3, 9, 11, 13, and 14. Literally "woman house," this word is used only here in Scripture, though the context makes its meaning fairly clear, especially when fleshed out with the term "concubines" in 2:14. This latter is a more common biblical word which, in this passage, means "women officially recognized as the king's mistresses, . . . having a lower status than his wife or wives." Since the queen candidates not chosen by Ahasuerus were eventually relegated to this group, "each woman's first night with the king was her initiation as a concubine."[19]

In fact, Fox asserts that the actual competition for the spot of queen is not a beauty contest, as is so often asserted, but rather "a *sex* contest."[20] Iain Provan agrees that as the king calls the women in night after night, "he tests them out sexually, one by one, until he finds a competition winner."[21] Karen Jobes adds: "Given the sensual atmosphere created by the author's description of the period of preparation . . . the reader can hardly avoid wondering just how she won Xerxes in just one night with him. Did God give her favor with Xerxes? The text does not explain it that way. However, it is certain that because this young Jewish virgin apparently did whatever it took to please a lascivious pagan king, she won the position of queen."[22]

This is all the more shocking when one considers what would have happened if Esther had not won the king's favor and thereby achieved royal office. In the "second harem" of Esther 2:14, what awaited these

---

18. Karen H. Jobes, *Esther*, The NIV Application Commentary (Grand Rapids: Zondervan, 1999), 101.

19. *ESV Study Bible*, 855.

20. Fox, *Character and Ideology in the Book of Esther*, 27–28.

21. Iain Provan, *Ecclesiastes, Song of Songs*, The NIV Application Commentary (Grand Rapids: Zondervan, 2001), 274.

22. Jobes, *Esther*, 111.

"also-rans" was "more like widowhood than marriage."[23] "After spending one night in the king's bed, the woman was returned to the harem of concubines, where she would spend the rest of her life in luxurious but desolate seclusion."[24] It is possible that Esther's eventual position was not much better, since at one point later she tells Mordecai, "I have not been called to come in to the king these thirty days" (Est. 4:11).

Perhaps the most surprising aspect of this passage is that Esther's narrator expresses no clear moral stance on her premarital night with the king, or on her subsequent marriage to a heathen with a sizable harem. It is all reported in perfectly direct prose, with Esther eventually becoming a national hero when she uses her position in the kingdom to prevent a Jewish genocide engineered by the king's adviser, Haman. Perhaps most remarkable of all is God's willingness to make providential use of premarital sex and pagan intermarriage to preserve the nation that would one day give rise to the Savior, Jesus Christ.

---

23. Joyce G. Baldwin, *Esther: An Introduction and Commentary*, Tyndale Old Testament Commentaries (Leicester, UK: Inter-Varsity, 1984), 67–68.
24. Jobes, *Esther*, 110.

6

"Be Drunk with Love!"

Intercourse and Marriage

THIS CHAPTER'S TITLE by no means aims to prescribe a suitable order for these two activities; but I do wish to reserve the exciting material on married sexuality for the end of this discussion—as the pinnacle and climax of God's intentions for physical intimacy.

Let's begin instead with the terminology for sexual relations— terms which, in modern American culture, are multifarious and often euphemistic: "go to bed with," "make love," "sleep with," even the slangy "hook up."

The Bible writers are no different, employing a wide array of mild or indirect terms, perhaps the politest of which is the New Testament's "have" and "has." This common verb is used in the Gospels when John the Baptist indicts Herod because "it is not lawful for you to have your brother's wife" (Mark 6:18; see also Matt. 14:4). The sexual overtones of "have" are subtly apparent in John 4, where Jesus speaks to a Samaritan woman: "You have had five husbands, and the one you now have is not your husband" (John 4:18). Clearest of all is 1 Corinthians 5, in which the apostle Paul condemns a church body because they have countenanced a man who "has his father's wife"; this is Paul's expression for a type of "sexual immorality" which, he says, "is not tolerated even among pagans" (1 Cor. 5:1).

More familiar to Bible readers—and much more widely used in Scripture—is the Old Testament verb "to know," once fairly famous in the King James Bible and now restored in the English Standard Version of 2001. This is the common Hebrew *yada*, used hundreds of times in its ordinary sense but appearing idiomatically for intercourse in such verses as Genesis 4:1 ("Adam knew his wife Eve, and she conceived") and about a dozen others—for instance, Genesis 24:16 ("a maiden whom no man had known") and Numbers 31:17 ("every woman who has known man by lying with him"). Derek Kidner points out that in this special sense, the word "conveys very well the fully personal level of true sexual union, although it can lose this higher content altogether,"[1] as it does in the Sodomite passage in Genesis 19:5–8 and the gang rape in Judges 19:25.

"Know" in the sexual sense also occurs in a fascinating passage from 1 Kings, where Israel's aged King David has become so frail that he can no longer keep himself warm; so a young virgin named Abishag is brought in to lie with him—but the text tells us that "the king knew her not" (1 Kings 1:4). Earlier in the passage, two other likely sexual euphemisms occur when David's servants suggest that the woman "wait on the king" and that she "lie in your arms." According to the *ESV Study Bible*, the first phrase is also used in Leviticus 18:23, where it "refers to availability for sexual intercourse; . . . and 'in your arms' has sexual overtones in Gen. 16:5 ('your embrace'); 2 Sam. 12:8; and Mic. 7:5." The text thus indicates that "Abishag is no doubt intended to interest David sexually," and his apparent lack of sexual vitality is enough to suggest that he has also become politically impotent—at which point David's son Adonijah determines to lead an insurrection.

In addition to "know," another ordinary verb phrase used for sexual union in Scripture is "went in" (or "go in"). Appearing about two dozen times in the Old Testament, this is not a literal reference to coital penetration; rather, it refers to approaching a woman for the purpose of sexual intercourse (perhaps actually "going in" to her tent or house). For example: Abraham "went in to Hagar, and she conceived" (Gen. 16:4); "they have gone in to her, as men go in to a prostitute" (Ezek. 23:44); and "David comforted his wife, Bathsheba, and went in to her and lay with her, and she bore a son" (2 Sam. 12:24).

That last example also includes the most common Old Testament term for intercourse, namely, "lie with" (or "lay with"), which occurs well

---

1. Derek Kidner, *Genesis: An Introduction and Commentary*, Tyndale Old Testament Commentaries (Leicester, UK: Inter-Varsity, 1967), 74.

over thirty times altogether. Similar to "know" and "go in," it appears quite commonly in its ordinary sense (lying down), but often refers to coitus, as in this brief but important law regarding intercourse: "If a man lies with a woman and has an emission of semen, both of them shall bathe themselves in water and be unclean until the evening" (Lev. 15:18).

While this stricture in Leviticus 15 would have applied largely to husbands and wives, most instances of the term "lie with" involve some sort of forbidden union, such as the narrative where Lot's daughters get their father drunk and have sex with him (Gen. 19:32–35); various sexual proscriptions in Leviticus 15, 19, and 20 (e.g., "if a man lies with a male as with a woman" in Lev. 20:13); and several other passages in 2 Samuel, including God's promised punishment for David's sexual sins: "Your neighbor . . . shall lie with your wives in the sight of this sun" (2 Sam. 12:11). Similar negative uses occur in Genesis 34:2–7, 1 Samuel 2:22, and Deuteronomy 27:20–23. Indeed, even though it "sounds like an innocent euphemism for sexual intercourse," nevertheless, "lie with" nearly always appears in the context of "illicit relationships."[2]

That may explain why this term—unlike "know" and "go in"—has a literal sense that is closely related to its euphemistic meaning; in most cases, a man really does "lie with" a woman when he has sex with her. This use of a blunter and less diplomatic term in negative contexts is even more apparent with the oft-occurring phrase "uncover nakedness," a term for sexual intercourse so frank that it scarcely qualifies as a euphemism.

As might be expected, it shows up most often in Leviticus's numerous laws against sexual perversity: "You shall not uncover the nakedness of your father's wife" (Lev. 18:8); "you shall not uncover the nakedness of your sister" (Lev. 18:9); "you shall not uncover the nakedness of your son's daughter" (Lev. 18:10). While these might at first sound like injunctions against viewing close relatives in the nude, the *ESV Study Bible* insists that "uncover nakedness" is an idiom for sexual intercourse,[3] as made clear in Leviticus 20: "If a man lies with his father's wife, he has uncovered his father's nakedness" (Lev. 20:11); and, "If a man lies with a woman during her menstrual period and uncovers her nakedness . . ." (Lev. 20:18).

2. Gordon J. Wenham, *Genesis 16–50*, Word Biblical Commentary, vol. 2 (Dallas: Word, 1994), 61.
3. *ESV Study Bible* (Wheaton, IL: Crossway, 2008), 240.

Ezekiel also clarifies the meaning of this phrase in some of the Bible's strongest language about sexual sin. After a bold condemnation of Israel for spiritual adultery—insisting, "You spread your legs to every passer-by" (Ezek. 16:25, NASB)—chapter 22 then indicts Jerusalem because "in you men uncover their fathers' nakedness; in you they violate women who are unclean in their menstrual impurity. One commits abomination with his neighbor's wife; another lewdly defiles his daughter-in-law . . ." (Ezek. 22:10–11).

Several Bible passages refer to intercourse between animals, strictly in the context of agriculture (Gen. 30:38–41; 31:10–12; Lev. 19:19). Though generally rendered in English by a form of "mate" or "breed," the original language of these passages also tends to be euphemistic, translating such common Hebrew verbs as "to go up," "to become warm" and "to be stretched out."

Aside from all the euphemisms and idioms, the Old Testament does offer a few rare words that refer unequivocally to sexual intercourse. One is *shekobeth*, closely derived from the common *shakab*, "to lie down"—the word so often used euphemistically in the passages described above. Literally defined as "copulation," *shekobeth* is found in only four Bible verses: Leviticus 18:20; 18:23; 20:15; and Numbers 5:20—all of which involve negative contexts such as adultery or bestiality.[4]

I have laid out all this terminology in detail to show that while the Bible is generally tasteful in referring to sexual intercourse, it can often be perfectly blunt; and in any case, it certainly isn't squeamish in discussing this vital aspect of human existence. The many uses of "have," "know," "go in," "lie with," "uncover nakedness"—together with the other passages below, plus some we have not discussed—comprise more than 120 direct references to coitus in the Holy Book.

And while the Bible is not especially prudish in its treatment of sexuality, neither is it primarily negative, as though sex were something shameful that we are not to mention or enjoy. After all, it is part of the very first command issued to humanity—"Be fruitful and multiply and fill the earth" (Gen. 1:28)—in accordance with which, the man and woman "shall become one flesh," both being "naked and . . . not ashamed" (Gen. 2:24, 25). And of course, all this is before the fall and the entry of sin into the world.

---

4. R. Laird Harris, Gleason L. Archer Jr., and Bruce K. Waltke, *Theological Wordbook of the Old Testament* (Chicago: Moody, 1980), 922.

For these reasons, we should not be surprised to find plenty of Scripture depicting marital sexuality in positive terms. In fact, two such passages, using a figurative parable, seem to involve God himself. In Ezekiel 16, for example, the prophet describes a budding young virgin who represents the nation of Judah as nurtured and cared for by Jehovah. Addressing her, God says that under his loving care, "You grew up and became tall and arrived at full adornment. Your breasts were formed, and your hair had grown. . . . When I passed by you again and saw you, behold, you were at the age for love, and I spread the corner of my garment over you and covered your nakedness; I made my vow to you and entered into a covenant with you, declares the Lord GOD, and you became mine. Then I bathed you with water and washed off your blood from you and anointed you with oil" (Ezek. 16: 7–9). Regarding the blood in this final clause, scholar Daniel I. Block writes, "Of course, the entire speech is metaphorical, but this image should probably be associated with virginal bleeding, the effects of the first coitus (Deut. 22:13–21)."[5] In other words, the passage first describes pubescence ("you were at the age for love") and then marriage ("my vow" and "covenant")—which is followed, naturally, by consummation.

Similarly, John the Baptist used a figure of speech in which he compared himself to a sort of first-century "best man" at the wedding of Christ and his church: "The one who has the bride is the bridegroom. The friend of the bridegroom, who stands and hears him, rejoices greatly at the bridegroom's voice" (John 3:29). Both contemporary scholar William Loader and German commentator Rudolf Schnackenburg assert that the "voice" of the groom here is a sexual cry indicating consummation. As Schnackenburg puts it: "Among the friends of the bride and groom (in Judea, at least), two had a position of trust regarding them and had to watch over the sexual relations of the young couple; they led the bride to the groom and kept watch outside the bridal chamber. The 'voice of the bridegroom' is thought to be 'the triumph shout by which the bridegroom announced to his friends outside that he had been united to a virginal bride.'"[6]

5. Daniel I. Block, *The Book of Ezekiel, Chapters 1–24*, New International Commentary on the Old Testament (Grand Rapids: Eerdmans, 1997), 484.

6. Rudolf Schnackenburg, quoted in George R. Beasley-Murray, *John*, Word Biblical Commentary, vol. 36 (Nashville: Nelson, 1999), 52–53. See also William Loader, *Sexuality in the New Testament: Understanding the Key Texts* (Louisville, KY: Westminster John Knox, 2010), 37.

If both of these readings seem somewhat shocking, we should recall the many Bible passages where God's people are referred to as his bride—passages such as Isaiah 62:4–5; Jeremiah 2:2; Hosea 2:16–20; Ephesians 5:25–32; and Revelation 19:7–9. In view of these, and of the many implications involved in this profound relationship, there should be nothing especially unsuitable about including consummation as part of the metaphor—provided, of course, that we insist it is indeed figurative and not to be thought of in some crude and literal manner. In the words of John Peck, "If a human being is made in the image of God, and if that image is fundamental to his being, then human sexuality is part of the image of God. We may conclude from this that sexual behavior is symbolic in that it reflects something about God's nature. One might even say that sex, in this sense, is sacramental."[7]

So we should not be surprised to find that many Bible texts treat sex in unequivocally positive terms. Among these, two of the most endearing are short passages in Genesis, the first of which has an aging Sarah learning that she is going to conceive a son: "So Sarah laughed to herself, saying, 'After I am worn out, and my lord is old, shall I have pleasure?'" (Gen. 18:12). The final word in Sarah's sentence occurs only here in the Bible; literally, it means "delight," and nearly every English translation renders it "pleasure"—partly because it is related to the Hebrew word for Eden.

A few chapters later, Sarah's promised son Isaac has not only arrived but also grown up and married Rebekah; the two have settled in Gerar, where Isaac tells the natives that Rebekah is his sister, because he fears they might be jealous. But then the local king, Abimelech, "looked out of a window and saw Isaac laughing with Rebekah his wife" (Gen. 26:7–8). The word rendered "laughing" here is related to the one used for Sarah's reaction in Genesis 18:12 (a form of it is also found in Isaac's name); but Abimelech then reproves Isaac for not telling the truth about Rebekah ("One of the people might easily have lain with your wife," v. 10); so the term is "clearly a euphemism for intimacy only proper between spouses."[8] For this reason, other English translations render it "caressing" (NASB), "showing endearment" (NKJV), "fondling" (*The Message*) or "hugging and kissing" (CEV).

7. John Peck, "Sex in Art—An Erotic Christian Imagination?" *Cornerstone* 30, 121 (2001).
8. Wenham, *Genesis 16–50*, 190.

Granted, we are not talking about intercourse in this latter instance; nonetheless, these two passages, with their emphasis on laughter, pleasure, and delight, suggest a glowing view of married sexuality even in old age, an approach that comports well with many other Bible passages.

Perhaps the most startling of these occur in Proverbs 5:15–19 and Song of Solomon 5:2, the latter of which has this charge for a newly-wed couple enjoying consummation: "Eat, friends, drink, and be drunk with love!" (Song 5:2). The expression "be drunk," sometimes translated "drink deeply," normally means "to become intoxicated," occurring as it does in Genesis 9:21; 1 Samuel 1:13–14; Isaiah 49:26; and many other places—and thus the Complete Jewish Bible renders this, "Drink, until you are drunk with love!"[9] A similar idea occurs in Proverbs 5, where the context once again is clearly physical lovemaking: "Rejoice in the wife of your youth. . . . Let her breasts fill you at all times with delight; be intoxicated always in her love" (Prov. 5:18–19). Here too "the writer is not prudish . . . , boldly encouraging the man to find consistent sexual satisfaction in his wife's body and consistent emotional attraction in her love, expressed physically."[10]

Quoting Michael V. Fox, writer Bruce K. Waltke indicates that the use of "intoxicated" conveys "no disapproval here, but perhaps it bears a slightly 'naughty' overtone by suggestions of 'straying' deliciously dazed in the ecstasies of lovemaking." Indeed, the *ESV Study Bible* notes that "intoxicated" can also mean "led astray," and thus it carries a sense of "being 'swept away' with delight in one's wife." In Waltke's words, "The quality of her lovemaking is totally satisfying, and its quantity unending," as indicated by the phrase "at all times," emphasizing that "the blessed wife's lovemaking should be always available to drench and intoxicate her thirsty husband." Fox also observes that the opening salvo in this passage—"Drink water from your own cistern, flowing water from your own well" (Prov. 5:15)—gives us imagery suggesting "cool, limpid refreshment for hot desires, which are slaked by 'drinking,' that is, lovemaking."[11]

---

9. G. Lloyd Carr, *The Song of Solomon: An Introduction and Commentary*, Tyndale Old Testament Commentaries (Leicester, UK: Inter-Varsity, 1984), 129.

10. Anthony Selvaggio, *A Proverbs Driven Life: Timeless Wisdom for Your Words, Work, Wealth and Relationships* (Wapwallopen, PA: Shepherd, 2008), 155.

11. Bruce K. Waltke, *The Book of Proverbs, Chapters 1–15*, New International Commentary on the Old Testament (Grand Rapids: Eerdmans, 2004), 317, 322. See also *ESV Study Bible*, 1143. The Fox quotes cited in Waltke are from Michael V. Fox, *Proverbs 1–9*, The Anchor Bible (New York: Yale University Press, 2000).

These are strong readings for strong words, but other passages in Song of Solomon also bear out the joy and excitement of married sexuality. Take Song of Solomon 6:5, for example, where the young bridegroom says to his wife, "Turn your eyes away from me, for they overwhelm me." Other modern English versions translate this final verb as "confuse," "disturb," "overcome," "dazzle," or "hold captive." Commentator Marvin Pope renders it "drives me wild," and Luther has "make me (sexually) ardent." G. Lloyd Carr says, "her glance 'turns him on' and makes him bold in his advances."[12] Carr also sees the idea of passionate arousal in Song of Solomon 4:9: "You have captivated my heart with one glance of your eyes." Both he and Pope cite the phrase "rising of the heart" from contemporary Mesopotamian literature, where it is used in a series of female "love incantations . . . intended to produce prolonged sexual excitement in the male, leading to extended intercourse."[13]

In the midst of all this excitement, I've saved for last a passage that is considerably more low-key, but absolutely crucial to understanding how the Bible approaches sex in the context of marriage. That would be 1 Corinthians 7:1-5, where Paul writes as follows to the church at Corinth:

> Now concerning the matters about which you wrote: "It is good for a man not to have sexual relations with a woman." But because of the temptation to sexual immorality, each man should have his own wife and each woman her own husband. The husband should give to his wife her conjugal rights, and likewise the wife to her husband. For the wife does not have authority over her own body, but the husband does. Likewise, the husband does not have authority over his own body, but the wife does. Do not deprive one another, except perhaps by agreement for a limited time, that you may devote yourselves to prayer; but then come together again, so that Satan may not tempt you because of your lack of self-control.

Once again, the passage offers polite idioms for coitus, prompting David E. Garland to observe that—as we have seen so often in this chapter— "Scripture does not use a verb that means 'to have sexual intercourse'

---

12. Marvin H. Pope, *Song of Songs: A New Translation with Introduction and Commentary*, The Anchor Bible 7C (Garden City, NY: Doubleday, 1977), 564; and Carr, *Song of Solomon*, 148. The quote from Luther is cited by Pope.

13. Pope, *Song of Songs*, 479–80. See also Carr, *Song of Solomon*, 120.

but employs euphemistic language instead."[14] He is referring principally to verse 1, where the actual Greek says, "It is good for a man not to touch a woman" (NASB), and to other terms later in the passage, such as "have" (see p. 43), "conjugal rights," and "come together."

You will notice too that the ESV puts quotation marks around the early sentence about not having sexual relations (v. 1). It is almost universally agreed that Paul is here quoting a slogan circulating in Corinth at that time, one about which the church there had apparently written to Paul for advice. In the first place, these words cannot possibly convey some frowningly negative attitude of Paul himself concerning sexuality, as that would contradict the tenor of the entire passage, which repeatedly exhorts husbands and wives to have sex. Furthermore, there is evidence of a movement against sexual activity at that time in the ancient world, one that may well have infiltrated the Corinthian church. Garland avers that "sexual asceticism was in the air during this period," quoting R. B. Hays's statement that "sexual abstinence was widely viewed as a means to personal wholeness and religious power."[15] In fact, "it is possible that some of the Corinthians thought it advisable for believers to have no sexual relations in marriage."[16] Gordon D. Fee suggests that if indeed Corinthian husbands were being deprived of their "conjugal rights," this might explain why some of them were going to prostitutes, as apparent from Paul's discussion of this problem in the preceding paragraph (1 Cor. 6:15–20).[17]

The main point here is that Paul flatly rejects any sort of false sexual asceticism in marriage. Although he later upholds the value of remaining celibate for the sake of God's kingdom (1 Cor. 7:32–38), he nevertheless classes both celibacy *and* marriage as "a gift from God" (v. 7). Furthermore, he does not even assume that the husband will show more interest in sex than the wife; on the contrary, verses 2, 3, 4, and 5 all contain grammatically equivalent commands to both spouses, with verse 3 putting the wife's "conjugal rights" first. "Paul

14. David E. Garland, *1 Corinthians*, Baker Exegetical Commentary on the New Testament (Grand Rapids: Baker, 2003), 254.

15. Ibid., 263.

16. Leon Morris, *The First Epistle of Paul to the Corinthians*, Tyndale New Testament Commentaries (Leicester, UK: Inter-Varsity, 1999), 102.

17. Gordon D. Fee, *The First Epistle to the Corinthians*, New International Commentary on the New Testament (Grand Rapids: Eerdmans, 1987), 271.

will have no truck with a view of marriage that leaves the sex act in the sole control of the male, nor with a view of marriage that sees sex as defiling."[18] Indeed, four times in this passage the apostle unequivocally commands husbands and wives to freely and regularly engage in sexual activity:

In verse 2, the phrase "should have his own wife" is "an imperative, a command, not a permission." In verse 3, the Greek verb "give"— sometimes translated "render" or "pay"—is in a tense that indicates "habitual duty," namely, that of meeting one another's "conjugal rights."[19] In verse 4, the phrase "have authority over" is the same Greek word Paul uses in 1 Cor. 6:12, where it is translated "enslaved." The word thus implies complete control over the spouse's body— "authority over something in such a way as to do with it as one sees fit." And finally, in verse 5, the Greek word translated "deprive" is the same one Paul uses in 1 Cor. 6:7–8, where he condemns the Corinthian believers for "defrauding" one another. Also translatable as "rob" or "steal," it is a "pejorative word for taking away what rightfully belongs to another."[20] Thus, in this verse, Paul "likens abandoning conjugal relations to reneging on a debt."[21]

In this key passage—Scripture's final word on married sexuality— the great apostle "affirms that marriage is to be a fully sexual relationship and does not hint that this state of affairs is unfortunate or regrettable. He does not lament the physical aspect of marriage but instead encourages it."[22] As such, the passage comports well with those above from Proverbs 5 and Song of Solomon, providing a healthy view of sex that is beautifully addressed in this passage from R. B. Laurin:

> It is a strange paradox that among those most vociferous about their belief in the Bible "from cover to cover" is often found an attitude that sex is "nasty." The Victorian embarrassment with sexual matters has not disappeared from the contemporary scene. The Bible should have given the lie to this kind of attitude. It is, to be sure, fully aware of lust and the misuse of sex; but at the same time it is forthright

18. Morris, *First Corinthians*, 103.
19. Ibid., 102–3.
20. Fee, *First Corinthians*, 281.
21. Garland, *1 Corinthians*, 260.
22. Ibid., 258.

in approving the wholesomeness of sex. The passionate, physical attraction between man and woman, who find in this the fulfillment of their deepest longings, is seen as a healthy, natural thing. . . . We are to remember that God established physical attraction between the sexes; this is not wrong. And in the marriage relationship, as the Song stresses, sex is to have its normal, healthy role in providing fulfillment and joy for both partners. It is not something to be shunned, but to be praised.[23]

23. R. B. Laurin, "The Song of Songs and Its Modern Message," *Christianity Today* 6 (1961–62): 1062, quoted in Pope, *Song of Songs*, 193–94.

7

"Your Lewd Whorings"

Adultery

CONCERNING ADULTERY, surely the Bible's best-known verse is also its earliest, occurring in the Ten Commandments: "You shall not commit adultery" (Ex. 20:14; see also Deut. 5:18).

Similar prohibitions include Leviticus 18:20, "You shall not lie sexually with your neighbor's wife," and 20:10, "If a man commits adultery with the wife of his neighbor, both the adulterer and the adulteress shall surely be put to death." Deuteronomy 22:22–27 repeats the latter injunction, also ordaining the death penalty in the case of an adulterous woman who was betrothed at the time—that is, if she was pledged to a type of premarital commitment "much more binding than modern engagement."[1] In keeping with these restrictions, Numbers 5:11–31 provides a test to be administered if a husband suspects his wife of marital unfaithfulness; if she is found guilty, she will become a barren outcast: "Her womb shall swell, and her thigh shall fall away, and the woman shall become a curse among her people" (Num. 5:27; "thigh" here probably refers to her reproductive organs—see p. 10).

The New Testament reaffirms this ban on extramarital sex when the seventh commandment is quoted verbatim by Jesus (Matt. 5:27; 19:18; see also Mark 10:19; Luke 18:20), by the apostle Paul (Rom. 13:9), and in the letter of James (2:11). And of course there are other verses along these

1. *ESV Study Bible* (Wheaton, IL: Crossway, 2008), 363.

lines, notably Hebrews 13:4: "Let the marriage bed be undefiled, for God will judge the sexually immoral and adulterous."

Jesus in fact clarifies the proscription against adultery by indicating that this sin also includes even unconsummated lust directed toward someone other than a spouse, as well as remarriage after divorce: "Everyone who looks at a woman with lustful intent has already committed adultery with her in his heart" (Matt. 5:28); and, "Everyone who divorces his wife, except on the ground of sexual immorality, makes her commit adultery, and whoever marries a divorced woman commits adultery" (Matt. 5:32; see also Matt. 19:9; Mark 10:11–12; Luke 16:18). Some first-century hearers may have felt that this approach to marital fidelity was much stricter than that found in the Old Testament laws; indeed, Christ's own disciples reacted to his teaching on divorce by exclaiming, "If such is the case of a man with his wife, it is better not to marry" (Matt. 19:10). Yet William Loader points out that the prohibition against lust was already present in the Decalogue, specifically in Exodus 20:17, which forbids coveting "your neighbor's wife,"[2] and Christ himself insisted that divorce was forbidden "from the beginning," specifically because in marriage the man and woman "become one flesh" (Matt. 19:4–5).

Surely the most famous Old Testament narrative showing the folly of adulterous sex involves King David's tryst with the wife of his loyal soldier Uriah, depicted in 2 Samuel. With the army off at war, David was on the roof one day and spied the lovely Bathsheba bathing nearby, "so David sent messengers and took her, and she came to him, and he lay with her. . . . And the woman conceived, and she sent and told David, 'I am pregnant'" (2 Sam. 11:2–5). The text adds that the woman's bath had been for the purpose of "purifying herself from her uncleanness" (v. 4), implying that she had just finished having her period and thus the child she now bore could not possibly have been sired by Uriah before he left; and of course, Uriah would almost certainly know this.

Walter Brueggemann observes that the narrator presents this episode very swiftly, indicting David's lascivious haste: "There is no adornment to the action. . . . There is no conversation. There is no hint of caring, of affection, of love—only lust. David does not call her by name, does not even speak to her. At the end of the encounter she is only 'the

2. William Loader, *Sexuality in the New Testament: Understanding the Key Texts* (Louisville, KY: Westminster John Knox, 2010), 67.

56

woman' (v. 5)."[3] As Peter J. Leithart points out, this crime was exacerbated by the fact that Bathsheba was probably a generation younger than the king, being "from David's own tribe, and the granddaughter of one of David's closest advisers (2 Sam. 15:12)"; thus, his deed appears as "the work of a dirty old man and leering voyeur, of a sexual predator whose lust was almost incestuous."[4]

To make matters worse, David tried to cover his sin by summoning Uriah back from the front and urging him to "go down to your house and wash your feet"—the final word being commonly associated with sexuality (see pp. 8–9). But Uriah, with the ark and his fellow soldiers in peril, refused "to lie with my wife," so David had him killed by surreptitiously ordering the unsuspecting husband to "the forefront of the hardest fighting" in an ensuing battle (2 Sam. 11:8–21). This double sin redounded to David's shame and disgrace when the king's own son, Absalom, later made a play for the throne and—perhaps on the very roof where David first spied Bathsheba—pitched a tent and then adulterously "went in to his father's concubines in the sight of all Israel" (2 Sam. 16:22).

Much more strident in their warnings against infidelity—and somewhat more graphic—are Proverbs 5 and 7, in which a solicitous father gives marital and sexual counsel to his son. In chapter 5, the youth is warned about the "forbidden woman" whose lips "drip honey" and whose "feet go down to death"; rather than "embrace the bosom of an adulteress," he is urged to "rejoice" in the wife of his youth: "Let her breasts fill you at all times with delight; be intoxicated always in her love" (Prov. 5:3–20).

Proverbs 7 takes these injunctions a step further by recounting a scenario in which a young man actually falls prey to a seductive woman: "Passing along the street near her corner," he finds an adulteress "dressed as a prostitute"; she "seizes him and kisses him," then urges him to accompany her home, using lavishly seductive imagery about what awaits him there: "I have spread my couch with coverings, colored linens from Egyptian linen; I have perfumed my bed with myrrh, aloes, and cinnamon. Come, let us take our fill of love till morning; let us delight ourselves with love. For my husband is not at home" (Prov. 7:6–19).

3. Walter Brueggemann, *First and Second Samuel: Interpretation* (Louisville, KY: John Knox Press, 1990), 273, quoted in Dale Ralph Davis, *2 Samuel: Out of Every Adversity*, Focus on the Bible (Fearn, UK: Christian Focus, 2002), 142.

4. Peter J. Leithart, *A Son to Me: An Exposition of 1 and 2 Samuel* (Moscow, ID: Canon, 2003), 217–18.

As Bruce K. Waltke puts it, having flattered the young man by insisting that she has been seeking him "eagerly" (Prov. 7:15), she now "further stimulates his sexual appetites by a sensual vision of the luxurious couch she prepared beforehand for the feast and lovemaking"—a vision heightened by the use of such then-common aphrodisiacs as myrrh, aloes, and cinnamon (see chap. 1). In verse 18, "let us take our fill" is literally "drink our fill," and Waltke links this passage with the idiom "to drink love," which is "probably related to the metaphors 'to drink water' for coitus and 'well water' for the vagina (see 5:15–18; 9:17)." (This idiom also shows up—though with a slightly different verb—in Song 5:1: "Eat, friends, drink, and be drunk with love!") And finally, says Waltke, the adulteress's phrase "till morning" shows that "she anticipates slowly passing the night while enjoying every form and delight of lovemaking."[5]

These warnings and injunctions take on a broader significance when we consider the vast number of Bible texts in which adultery serves as a metaphor highlighting the spiritual infidelities of God's people. There are dozens of such passages, including Judges 2:17, Isaiah 57:3–10, Matthew 12:39, and James 4:4, but most of them occur in Jeremiah, Ezekiel, and Hosea, with Jeremiah 13:27 serving as a typical example: "I have seen your abominations, your adulteries and neighings, your lewd whorings, on the hills in the field. Woe to you, O Jerusalem!"

Jeremiah 3:1–13 is worth quoting at length in this regard, as it clarifies the figurative use of God-as-covenant-husband, with his people as an unfaithful wife:

> If a man divorces his wife and she goes from him and becomes another man's wife, will he return to her? . . . You have played the whore with many lovers; and would you return to me? declares the LORD. . . . Where have you not been ravished? By the waysides you have sat awaiting lovers like an Arab in the wilderness. . . . "Have you seen what she did, that faithless one, Israel, how she went up on every high hill and under every green tree, and there played the whore? And I thought, 'After she has done all this she will return to me,' but she did not return, and her treacherous sister Judah saw it. She saw that for all the adulteries of that faithless one, Israel, I had sent her away with a decree of divorce. Yet her treacherous sister Judah did not fear, but she too went and played

5. Bruce K. Waltke, *The Book of Proverbs: Chapters 1–15*, New International Commentary on the Old Testament (Grand Rapids: Eerdmans, 2004), 378–80.

the whore . . . she polluted the land, committing adultery with stone and tree . . . you rebelled against the LORD your God and scattered your favors among foreigners under every green tree."

The stones, trees, and hills cited here refer to pagan shrines and idols, with the people of Israel and Judah bowing down to worship and serve such local gods as Asherah (2 Kings 17:16), Molech (2 Kings 23:10), and Baal-berith (Judg. 8:33). A particularly strong condemnation of such heathen worship is found in Jeremiah 2, where Israel, in her desire for these foreign deities, is compared to a wild donkey in heat, "sniffing the wind" in unrestrained lust: "None who seek her need weary themselves; in her month they will find her" (Jer. 2:24). J. A. Thompson tells us that "the female ass in heat is almost violent. She sniffs the path in front of her trying to pick up the scent of a male (from his urine). Then she races down the road in search of the male. One Arab proverb runs, 'She is intoxicated with the urine of the male.'"[6] Thus, the male donkeys need not seek her, for she, like God's people, is bent on "running to and fro in the dust looking feverishly for satisfaction from a mate."[7]

Jeremiah introduces Israel's behavior here by that saying she "bowed down like a whore" (Jer. 2:20), a word used often in these passages on the faithlessness of God's people (cf. "played the whore" in Jer. 3 above). This unpleasant English word translates the Hebrew *zanah*, which is not the standard Old Testament term for adultery (that would be *naaph*, discussed below). Yet *zanah* in its various forms is used almost exclusively in the three broadest treatments of Israel-as-adulteress—Hosea 1–3 and Ezekiel 16 and 23. So it might be helpful to examine this term more closely before proceeding to those key passages.

The English word used most often in these three texts is "whore," which can mean either "slut" (loose woman) or "prostitute" (one who takes money for sex); as such, it accurately reflects the meaning of *zanah*, a broad term that is used with considerable flexibility. Meaning "to commit fornication, be a harlot," *zanah* refers to an actual prostitute in such passages as Deuteronomy 23:18, Isaiah 23:17–18, and Micah 1:7, which all talk about a "fee" or "wages." Some passages use *zanah* in the context of

6. J. A. Thompson, *The Book of Jeremiah*, New International Commentary on the Old Testament (Grand Rapids: Eerdmans, 1980), 179.
7. R. K. Harrison, *Jeremiah and Lamentations: An Introduction and Commentary*, Tyndale Old Testament Commentaries (Leicester, UK: Inter-Varsity, 1973), 60.

literal adultery: in Judges 19:2, for example, a Levite's wife is said to have "played the harlot [*zanah*] against him" (NASB); and the term is also used for the adulteress in Proverbs 7:10 ("The woman meets him, dressed as a prostitute").

More often, *zanah* refers to "wanton sexual immorality."[8] In a few instances, this describes literal promiscuity, as in Deuteronomy 22:21, where a newlywed husband discovers that his young bride has already lost her virginity by "whoring in her father's house." However, in nearly every case where the word describes promiscuity—almost one hundred instances all told—*zanah* functions as it does in Jeremiah, Ezekiel, and Hosea: as a metaphor for spiritual adultery.

All of these passages emphasize the way Israel has broken the marriage covenant God made with her; yet the specific Hebrew word for adultery—*naaph*—does not occur nearly as often in these contexts as *zanah*, and indeed, it is used less frequently in Scripture as a whole.

In its literal sense of betraying an actual spouse, *naaph* appears in the commandments against this sin (Ex. 20:14; Lev. 20:10; Deut. 5:18) and a few other places (e.g., Job 24:15; Ps. 50:18; Prov. 30:20; Mal. 3:5). However, the word is also used for spiritual adultery in Jeremiah 3:8–9 (above) and in Ezekiel 23:37. In Jeremiah 5, it appears in close conjunction with *zanah*: "They committed adultery and trooped to the houses of whores" (Jer. 5:7). Most significantly, Hosea uses the two words as synonyms in the classic parallel structure so common in Old Testament writings: "Plead with your mother, . . . that she put away her whoring from her face, and her adultery from between her breasts. . . . Your daughters play the whore, and your brides commit adultery; I will not punish your daughters when they play the whore, nor your brides when they commit adultery" (Hos. 2:2; 4:13–14). It's clear from this passage that the "daughters" are whores and the "brides" adulteresses; nonetheless, "the words are sufficiently parallel . . . that they can be used for the same person," as they are in Hosea 3:1 ("adulteress") and 3:3 ("whore").[9] (See also Ezek. 16:32–36.)

In other words, the terms used to describe a slut, an adulteress, and a prostitute are somewhat interchangeable in Old Testament usage, a dynamic that aptly reflects the similar nature of these sins. As scholar

8. *ESV Study Bible*, 1520.

9. R. Laird Harris, Gleason L. Archer Jr., and Bruce K. Waltke, *Theological Wordbook of the Old Testament* (Chicago: Moody, 1980), 246.

Daniel I. Block asserts in his study of Ezekiel, "Apart from the marital covenant commitment, all sexual activity is prostitution."[10] In some ways, of course, all such illicit activity qualifies as adultery as well.

This linguistic study is necessary before proceeding to our next example of spiritual adultery—namely, that involving Gomer, wife of the Old Testament prophet Hosea. Because *zanah* is the primary word used for Gomer in that book, she has sometimes been viewed as a prostitute, and thus it may surprise some readers to find her here, rather than in the later chapter on prostitution; but as we shall see, the emphasis in Hosea is not on the woman's trade or profession, but rather on her profoundly symbolic sexual treachery toward her husband.

Of course, one might suggest that Hosea asked for it—but then, he was merely obeying a direct command from God, who told the prophet, "Go, take to yourself a wife of whoredom and have children of whoredom, for the land commits great whoredom by forsaking the Lord" (Hos. 1:2). Thus Hosea's troubled marriage was to serve as an object lesson to Israel, with Hosea—like God himself—pledged by covenant to a mate who either was promiscuous already, or who would one day surely be so. As for the order to have "children of whoredom," that was fulfilled in relatively short order.

Responding to God's mandate, Hosea "went and took Gomer, . . . and she conceived and bore him a son" (Hos. 1:3); so the first child was clearly Hosea's. However, when two more children arrive later, the prophet omits the pronoun "him," stating that "she conceived again and bore a daughter" (1:6) and "she conceived and bore a son" (1:8). In addition to the different wording, God commanded Hosea to name these two children *Lo-ruhama* and *Lo-ammi*—literally, "No Mercy" and "Not My People"—cementing the suggestion that Gomer had conceived them with someone other than her husband.

Apparently, Gomer then added insult to injury by leaving Hosea, perhaps returning to her father's house, as the Levite's concubine did after being unfaithful in Judges 19:1–3. More likely, she somehow got herself enslaved to another man, probably one of her lovers. In any case, the prophet later receives an additional command from the Lord and thereafter brings back—or redeems—his faithless wife: "And the LORD

10. Daniel I. Block, *The Book of Ezekiel: Chapters 1–24*, New International Commentary on the Old Testament (Grand Rapids: Eerdmans, 1997), 764.

said to me, 'Go again, love a woman who is loved by another man and is an adulteress. . . . ' So I bought her for fifteen shekels of silver and a homer and a lethech of barley. And I said to her, 'You must dwell as mine for many days. You shall not play the whore, or belong to another man'" (Hos. 3:1–3).

Most commentators agree that even if Gomer did sometimes engage in literal prostitution—perhaps to the point of permanently selling herself in the passage above—nonetheless, the emphasis in Hosea is on "a married woman being unfaithful to her husband,"[11] with the word "adulteress" in Hosea 3:1 being a participle that suggests "she became completely enslaved to licentious behavior."[12]

This sort of strong language has created difficulties for interpreters of Hosea, starting with the fact that Leviticus forbids priests to marry "a woman who has been defiled, or a prostitute" (Heb. *zanah*); rather, "he shall take as his wife a virgin of his own people, that he may not profane his offspring" (Lev. 21:14–15). Though Hosea was not actually a priest and therefore did not technically violate this regulation, nonetheless his marriage to a "wife of whoredom" has troubled readers so much that some attempt to give it a different slant using one of two arguments.

On one hand is the "merely symbolic" explanation, with writers such as John Calvin, C. F. Keil, and Edward J. Young asserting that Hosea's marriage is hypothetical, or allegorical, rather than actual; similarly, a few insist that "whoredom" does not refer to literal promiscuity but only to the wife's *spiritual* harlotry and wickedness. This latter spiritual reading of "whoredom," however, does not solve the problem of commanding a godly man to marry a profane woman; and as for the symbolic or allegorical interpretation espoused by Calvin and others, Michael P. V. Barrett observes that "there seems to be nothing in the text to suggest symbolic language."[13] On the contrary, Hosea uses particular and realistic details like Lo-ruhama's weaning (Hos. 1:8) and the specific amounts of silver and barley used to redeem Gomer (Hos. 3:2).

David Allan Hubbard agrees that Hosea's marriage is "literal, not allegorical," averring that "something of the poignancy, power and pathos

---

11. *ESV Study Bible*, 1623.

12. Michael P. V. Barrett, *Love Divine and Unfailing: The Gospel according to Hosea*, The Gospel according to the Old Testament (Phillipsburg, NJ: P&R Publishing, 2008), 81.

13. Ibid., 77.

is drained from the book, if we are not dealing with an actual story where a suffering prophet learns and teaches volumes about the pain of a God whose people have played false with him."[14] Thomas E. McComiskey adds that if Hosea did indeed marry a woman who was already a whore, and perhaps even serve as father to her illegitimate children, "it is one of the most remarkable depictions of grace in the Old Testament. Hosea sacrificed a normal married life to call Israel to recognize its sin."[15]

Somewhat more tenable than these allegorical readings is the so-called "proleptic," or *predictive*, approach, in which the phrase "wife of whoredom" is viewed as foretelling Gomer's future unfaithfulness rather than indicating that she was already a whore at the time Hosea married her. The *ESV Study Bible* sums up this theory nicely, stating that Hosea relates "the tragedy of a marriage that began well but went bad."[16] Hubbard is more specific: "When Gomer married Hosea she was an ordinary Israelite woman who later became an adulteress and a prostitute." In support of this view, Hubbard points out that in Hosea 1:2, "wife of whoredom" is predictive in the same way as "children of whoredom": both indicate future things that Hosea is going to have.[17] This argument is strengthened by the fact that the original Hebrew of 1:2 has only one verb to govern both of these phrases—literally, "take to yourself a wife of whoredom and children of whoredom." Furthermore, the Hebrew word for "wife" in 1:2 is the ordinary term for a married or betrothed woman.[18] Only later, when the infidelity has definitely occurred, is Hosea ordered to go and reestablish his relationship with this "adulteress" (Hos. 3:1).

McComiskey tells us that "the majority of commentators have espoused the proleptic view of Hosea's marriage"; but Barrett insists that "it does not do justice to the exact wording of Hosea 1:2." McComiskey agrees, asserting that the grammar used in 1:2 always describes a "present state": "To 'take a woman' is to marry. To 'take a woman of fornications' is to marry a promiscuous woman. . . . It is difficult to conceive of a more

---

14. David Allan Hubbard, *Hosea: An Introduction and Commentary*, Tyndale Old Testament Commentaries (Leicester, UK: Inter-Varsity, 1989), 52.

15. Thomas Edward McComiskey, *Hosea*, in *The Minor Prophets: An Exegetical and Expository Commentary*, vol. 1: *Hosea, Joel, and Amos*, ed. Thomas Edward McComiskey (Grand Rapids: Baker, 1992), 17.

16. *ESV Study Bible*, 1623.

17. Hubbard, *Hosea*, 54.

18. McComiskey, *Hosea*, 11.

succinct way to express legal marriage to a promiscuous woman than the words in this command."[19]

More broadly, we might ask what light is shed on this issue by the symbolic nature of Gomer's infidelity. Hosea 1:2 clearly indicates that her unfaithfulness, as so often in Scripture, serves as a metaphor for the adulterous practices of Israel. So: Was the nation of Israel already idolatrous when God committed himself to her, or did she begin in a state of "virginal" innocence? The book of Hosea itself sometimes hints at original purity, where God recalls good relations with Israel "in the days of her youth, . . . when she came out of the land of Egypt" (Hos. 2:15), and where Israel declares, "I will go and return to my first husband, for it was better for me then than now" (Hos. 2:7). And the lengthy wife-turned-adulteress passage in Ezekiel 16 (discussed below) starts out with God's people in a state of youthful spotlessness—washed, anointed, decked out with lovely garments and jewels, "perfect through the splendor that I had bestowed on you" (Ezek. 16:8–14).

Yet McComiskey points out that when God called Israel out of Egypt and set her up as a nation with its own laws and regulations, the first two commandments she received both suggest some experience with idolatry that the people were now to forsake, having "no other gods" and not worshiping any "carved image" (Ex. 20:3–4). These extant pagan propensities manifested themselves even before the finalized law could be delivered, when Israel made and worshiped a golden calf just a few chapters later (Ex. 32:1–6). "These two traditions [the law and the calf] support the surprising fact that when Yahweh entered into a relationship with his people at Sinai, he married a people already tainted with idolatry; they were guilty of spiritual fornication."[20]

The idea that God pledges himself to people already corrupt and depraved comports well with the many New Testament passages about salvation of sinners, such as Romans 5:8 ("While we were still sinners, Christ died for us") and Colossians 1:21 ("And you, who once were alienated and hostile in mind, doing evil deeds, he has now reconciled"). Accordingly, it seems probable that Gomer, like God's people, was already adulterous when Hosea claimed her and that this adultery was literal, not merely figurative or metaphorical.

---

19. McComiskey, *Hosea*, 11–13; Barrett, *Love Divine and Unfailing*, 79.
20. McComiskey, *Hosea*, 14.

Yet even if we view God's command to Hosea as merely predictive, this does not really eliminate the moral difficulties of the passage. Barrett tells us that the phrase "of whoredom" in Hosea 1:2 implies a "latent bent toward immorality" and that even if she was at first innocent of sexual misconduct, nonetheless "Hosea knew both what she was capable of doing and what she would most likely do."[21] How much more acceptable is it to marry a woman who is guaranteed to commit adultery than to marry one who already has? And even if it is somewhat more acceptable, and we thus manage to "tone down" the moral outrage of Hosea 1:2, doesn't this problem simply reassert itself in 3:1–3, when Hosea is commanded to marry a woman who has already been "loved by another man and is an adulteress"?

As in the case of prophets being commanded to go naked (see pp. 29–30), when it comes to saving his people from idolatry and destruction, God is apparently willing to employ not only strong language, but strong public actions as well.

As we have already seen, by far the longest and most graphic treatment of Israel's "whoredom" occurs in Ezekiel 16 and 23. In these two passages, the conduct of two sister-nations—Judah in the south (represented by her capital, Jerusalem) and Samaria in the north—is repeatedly and emphatically likened to that of a whore, prostitute, and adulteress. In chapter 16, which specifically addresses Jerusalem, this sluttish behavior is exacerbated by the way her divine husband cared for the nation from her youth: On the day she was born, when the Lord saw her wallowing in blood with no one to care for her, he took her up, saying "Live!"; and with his loving provision, she grew into a young woman who had reached "the age for love, and I spread the corner of my garment over you and covered your nakedness; I made my vow to you and entered into a covenant with you, declares the Lord GOD, and you became mine" (Ezek. 16:1–8). Yet in spite of the way he adorned her with fine linen and silk and jewelry, in spite of his providing her with "fine flour and honey and oil," in spite of the fact that her beauty "was perfect through the splendor that I had bestowed on you," nonetheless, God tells her, "You trusted in your beauty and played the whore because of your renown. . . . At the head of every street you built your lofty place and made your beauty an abomination, offering yourself to any passerby and multiplying your

21. Barrett, *Love Divine and Unfailing*, 80.

65

whoring" (Ezek. 16:13–25). The ESV is a bit too diplomatic with the phrase "offering yourself," which in Hebrew is literally "spreading your legs" (as in the NASB). Worse yet, Israel made unwise political and spiritual alliances with pagan nations: "You also played the whore with the Egyptians, your lustful neighbors, multiplying your whoring. . . . You played the whore also with the Assyrians, because you were not satisfied; yes, you played the whore with them, and still you were not satisfied. You multiplied your whoring also with the trading land of Chaldea, and even with this you were not satisfied" (Ezek. 16:26–29).

In chapter 23, Ezekiel's attack is broadened to include both sister-states, who are given the names Oholah (Samaria) and Oholibah (Jerusalem): "Oholah played the whore while she was mine, and she lusted after her lovers. . . . She bestowed her whoring upon them, the choicest men of Assyria all of them, and she defiled herself with all the idols of everyone after whom she lusted. She did not give up her whoring that she had begun in Egypt; for in her youth men had lain with her and handled her virgin bosom and poured out their whoring lust upon her" (Ezek. 23:5–8).

As for Oholibah, God declares that

> the Babylonians came to her into the bed of love, and they defiled her with their whoring lust. And after she was defiled by them, she turned from them in disgust. When she carried on her whoring so openly and flaunted her nakedness, I turned in disgust from her, as I had turned in disgust from her sister. Yet she increased her whoring, . . . and lusted after her paramours there, whose members were like those of donkeys, and whose issue was like that of horses. Thus you longed for the lewdness of your youth, when the Egyptians handled your bosom and pressed your young breasts. (Ezek. 23:17–21)

As the ESV footnotes indicate, "breasts" in this passage can be rendered "nipples"; and as we saw in chapter 2, the final description of the "paramours" above seems to refer specifically to the large penises and copious seminal emissions of these lovers (see pp. 12–13). Thus, "in her lust, she was not even limited by natural relationships; instead, she sought those whose sexual capacities were not merely superhuman but positively bestial."[22]

22. Iain M. Duguid, *Ezekiel*, The NIV Application Commentary (Grand Rapids: Zondervan, 1999), 304.

Several commentators have remarked on the shocking nature of Ezekiel 16 and 23. Daniel I. Block notes, "The obscenity of the description accords with the unrestrained prurience of Oholibah's actions"; the prophet employs "an intentional rhetorical strategy, designed not only to shock the audience but also to reflect Yahweh's disgust with Oholibah's behavior."[23] John B. Taylor says that modern-day Christian readers may "feel nauseated at the indelicate realism of Ezekiel's language, but Ezekiel meant it that way. He was telling of ugly sins and he made the parable fit the facts." Indeed, the passages feature "repulsive detail" and "the crudest of terms," together with "language of unspeakable disgust"; yet in these expressions we should see "Ezekiel's passion for God's honour and his fury at the adulterous conduct of his covenant people. The feeling of nausea which a chapter like this arouses must be blamed not on the writer ... but on the conduct which had to be described in such revolting terms."[24] And Iain M. Duguid comments that in chapter 16, Jerusalem is "a thoroughly depraved and degraded prostitute" whose description is "beyond the reaches of even the most fevered imagination of the tabloid press." Indeed, the "shockingly explicit language" throughout these passages produces "an 'in-your-face' effect, whose emotional impact is far greater than a similar indictment in dry legal terminology."[25]

As we noted in the introduction to this volume, the nineteenth-century preacher C. H. Spurgeon said of this description, "A minister can scarcely read it in public." Yet Duguid wonders "if contemporary Christians need to be as shielded from unpleasant realities as we tend to think":

> Is it possible to teach this passage "with decorum" and not lose an essential element of its meaning? There are no new *facts* here about Israel's history, and if we read it simply as a historical catalog of crime like 2 Kings 17, we lose all that this passage *distinctively* contributes to the message of Scripture. The whole point is the lack of decorum in Ezekiel's manner. He will not "be polite" about Israel's history of sin; instead, he is instructed to expose it in its full ugliness in the most graphic manner possible. Only thus can he get his point across.[26]

23. Block, *Ezekiel 1–24*, 746–47.

24. John B. Taylor, *Ezekiel: An Introduction and Commentary*, Tyndale Old Testament Commentaries (Leicester, UK: Inter-Varsity, 1969), 133, 170–71.

25. Duguid, *Ezekiel*, 212, 301.

26. Ibid., 215–16.

8

"The Wages of a Dog"

Prostitution

ANCIENT HEBREW has two words for "prostitute." One of them, *qadesh*, nearly always refers specifically to a cult prostitute serving in or near a pagan shrine—a fairly common usage that we shall examine later in this chapter. We'll begin our study here with uses of the other word—*zanah*. As we saw in the previous chapter, this term can describe a variety of sexual sins, including adultery and promiscuity (see pp. 59–61); but in a few cases, the context for *zanah* suggests literal prostitution—that is, providing sexual services in exchange for money.

As has been the case with so much of the other sexuality we've discussed, the actual mechanics of prostitution are not described with much detail by the writers of Scripture; instead, a few key characters are simply identified as such, including two women in 1 Kings 3 who came to King Solomon to determine the ownership of a disputed baby.

Apparently each of these prostitutes had an infant, and one of them accidentally lay on hers and smothered it while sleeping—after which she surreptitiously took the other woman's baby and claimed it as her own. Solomon proposed a clever solution to their dispute over whose baby the remaining child really was: he threatened to split the child in two and give half to each woman, an idea that pleased one woman and terrified the other, thereby identifying the true parent (1 Kings 3:16–28). Though it doesn't tell us too much about prostitution itself, this fascinating story does at least remind us that pregnancy and the trials of single parenthood were occupational hazards in what has been called "the oldest profession."

Other instances in the Old Testament: Joel's condemnation of those who "have traded a boy for a prostitute" (Joel 3:3); the woman of Gaza whom Samson visited in Judges 16:1; the prostitutes who bathed where the blood of King Ahab was washed out of his chariot (1 Kings 22:38); and Tamar, whose appearance in Genesis 38 marks the Bible's first use of *zanah*.

As we shall see when we examine the early part of this incident (see chap. 18 below), Tamar's tale involves unjust treatment at the hands of her father-in-law, Judah, who promised to wed her to his third son after the deaths of her first two husbands (both also Judah's sons). When this promise went unfulfilled, Tamar, learning that her father-in-law was visiting his sheep shearers, "covered herself with a veil" and sat beside the road—and "when Judah saw her, he thought she was a prostitute" (Gen. 38:14–15). This was a fair assumption on his part, since the veil was standard professional apparel for these women, providing protective anonymity; and furthermore, prostitutes did sometimes solicit business among shepherds. (This is probably the sense in Song of Solomon 1:7, where the young woman insists on knowing exactly where her lover pastures his flocks, lest she be mistaken for a harlot seeking business among shepherds—that is, "one who veils herself beside the flocks of your companions.")[1]

At any rate, when Judah decided to patronize Tamar, we do get a glimpse of the monetary exchange associated with harlotry in ancient times:

> He turned to her at the roadside and said, "Come, let me come in to you," for he did not know that she was his daughter-in-law. She said, "What will you give me, that you may come in to me?" He answered, "I will send you a young goat from the flock." And she said, "If you give me a pledge, until you send it—" He said, "What pledge shall I give you?" She replied, "Your signet and your cord and your staff that is in your hand." So he gave them to her and went in to her, and she conceived by him. (Gen. 38:16–18)

1. Iain Provan, *Ecclesiastes, Song of Songs*, The NIV Application Commentary (Grand Rapids: Zondervan, 2001), 268–69; see also G. Lloyd Carr, *The Song of Solomon: An Introduction and Commentary*, Tyndale Old Testament Commentaries (Leicester, UK: Inter-Varsity, 1984), 80.

Later, Judah learned that his daughter-in-law was pregnant; still unaware of his own role in the matter, he declared, "Bring her out, and let her be burned." Tamar then produced the cord, staff, and signet (the latter would have clearly identified its owner), saying, "By the man to whom these belong, I am pregnant" (vv. 24–25). After Judah admitted his sins of sexual immorality and breach of promise ("She is more righteous than I," v. 26), Tamar gave birth to twins named Zerah and Perez, the latter earning her a spot in Christ's genealogy: "Judah the father of Perez and Zerah by Tamar" (Matt. 1:3).

Surprisingly, Tamar is not the only woman of this sort found in Matthew's account of the Messianic bloodline. The adulterous Bathsheba is there, too (Matt. 1:6), as is Rahab, a prostitute in the ancient city of Jericho. Probably the best-known Old Testament whore, Rahab sheltered two spies sent out in advance of the invading Israelite army, was spared when the city fell, and eventually joined the community of God's people (Josh. 2:1–21; 6:25). Despite her questionable occupation—once again, described with the word *zanah*—Rahab is extolled by several New Testament writers: she appears on the list of Old Testament heroes in Hebrews 11 (v. 31), and the first-century church leader James praises her as an example of good works demonstrating valid faith (James 2:25); Rahab is also found in the genealogy of Jesus Christ, being the mother of Boaz and thus the great-great-grandmother of King David (Matt. 1:5).

When Rahab is mentioned in Hebrews and James, the writers call her "Rahab the prostitute," using the Greek word *porne*, discussed at length in chapter 5 (see pp. 35–36). Though the *porne* word group covers many sexual sins, James and Hebrews demonstrate that it is the New Testament term for "prostitute," clarifying such other instances as Luke 15:30, in which the prodigal son is said to have wasted his inheritance on prostitutes, and Matthew 21:31–32, which makes it clear that Jesus Christ had great appeal for such social outcasts as "the tax-collectors and the prostitutes."

The two principal New Testament references to prostitution are similarly straightforward. In 1 Corinthians 6, the apostle Paul responds in no uncertain terms to men at Corinth who appear to have been arguing for the right to visit prostitutes, based on the widespread heresy that what one did with one's physical body was not important. Paul disagrees vehemently: "Do you not know that your bodies are members of Christ?

Shall I then take the members of Christ and make them members of a prostitute? Never! Or do you not know that he who is joined to a prostitute becomes one body with her? . . . Flee from sexual immorality" (1 Cor. 6:15–18).

The final chapters of Revelation take up the concept of prostitution as a metaphor for slavish devotion to pagan immorality, contrasted with service to the one true God. In chapters 17 and 19, the figurative nation of Babylon, representing earthly kingdoms opposed to God's rule, is called "the great prostitute" and the "mother of prostitutes," a seductress with whom "the kings of the earth have committed sexual immorality" (Rev. 17:1–5).

This, of course, is an idea we have seen before, specifically, in chapter 7 above, where the word *zanah*, or "whore," was often seen to describe Israel's spiritual infidelity to her covenant husband, Yahweh. In that chapter, I argued that most *zanah* passages—despite the fact that the word can mean "prostitute"—have this underlying sense of metaphorical faithlessness, and that the term can serve as a synonym for adultery. Nevertheless, several instances of this spiritual adultery—including a few that use *zanah*—link Israel's whorish behavior to the notion of sex for money, and thus they merit discussion in this chapter as well.

Leviticus 19 is a case where literal and metaphorical prostitution seem joined in one prohibition: "Do not profane your daughter by making her a prostitute, lest the land fall into prostitution and the land become full of depravity" (Lev. 19:29). On the surface, the first clause forbids hiring a woman out for sex; yet the rest of the sentence portrays whoredom of a general kind—adulterous betrayal by the whole nation. This idea of a more widespread, spiritual unfaithfulness is supported by the context, with this verse surrounded by laws against fortune-telling, tattoos, body piercing, necromancy, and eating flesh with blood—all practices common among the pagan nations around Israel at that time.

Ezekiel 16 was covered earlier under "adultery" because its parable of a sluttish woman is used to depict Israel's covenant faithlessness. Yet this passage does sometimes play on literal prostitution as well. For example, Ezekiel 16:16 excoriates the woman because "you took some of your garments and made for yourself colorful shrines, and on them played the whore." Commentator Daniel I. Block posits that "shrines" may refer to "raised pedestals on which prostitutes performed their services," with colorful clothing draped over the platform to attract passersby and provide a covering for their "bed of love."[2]

Block asserts that Ezekiel 16 uses *zanah* ("whore") rather than *naaph* ("adultery") in order to link Israel's conduct with that of a professional whore through the multiplicity of partners and the habitual, recurring nature of the sin; Ezekiel also uses "whore," says Block, to suggest that Israel is even worse than a common prostitute because she refused payment! Verses 32–34, for instance, indict God's people as follows: "Adulterous wife, who receives strangers instead of her husband! Men give gifts to all prostitutes, but you gave your gifts to all your lovers, bribing them to come to you from every side with your whorings. . . . No one solicited you to play the whore, and you gave payment, while no payment was given to you; therefore you were different." Block explains: "Whereas prostitutes generally follow their professions as a means of livelihood, Jerusalem has scorned the payment for a woman's sexual favors. Worse yet, she has bribed them to satisfy her lusts, . . . inverting the normal roles of prostitute and client."[3] (See Hos. 8:9 for a similar condemnation.)

Block adds that the use of *zanah* does nonetheless highlight the way these adulterers are driven by a sense of personal gain, rather than a mere desire for casual sex: the prostitution metaphor, he says, is very appropriate because the local pagan deities pursued by Israel are "lusty young fertility gods" whose worship practices "offered exciting and often erotic cult rituals"[4]—a payment that was, to their corrupt hearts, perhaps even more desirable than cash.

As it happens, these heathen rituals often involved sacred prostitution, which is usually indicated in Scripture not with *zanah* but with *qadesh*, a technical term occurring in about a dozen Old Testament passages.

Traditional secular prostitution of the kind described above is condemned not only in Leviticus 19:29 ("Do not profane your daughter by making her a prostitute"), but also by the ritual laws declaring unclean anyone who had recently participated in sexual intercourse (Lev. 15:18); this mandate placed prostitutes in a "continuous state of

2. Daniel I. Block, *The Book of Ezekiel: Chapters 1–24*, New International Commentary on the Old Testament (Grand Rapids: Eerdmans, 1997), 488.
3. Ibid., 128, 497.
4. Ibid., 129.

ceremonial uncleanness" and effectively excluded them from public life and worship.[5]

However, the sacred prostitution indicated by *qadesh* seems to have created far greater problems throughout Israel's history despite the regulation against it in Deuteronomy: "None of the daughters of Israel shall be a cult prostitute, and none of the sons of Israel shall be a cult prostitute. You shall not bring the fee of a prostitute or the wages of a dog into the house of the LORD your God in payment for any vow, for both of these are an abomination to the LORD your God" (Deut. 23:17–18).

The purpose of this ordinance was to prevent Israel from imitating or importing the practices of nearby pagan cultures—particularly the Canaanites—which often involved sexual activity as part of religious worship. This was, quite literally, ritual intercourse founded on the idea that the forces of nature could be "revived through the union of a god and goddess"; such a union, "insuring the fertility of the crops and of the wombs," was thought to be achieved by "sympathetic magic" involving actual sex with a cult prostitute.[6] In other words, worshipers at pagan shrines would make offerings and then copulate with temple prostitutes in a rite that supposedly encouraged or stimulated fertility gods to make the land fruitful. As part of the package, same-sex prostitutes were provided for homosexual devotees.[7] "The cult prostitute's wages were analogous to a bride-price and provided the chief source of revenue for the shrines."[8] Thus, the Deuteronomy passage above is designed to keep such abhorrent activities—and such fees—out of Israel's religious practices.

But like so many other laws laid down in the Old Testament, this regulation did little to prevent pagan sex rites. We later find "male cult prostitutes in the land" in the days of King Rehoboam (1 Kings 14:24), and these repeatedly had to be "put away" or "exterminated" by such later kings as Asa (1 Kings 15:12), Jehoshaphat (1 Kings 22:46), and, most notably, Josiah (2 Kings 23:7). Ongoing struggles with this particular sin are also clear in Micah 1:7, which condemns making idols "from the fee of a prostitute." And in the words of David Allan Hubbard, Hosea 4:14

5. R. K. Harrison, *Leviticus: An Introduction and Commentary*, Tyndale Old Testament Commentaries (Leicester, UK: Inter-Varsity, 1980), 166.

6. Bruce K. Waltke, *A Commentary on Micah* (Grand Rapids: Eerdmans, 2007), 59–60.

7. Douglas Stuart, *Hosea–Jonah*, Word Biblical Commentary, vol. 31 (Waco, TX: Word, 1987), 83.

8. Waltke, *Micah*, 59.

shows us "the male members of the priestly clan" slipping away from the throngs and into "the shady glades where copulation with harlots and carousing with temple prostitutes seem a part of the prosperity of God's gifts to them."[9] These practices may have begun to infiltrate God's chosen people as early as Genesis, since the word *qadesh* makes its first appearance in the story of Judah and Tamar, when Judah's friend Hirah assumes that Tamar was a cult prostitute soliciting business among the shepherds (Gen. 38:21).

Scripture itself is virtually silent on the actual nature of these activities, and thus nearly all the information above comes from historical and archeological sources; nonetheless, Beatrice Brooks has compiled a variety of Bible passages by which she not only demonstrates several characteristics of these women, but also—by citing numerous Bible books—shows how widespread the problem was: "They arrayed themselves elaborately and flashily with scarlet garments and much jewelry and cosmetics (Jer 4:30; Ezek 23:40). . . . Possibly they sang to attract attention (Isa 23:16), and had a special mark on the forehead (Jer 3:3). . . . They were found by the wayside (Tamar, Ezek 16:25 and Prov 7:12), 'on every high hill and under every green tree' (Jer 2:20), by the shrines (Ezek 16:23), and at the threshing floor (Hos 9:1)."[10]

So the problem persisted, and even flourished, despite specific laws against it; that is also the case with some of the more flagrant sins discussed in our next chapter.

9. David Allan Hubbard, *Hosea: An Introduction and Commentary*, Tyndale Old Testament Commentaries (Leicester, UK: Inter-Varsity, 1989), 106.

10. Beatrice Brooks, "Fertility Cult Functionaries in the Old Testament," *Journal of Biblical Literature* 60 (1941): 227–53, quoted in Waltke, *Micah*, 60.

9

"You Shall Not"

Bestiality, Voyeurism, Incest, and Homosexuality

ACCORDING TO *WIKIPEDIA*, bestiality—or sex with animals (also known as zoophilia)—is not explicitly condoned by any society; in most countries it is illegal, falling under animal abuse laws or "crimes against nature."[1] So we should not be surprised to find it bluntly condemned in Scripture: "Cursed be anyone who lies with any kind of animal" (Deut. 27:21). Also: "You shall not lie with any animal and so make yourself unclean with it, neither shall any woman give herself to an animal to lie with it: it is perversion" (Lev. 18:23). In Exodus, zoophilia is listed as a capital crime: "Whoever lies with an animal shall be put to death" (Ex. 22:19); Leviticus broadens this by stipulating the death of the animal as well (Lev. 20:15–16).

Commentator R. K. Harrison points out that bestiality was occasionally practiced by some of the ancient peoples surrounding Israel—including Babylon, Egypt, and Canaan—and that the Bible's prohibitions refer to "actual coition with animals, and not merely their manual stimulation" (the latter may occasionally have been used legitimately in conjunction with agricultural breeding practices). As such, these pronouncements against bestiality comprise "the most specific statements of their kind in the whole of ancient near Eastern legal literature."[2]

1. "Zoophilia," *Wikipedia*, accessed September 25, 2012, http://en.wikipedia.org/wiki/Bestiality.
2. R. K. Harrison, *Leviticus: An Introduction and Commentary*, Tyndale Old Testament Commentaries (Leicester, UK: Inter-Varsity, 1980), 193.

Instances of this shocking depravity "were not too bad to be anticipated by the Lord, who knew the heart."[3] Nevertheless, Scripture contains no narrative account of this sin occurring in either Israel or the New Testament church.

Voyeurism, by contrast, is not specifically forbidden in the Old Testament, though it is implied in the proscription against coveting a neighbor's wife (Ex. 20:17). In the New Testament, Jesus' condemnation of looking "with lustful intent" points right to this sin (Matt. 5:28), which *Merriam-Webster's* defines as "obtaining sexual gratification from observing unsuspecting individuals who are partly undressed, naked or engaged in sexual acts."[4] Though the individuals in pornography could hardly be described as "unsuspecting," nonetheless Christ's injunction clearly prohibits the use of pornography, which is not otherwise mentioned in Scripture.

Likewise, Jesus' insistence that lustful looks are tantamount to physical adultery posits a link between voyeurism and actual sex, as though the former can sometimes lead to the latter; this is certainly the case in the Old Testament story of King David, who wound up committing both adultery and murder after observing an "unsuspecting" neighbor at her bath (2 Kings 11; see chap. 7 above).

This link between looking and doing could also be a factor in Scripture's clearest case of voyeurism—Genesis 9, which concerns Noah and his family after the great flood. Having planted a vineyard, Noah harvested grapes, made wine, and then drank too much, after which he fell asleep with no clothes on—that is, he "lay uncovered in his tent." Ham, one of Noah's sons, "saw the nakedness of his father and told his two brothers outside," but instead of joining in their sibling's dishonorable conduct, the other sons "took a garment, laid it on both their shoulders, and walked backward and covered the nakedness of their father. Their faces were turned backward, and they did not see their father's nakedness." When Noah later awoke and "knew what his youngest son had done to him," he cursed Ham's descendants with eternal servitude (Gen. 9:20–25).

As Gordon J. Wenham observes, "Westerners who are strangers to a world where discretion and filial loyalty are supreme virtues have

---

3. Andrew A. Bonar, *A Commentary on Leviticus* (Edinburgh: Banner of Truth, 1989), 337.
4. *Merriam-Webster's Collegiate Dictionary*, 11th ed. (Springfield, MA: Merriam-Webster, 2004).

often felt that there must be something more to Ham's offense than appears on the surface."[5] It is not, however, mere cultural distance, but rather principally the passage's language that leads to speculation about whether Ham committed some other offense besides voyeurism.

One indicator is the verb phrase about what Ham had "done to" Noah, which seems to imply something more active than mere looking. More to the point, the text refers to "seeing someone's nakedness," an idiom used to describe incestuous sex in Leviticus 20:17. There, it appears in parallel structure with "uncover nakedness," yet another common Hebrew sex idiom that makes its way into this passage (vv. 21 and 23; see pp. 45–46 for a discussion of this expression). "Very possibly," writes O. Palmer Robertson, "Ham committed a homosexual act with his father, evoking his father's curse. The depravity of Ham's action would explain the severity of the curse," which seems disproportionate to a possibly inadvertent act of voyeurism.[6]

In a careful study of this passage originally published in the *Journal of Biblical Literature*, John Bergsma and Scott Hahn also point out its similarity to Genesis 19:31–35, an incident that unequivocally involves parental incest—in that case, between Lot and his two daughters (see below). Not only do both episodes feature a father drunk on wine, but each also follows a catastrophic judgment (the flood in Gen. 6–8, the destruction of Sodom and Gomorrah in Gen. 19); and each is tied to a race of future enemies of Israel: Ham's son Canaan is cursed to servitude (Gen. 9:25), and Lot's incest produces the well-known oppressors of Israel—Moab and Ammon (19:37–38).[7]

However, while explaining why many readers see homosexual incest in Genesis 9, Bergsma and Hahn nonetheless conclude with a lengthy argument for *maternal* incest in this passage. In other words, Ham had sex with Noah's wife. Their surprising case rests on several factors, perhaps the chief being that numerous Old Testament laws use the phrase "uncover your father's nakedness" to describe intercourse

5. Gordon J. Wenham, *Genesis 16–50*, Word Biblical Commentary, vol. 2 (Dallas: Word, 1994), 200.

6. O. Palmer Robertson, *The Genesis of Sex: Sexual Relationships in the First Book of the Bible* (Phillipsburg, NJ: P&R Publishing, 2002), 121.

7. John Sietze Bergsma and Scott Walker Hahn, "Noah's Nakedness and Curse on Canaan (Genesis 9:20–27)," 2005, Chronicles of the Nephilim: Links, *Godawa.com*, http://www.godawa .com/chronicles_of_the_nephilim/Articles_By_Others/Bergsma- Noahs_Nakedness_And _Curse_On_Canaan.pdf?.pdf, 5.

with a "father's wife." Leviticus 18:8, for example, states, "You shall not uncover the nakedness of your father's wife; it is your father's nakedness" (see also Lev. 18:16; 20:11; 20:21; Deut. 22:30; 27:20). Bergsma and Hahn point out further that the phrase "uncover nakedness" always describes heterosexual encounters, whereas laws on homosexuality exclusively use "lie with" (Lev. 18:22; 20:13).[8]

The maternal-incest interpretation, they argue, would explain why the passage repeats the phrase "Ham, the father of Canaan"; specifically, Canaan must have been the product of this incestuous match, which would likewise explain why he and his descendants were cursed. Bergsma and Hahn even offer a rationale for Ham's act. Whereas it is hard to conceive of a reason for homosexual incest, having sex with a father's wife is well attested as a power play in ancient literature and even in the Bible itself. For instance, Absalom had public intercourse with the concubines of his father, David, whom he was seeking to unseat (2 Sam. 16:20–22; see also Gen. 35:22; 49:3–4; 1 Kings 2:13–25; 2 Sam. 12:8).[9]

As careful as these arguments are, however, theories of incestuous sex collapse under several weighty considerations. First, the act of Ham's brothers in covering up their father clearly indicates that Noah's nakedness was literal, and not a figurative or idiomatic expression for indecent sexual activity.[10] Second, if some sort of scandalous sex is involved here, why doesn't the narrator just say so? He has no qualms about mentioning the incest of Lot (Gen. 19:31–35) and of Jacob's son Reuben (Gen. 35:22), nor about discussing various other frankly sexual encounters, such as Judah having intercourse with his daughter-in-law (Gen. 38:12–19) and Onan wasting "his semen on the ground" (Gen. 38:9). Additionally, if Canaan was the product of an incestuous union between Ham and his mother, then how and why did Noah curse him immediately after the act? As the passage tells us, "When Noah awoke from his wine and knew what his youngest son had done to him, he said, 'Cursed be Canaan...'" (vv. 24–25). Needless to say, this seems unlikely nine months before Canaan's birth.[11]

Commentators Bruce K. Waltke and Cathi J. Fredricks are among many writers who reject an overly sexualized reading of the encounter

8. Ibid., 7.
9. Ibid., 8–10.
10. Ibid., 6.
11. Ibid., 10.

between Ham and Noah. Finding sufficient sin in the distasteful act of parental voyeurism, they write that the Hebrew used in that verse "means 'to look at (searchingly)' (Songs 1:6; 6:11b), not a harmless or accidental seeing. Rabbinical sources think either that he castrated his father or that he committed sodomy. However, they are guilty of adding to the text.... Probably just Ham's 'prurient voyeurism' is meant. . . . His voyeurism, however, is of the worse sort. Voyeurism in general violates another's dignity and robs that one of his or her instinctive desire for privacy. . . . It is a form of domination."[12] And a particularly vile type of domination at that, since this voyeurism is also both incestuous and homosexual.

Speaking of incest, here is another crime that, like bestiality, is "one of the most common of all cultural taboos."[13] The Old Testament is extraordinarily specific in its regulations on this topic and fairly broad in terms of which family relationships are prohibited: Leviticus 18 introduces a lengthy section on incest by insisting, "None of you shall approach any one of his close relatives to uncover nakedness"; the chapter then proceeds to forbid sex with one's father, mother, stepmother, sister, half sister, stepsister, granddaughter, aunt, uncle, uncle's wife, daughter-in-law, and sister-in-law—also enjoining relations with a woman and her daughter, and with a woman and one of her grandchildren (Lev. 18:6–18; see also Deut. 27:20–23). Leviticus 20 repeats many of these ordinances, with specific punishments in several cases: banishment for sex with a sister or half sister, childlessness in the case of an aunt or sister-in-law, and the death penalty for relations with a father's wife, a daughter-in-law, or with both a woman and her daughter (Lev. 20:11–21).

R. K. Harrison makes several helpful observations on these passages. First, their specific and explicit nature "reflects the unselfconscious attitude of the Hebrews, and indeed of all ancient near Eastern peoples, towards sexual activity"; along the same lines, these clear guidelines are vital if illicit sex is to be prevented "in a nomadic society where family members are necessarily in close contact on regular occasions." Furthermore, despite the great number of unions condemned here, these are nonetheless only representative cases and "do not exhibit all the possible illicit combinations." (Indeed, all such cases—including direct

12. Bruce K. Waltke and Cathi J. Fredricks, *Genesis: A Commentary* (Grand Rapids: Zondervan, 2001), 149.

13. "Incest," *Wikipedia*, accessed September 25, 2012, http://en.wikipedia.org/wiki/Incest.

father-daughter incest, which is not specifically named in these texts—
are covered by the term "close relatives" in Lev. 18:6.) And finally, "Laws
relating to incest are found in various forms of human society, but those
contained in this chapter [Lev. 18] are by far the most detailed written
material of their kind."[14]

Such regulations, coming just after Israel's exodus from Egypt, may
have been necessitated partly by the number of incestuous relationships
that had already made an appearance in the lives of God's people before
the days of Moses. In ancient times, for instance, Abraham's brother,
Nahor, married his niece, the daughter of a third brother named Haran
(Gen. 11:29). Discussed in the same passage, Abraham's marriage to Sarah
would also have fallen under the prohibitions in Leviticus 18, since she
was his half sister, the daughter of his father, Terah, by a different mother
(Gen. 20:12). Similarly incestuous is Genesis 29, with the simultaneous
marriage of Jacob to two different sisters, Leah and Rachel, a relation
specifically forbidden in Leviticus 18:18: "You shall not take a woman
as a rival wife to her sister, uncovering her nakedness while her sister
is still alive."

We have already discussed the shocking passage in which Judah had
sex with his own daughter-in-law, Tamar, thinking she was a prostitute
(Gen. 38:12–19; see chap. 8); and of course there's also Reuben, who had
intercourse with his father's concubine in Genesis 35:22, a crime for which
Jacob later revoked Reuben's status as firstborn son, saying, "You went
up to your father's bed; then you defiled it—he went up to my couch!"
(Gen. 49:4). But surely the most appalling among these pre-Mosaic cases
involves Lot and his two daughters.

Having escaped the destruction of Sodom and Gomorrah that killed
Lot's wife and both girls' fiancés, Lot and his daughters were living in a
cave when the older daughter expressed to the younger a fear that they
would never find new husbands and produce descendants to carry on
their father's line. The rest of the passage is worth quoting at length for
the blunt way it deals with this depraved exchange, accompanied by no
moral or editorial comment whatsoever from the narrator:

> "Come, let us make our father drink wine, and we will lie with him,
> that we may preserve offspring from our father." So they made their

14. Harrison, *Leviticus*, 185–85, 194–95.

father drink wine that night. And the firstborn went in and lay with her father. He did not know when she lay down or when she arose. The next day, the firstborn said to the younger, "Behold, I lay last night with my father. Let us make him drink wine tonight also. Then you go in and lie with him, that we may preserve offspring from our father." So they made their father drink wine that night also. And the younger arose and lay with him, and he did not know when she lay down or when she arose. Thus both the daughters of Lot became pregnant by their father. (Gen. 19:32–36)

Though the writer passes no judgment on these degraded actions, he does point out in later verses that the two unions here yielded the Moabite and Ammonite races, both of which were to remain long-term enemies of Israel throughout its subsequent history.

All this is scandalous enough; yet even after the laws against incest had been clearly set forth for God's people, this widely acknowledged crime continued to manifest itself in their ranks. In 2 Samuel, for example, one of David's sons, Amnon, became obsessed with his half sister Tamar, David's daughter by a different mother. Through a complex maneuver that we shall examine more fully in chapter 12, Amnon managed to get Tamar alone with him, at which point "he violated her and lay with her" (2 Sam. 13:14), an act that should have resulted in banishment from the kingdom (Lev. 20:17). A short time later, another of David's sons, Absalom, made a play for his father's throne, advancing this agenda in part by bedding David's concubines in a rooftop tent "in the sight of all Israel" (2 Sam. 16:20–22); by this action he was "invading his father's most intimate and private world, and doing so blatantly and publicly."[15] And furthermore, in the later book of Amos, God vehemently protests the spurning of his laws against fathers and sons sharing sexual partners: "A man and his father go in to the same girl, so that my holy name is profaned" (Amos 2:7); because the other sins condemned in this passage involve oppression and abuse of power, it seems likely that in this case, the young man's father is wickedly using his superior position to force himself on his daughter-in-law.[16]

15. Joyce G. Baldwin, *1 and 2 Samuel: An Introduction and Commentary*, Tyndale Old Testament Commentaries (Leicester, UK: Inter-Varsity, 1988), 264–65.

16. David Allan Hubbard, *Joel and Amos: An Introduction and Commentary*, Tyndale Old Testament Commentaries (Leicester, UK: Inter-Varsity, 1989), 142.

In the New Testament, Israel's detailed laws against incest must surely have fueled John the Baptist's run-in with Herod the tetrarch, a conflict that eventually led to the prophet's execution. Herod—one of several New Testament figures who share that name—was in this case a Roman administrator in the Palestinian regions called Perea and Galilee, where, at the time of John's preaching, he had married Herodias, the ex-wife of his brother (each had been divorced in order to wed the other). "In addition to being the wife of his half brother Herod Philip, she was also, through a complex of familial intermarriage that was typical of the Herods, his niece."[17] In a story recounted in all three Synoptic Gospels, Herod arrested and imprisoned John because John had been telling him, "'It is not lawful for you to have your brother's wife.' And Herodias had a grudge against him and wanted to put him to death." She was able to carry out her desire after the foolish king, carried away by an alluring dance during a party on his birthday, promised Herodias's daughter virtually anything she asked for—which turned out to be John's head on a platter (Mark 6:17-29; see also Matt. 14:3-12; Luke 3:19-20).

The only other New Testament occurrence of incest is 1 Corinthians 5, where the apostle Paul rebukes the Corinthian church for countenancing this sin in one of its members: "It is actually reported that there is sexual immorality among you, and of a kind that is not tolerated even among pagans, for a man has his father's wife. . . . Let him who has done this be removed from among you" (1 Cor. 5:1-2). Most commentators agree that the woman in question was not the man's biological mother, but rather a stepmother. Leon Morris speculates that he may have seduced her, or she may have been divorced or widowed.[18] In any case, such a sexual relation is clearly forbidden in Leviticus 18:8 ("You shall not uncover the nakedness of your father's wife"); indeed, writer Gordon D. Fee insists that Paul uses this phrase—"father's wife"—as a deliberate reference to the Old Testament ordinance; the apostle's indirect verb "has" could mean that they had married or that she had become a sort of mistress, but in any case it is "a euphemism for an enduring sexual relationship."[19] Paul's

17. Leon Morris, *The Gospel according to Matthew*, Pillar New Testament Commentary (Grand Rapids: Eerdmans, 1992), 370.

18. Leon Morris, *The First Epistle of Paul to the Corinthians*, Tyndale New Testament Commentaries (Leicester, UK: Inter-Varsity, 1999), 83.

19. Gordon D. Fee, *The First Epistle to the Corinthians*, New International Commentary on the New Testament (Grand Rapids: Eerdmans, 1987), 200.

phrase "sexual immorality" is, in the original Greek, the common word *porneia*, "a flexible term that covers all prohibited sexual intercourse" (see pp. 35–36); rather than "sexual immorality," an English rendering of "whoredom" would better express the "shock, amazement and horror" of the apostolic writer in this passage.[20]

These three nouns might also describe Paul's feelings about homosexuality, a topic that has become controversial in the church today. In fact, in his recent book *Sexuality in the New Testament: Understanding the Key Texts* (Westminster John Knox, 2010), William Loader acknowledges the hot-button nature of this issue by placing his chapter on homosexuality first among the many subjects covered. The controversy, of course, stems from the current move to accept and even promote the gay lifestyle as perfectly normal, making Scripture's attitude seem outmoded at best. In conjunction with this, many writers have undertaken to suggest that God does not in fact condemn homosexuality per se, that the Old Testament prohibitions have been abrogated (particularly by Jesus' apparent silence on the matter), and that such New Testament passages as Romans 1:26–27 and 1 Corinthians 6:9 condemn only certain types of homosexual behavior, such as prostitution, pederasty, and exploitation.

Whole books have been written on this matter (see, for instance, Dan O. Via and Robert A. J. Gagnon, *Homosexuality and the Bible: Two Views* [Fortress Press, 2009]), and I will not spend a lot of time attempting to resolve the issue here. My approach will be simply to examine the passages as they've been read and understood by the church for nearly 2,000 years (and by the Jewish community for another 1,300 years before that)—particularly as this approach continues to be upheld by the conservative and evangelical scholars on whom I have relied. Rather than holding, as many do today, that traditional interpretations have been biased or blinded by an outdated "homophobia," it is my contention that contemporary redactors are themselves prejudiced by their own "modern" attitude, making them anxious to deny or recolor the plain sense of texts that, until quite recently, have not been seen as problematic or controversial.

With this in mind, let us turn to the original prohibitions in Leviticus, which are so blunt and clear that they require no additional comment

---

20. David E. Garland, *1 Corinthians*, Baker Exegetical Commentary on the New Testament (Grand Rapids: Baker, 2003), 156–57.

or interpretation: "You shall not lie with a male as with a woman; it is an abomination" (Lev. 18:22); and, "If a man lies with a male as with a woman, both of them have committed an abomination; they shall surely be put to death" (Lev. 20:13). To these strictures we might add Deuteronomy 22:5, which condemns cross-dressing: "A woman shall not wear a man's garment, nor shall a man put on a woman's cloak, for whoever does these things is an abomination to the LORD your God." The Hebrew word "abomination" here—also meaning "loathsome" or "detestable"—is so strong that it "may also suggest transvestite practices associated with pagan temple worship."[21]

Actual instances of homosexual practice are rare in Bible narratives; they are restricted largely to two well-known passages in Genesis and Judges. The first of these involves the pagan city of Sodom and a visit by two angels who planned to spend the night in its town square; but Abraham's nephew, Lot, who lived in that city, urged the strangers to stay overnight in his home instead. Lot's insistence was typical of ancient Middle Eastern hospitality, but he may also have been considering what treatment the men might find in the town's open square; for later that evening, "the men of Sodom, both young and old, all the people to the last man, surrounded the house. And they called to Lot, 'Where are the men who came to you tonight? Bring them out to us, that we may know them'" (Gen. 19:1–5).

Sadly, the verb "know" here does not indicate a friendly overture to become better acquainted with these visitors. In the first place, "know" is a common Hebrew idiom for sexual intercourse (Gen. 4:1; 24:16; Num. 31:17; 1 Kings 1:4; see pp. 43–44). More significantly, Lot's response shows he was well aware that these importunate Sodomites were seeking sex, especially since he repeats their verb: "Behold, I have two daughters who have not known any man. Let me bring them out to you, and do to them as you please" (Gen. 19:8). In other words, the men of Sodom are proposing "homosexual gang rape . . . , something completely at odds with the norms of all oriental hospitality."[22] Lot, of course, has compounded the horror of this passage by offering his virgin daughters to the men instead, an action the *ESV Study Bible* calls "shocking, cowardly and inexcusable"—and one that is surely also well beyond the bounds of traditional "hospitality."

21. *ESV Study Bible* (Wheaton, IL: Crossway, 2008), 362.
22. Wenham, *Genesis 16–50*, 55.

Even more shocking is a reprise of this episode in Judges 19, where a traveling Levite priest, staying overnight in Gibeah, was urged to spend the night in a local home; once again, the native man told his visitor, "Do not spend the night in the square," probably worrying what might happen if he did. And sure enough, just as in Sodom, later that evening "the men of the city, worthless fellows, surrounded the house, beating on the door. And they said to the old man, the master of the house, 'Bring out the man who came into your house, that we may know him,'" at which point, the host offered instead his own virgin daughter and the Levite's concubine, saying, "Violate them and do with them what seems good to you, but against this man do not do this outrageous thing" (Judg. 19:16–24). In this case, the importunate men accepted the offer of the concubine; so we will discuss this passage more thoroughly in a later chapter on rape.

By contrast, Lot's loathsome offer of his two virgin daughters did not appease the men of Sodom, for "they pressed hard against the man Lot, and drew near to break the door down." Indeed, their lust was so all-consuming that even after the two angels struck them with blindness, "they wore themselves out groping for the door" (Gen. 19:9–11). Such a blatant preference for same-sex intercourse is probably why the locale of this narrative has given us the word "sodomy," a term for oral and anal sex that is still in occasional use today.

Fittingly, this instance of hard-headed commitment to homosexuality is condemned by the New Testament writer Jude, who says that the men of Sodom "indulged in sexual immorality and pursued unnatural desire" (Jude 1:7). In the second phrase here, the Greek literally means "went after other flesh" (or "strange flesh," NASB)—stressing the abnormal nature of their lust, and perhaps also alluding to the way, in both Genesis and Judges, these men seem to pounce on an opportunity to have sex with someone new. (Writers such as Richard J. Bauckham opine that "unnatural desire" actually refers to the Sodomites' eagerness to have sex with angels, a reading supported by the context in Jude, which discusses angelic beings.[23])

In any case, once the angels in Sodom had stricken their attackers with blindness—and after the celestial visitors had also warned of

23. Richard J. Bauckham, *Jude, 2 Peter*, Word Biblical Commentary, vol. 50 (Nashville: Nelson, 1983), 54.

approaching catastrophe—Lot and his daughters fled, just as God "rained on Sodom and Gomorrah sulfur and fire from the LORD out of heaven," thereby destroying the entire region. Even for Lot's family, however, the story did not end happily: Lot's wife and the daughters' fiancés, hesitating to flee, were all killed in the disaster (Gen. 19:15–26); and Gordon J. Wenham also points out the irony of how Lot's daughters, though saved from the gang rape implicit in their father's desperate offer, soon afterward sacrificed their virginity anyway (and their father's honor too) by committing incest with him even when there was no actual danger (see above discussion).[24]

Sadly, a thorough discussion of homosexuality in the Old Testament would probably be incomplete unless we also examine the emergent "gay reading" of the relationship between David and Jonathan in 1 Samuel. Not yet king of Israel, young David was at the time a right-hand man to King Saul and very close friends with Saul's son, Jonathan: "The soul of Jonathan was knit to the soul of David. . . . Then Jonathan made a covenant with David, because he loved him as his own soul. And Jonathan stripped himself of the robe that was on him and gave it to David, and his armor, and even his sword and his bow and his belt" (1 Sam. 18:1–4). Later, the writer tells us that Jonathan "delighted much in David" (1 Sam. 19:1), even to the point of helping David escape the murderous plots of his father, Saul, who was jealous of the younger man's success and popularity.

Once David had been warned of this and had determined to flee from the kingdom, the two friends "kissed one another and wept with one another, David weeping the most. Then Jonathan said to David, 'Go in peace, because we have sworn both of us in the name of the LORD, saying, "The LORD shall be between me and you, and between my offspring and your offspring, forever"'" (1 Sam. 20:41–42). Later, when Jonathan had been killed, David reacted by apostrophizing his lost friend: "Very pleasant you have been to me; your love to me was extraordinary, surpassing the love of women" (2 Sam. 1:26)—leading some readers to insist that "they were essentially bisexual men."[25] Jennifer Wright Knust cites Saul's reproof to Jonathan—"You have chosen the son of Jesse . . .

24. Wenham, *Genesis 16–50*, 61.
25. Ben Edward Akerley, *The X-Rated Bible: An Irreverent Survey of Sex in the Scriptures* (Los Angeles: Feral, 1998), 39. See also Teresa J. Hornsby, *Sex Texts from the Bible: Selections Annotated and Explained* (Woodstock, VT: SkyLight, 2007), 70.

to the shame of your mother's nakedness" (1 Sam. 20:30)—as proof that "Jonathan's disgrace is sexual as well as political, at least from the king's perspective."[26]

Conservative commentators are virtually unanimous in rejecting this sexualization of what appears to be a deeply compassionate and entirely platonic friendship. Sure, Jonathan "stripped" himself and gave the clothes to David; but Ralph W. Klein points out that in doing so, the king's son was "tacitly handing over to him the right of succession"—that Jonathan's robe may well have been a royal one, and that giving the bow and armor falls in line with nearby passages where receiving someone else's weapons indicates precedence, victory, or honor (1 Sam. 17:38–39, 50–51; 21:9).[27] Yes, Jonathan and David kissed each other; but so did many males in both the Old and New Testaments. Sometimes these men were fathers and sons (Gen. 27:27; 2 Sam. 14:33; 1 Kings 19:20; etc.), or other close relatives (Gen. 29:13; 33:4; 45:15; Ex. 4:27; 18:7). On many occasions, however, they were mere friends or associates (as in 1 Sam. 10:1; 2 Sam. 15:5; 19:39; 20:9; Matt. 26:48–49; Luke 7:45; Rom. 16:16; 1 Peter 5:14; and many other passages).

The accusation about Jonathan shaming the "nakedness" of his mother is a quote from King Saul—hardly the most trustworthy source of information in Old Testament narratives. And as for David's eulogy of Jonathan in 2 Samuel 1, his praise seems to indicate that their friendship was something different than romance—something loftier, nobler, more exalted—and not that it constituted an alternate type of sexual love. Commentator Joyce G. Baldwin suggests that in siding with David instead of with his father the king, Jonathan had put their friendship before his own royal interests and that this "selfless, transparent goodness" lay behind David's encomium to his beloved friend.[28] Perhaps the young king's eulogy means that he had not seen this sort of sacrificial love in any of his marriages. But of course, we lose all this if we try to give some sort of hidden sexual meaning to David's statement.

Regarding this passage, Peter J. Leithart writes that if the two men really were lovers, then "either the writer of 1–2 Samuel was ignorant of

26. Jennifer Wright Knust, *Unprotected Texts: The Bible's Surprising Contradictions about Sex and Desire* (New York: HarperOne, 2011), 42.

27. Ralph W. Klein, *1 Samuel*, Word Biblical Commentary, vol. 10 (Waco, TX: Word, 1983), 182.

28. Baldwin, *1 and 2 Samuel*, 181.

David's sin or cynically brushed it aside. Neither option is plausible. A writer who knew the inside story of David, Bathsheba, and Uriah would have known about a youthful homosexual fling, and a writer willing to present David's adultery without evasion or excuse would not be willing to treat sodomy as a peccadillo."[29]

Turning to the New Testament, we find a rare Greek word, *arsenokoites*, in two key passages—1 Timothy 1 and 1 Corinthians 6. Translated "homosexuals" (NASB), "perverts" (NIV), or "men who practice homosexuality" (ESV), *arsenokoites* is a compound of one Greek term for "male" and another meaning "bed." This Greek word "bed" is in turn a common euphemism for sexual intercourse; it occurs elsewhere in such contexts as Hebrews 13:4 ("let the marriage bed be undefiled") and Romans 9:10, where it is used in the phrase "Rebekah had conceived children." Appearing in both 1 Corinthians 6:9 and 1 Timothy 1:10, *arsenokoites* does not occur elsewhere in the New Testament or in any Greek writings before Paul's time.[30] It is probably a term coined to give a negative slant on homosexuality, since both of its Greek component words echo language in the Old Testament laws against same-sex intercourse—that is, they echo Leviticus 18:22 and 20:13 as these verses appear in the Septuagint, a Greek translation of the Old Testament familiar to some of Paul's first-century readers. As such, the compound "bed-male" probably refers to "all kinds of homosexual conduct."[31] In 1 Timothy 1:10, the coinage appears in conjunction with general sexual sin: Paul describes "the lawless and disobedient" as a group that includes "the sexually immoral" (Greek *pornos*) and "men who practice homosexuality" (*arsenokoites*).

The use of this term in 1 Corinthians 6:9, however, is more complicated. Like 1 Timothy, the Corinthian passage places *arsenokoites* in a list of other dangerous sins such as greed, idolatry, theft, and drunkenness; while the ESV for 1 Corinthians 6:9 uses the same phrase found in 1 Timothy ("men who practice homosexuality"), the actual Greek in the Corinthian passages consist of two separate words: *malakos* and *arsenokoites*. The former, translated in the NASB as "effeminate," appears elsewhere in the New Testament as "soft," so that the two words taken together indicate "the passive and active partners in consensual homo-

29. Peter J. Leithart, *A Son to Me: An Exposition of 1 and 2 Samuel* (Moscow, ID: Canon, 2003), 101.
30. Garland, *1 Corinthians*, 212.
31. *ESV Study Bible*, 2336.

sexual acts."[32] Garland translates them frankly as "males who are penetrated sexually by males" and "males who sexually penetrate males."[33]

Garland also suggests that this terminology highlights the unnatural quality of these sins, since "one of the males must act like a woman"; and he pairs the Corinthian passage with Romans 1, where "one of the women must act like a male."[34] Indeed, Romans 1 is certainly the key New Testament passage on same-sex activity, since it embraces two full verses rather than just a word or two as above—and furthermore, it is the one and only Bible passage that clearly references lesbianism.

Speaking of those who suppress the truth of God's existence, Paul asserts that as a consequence of their deliberate unbelief, "God gave them up to dishonorable passions. For their women exchanged natural relations for those that are contrary to nature; and the men likewise gave up natural relations with women and were consumed with passion for one another, men committing shameless acts with men and receiving in themselves the due penalty for their error" (Rom. 1:26–27). Paul's language here reveals much about his attitude toward this sin. The mechanics of homosexual activity are at least hinted at in 1 Corinthians 6:9 (e.g., passive and active males), but there is no such discussion here. Nevertheless, Paul's term "shameless" is a strong one, occurring in the Bible only here and in Revelation 16:15, where it clearly refers to private parts ("lest he walk about naked and men see his shame," NASB).

More significantly, Paul mentions women first, probably because "they are always the last to be affected in the decay of morals, and their corruption is proof that all virtue is lost."[35] Yet even in this case there is some restraint, for Paul's description of male activity provides additional details ("men committing shameless acts with men"), whereas his reference to lesbianism politely avoids a similar "women-with-women" phraseology; Paul is content to observe only that they "exchanged natural relations." John Murray notes that "it is likely that delicate feeling dictated this restraint."[36]

32. Ibid., 2198.
33. Garland, *1 Corinthians*, 211.
34. Ibid., 214.
35. Charles Hodge, *A Commentary on the Epistle to the Romans* (1864), 42, quoted in Geoffrey B. Wilson, *Romans: A Digest of Reformed Comment*, New Testament Commentaries (Aylesbury, UK: Banner of Truth, 1969), 31.
36. John Murray, *The Epistle to the Romans*, vol. 1 (Grand Rapids: Eerdmans, 1959, repr. 1982), 47.

These three passages from Romans, 1 Corinthians, and 1 Timothy constitute the sum total of direct New Testament teaching on homosexuality. Much has been made of Christ's silence on the matter; but of course, Christ was also silent on rape, incest, pedophilia, and bestiality—which hardly constitutes permission or endorsement. His brief discourse on marriage upholds the Old Testament tradition that "he who created them from the beginning made them male and female," and that "a man shall . . . hold fast to his wife" (Matt. 19:4–5). If anything, Christ reveals not a more liberal attitude toward sexuality, but rather one that strengthens the Old Testament's conservative approach; he condemns divorce (Matt. 5:31–32; 19:3–9), expands the meaning of adultery to include the actions of the eyes and the mind (Matt. 5:27–28), and mentions those "who have made themselves eunuchs for the sake of the kingdom of heaven" (Matt. 19:12).[37] Surely if Christ had meant to overturn 1,300 years of Jewish teaching on homosexuality, he would have done more with the subject than merely to affirm the indissoluble male/female nature of marriage. Just think how much time and effort he expended to revise Jewish views of the Sabbath!

37. William Loader, *Sexuality in the New Testament: Understanding the Key Texts* (Louisville, KY: Westminster John Knox, 2010), 34, 64–65.

PART 2

"The Blood Gushed Out"—Violence

10

"I Will Drench the Land"

Blood and Gore

THE WORD *BLOOD* appears more than 350 times in the Old Testament, and nearly 100 in the New. Roughly one-fourth of the Old Testament uses occur in the regulations on sacrifice and purification described in Exodus, Leviticus, and Numbers; so as we turn to a consideration of violence in Scripture, let's begin with these lengthy, detailed, and sometimes gory passages.

Israel's sacrificial system was far too vast and complex to describe in great detail here; but essentially it involved killing, cutting up, and burning animals as an offering to the Lord (though the system also allowed use of oil, wine, money, and various grains—not all of which were burned, obviously!). Such offerings could express gratitude, penitence, or commitment toward God, or they could represent expiation, with the animal being "punished" as a substitute, thus propitiating divine wrath and pointing to the later atoning sacrifice of Jesus Christ for the sins of God's chosen people. In addition, the sprinkled blood of these sacrificed animals was used symbolically in purification rites and covenants—particularly the covenant between Yahweh and his people. In many cases, once the animal's blood had served in this way—or once specified parts of the creature had been burned as an offering—the remainder was then used for meals; this system helped provide regular sustenance for Levites and priests who served in the temple and helped oversee the sacrifices.

Throughout the previous section of this book, we often observed that the Bible writers avoided the detailed mechanics of intercourse, prostitution, and other sexual matters. But there is little of this vagueness and indirection when it comes to sacrificial rites. Instructions for offering animals in the Old Testament are extraordinarily detailed and often quite gruesome. The priest, for example, is commanded to "flay the burnt offering and cut it into pieces" and to "arrange the pieces, the head, and the fat on the wood . . . ; but its entrails and its legs he shall wash with water" (Lev. 1:6–9). Later, the priest is instructed to "offer the fat covering the entrails and all the fat that is on the entrails, and the two kidneys with the fat that is on them at the loins, and the long lobe of the liver that he shall remove with the kidneys" (Lev. 3:3–4).

These graphic stipulations are repeated at length in several passages (Lev. 3:14–15; 4:8–9; 7:3–4), with occasional variations: "Remove the whole fat tail, cut off close to the backbone" (Lev. 3:9); and, "The flesh of the bull and its skin and its dung you shall burn with fire outside the camp" (Ex. 29:14). Most of these rules pertain to bulls, sheep, and goats, but if the offering is a bird, the priest is to "wring off its head and burn it on the altar. Its blood shall be drained out on the side of the altar. He shall remove its crop with its contents. . . . He shall tear it open by its wings, but shall not sever it completely" (Lev. 1:15–17).

Such detail may have been necessary in part to prevent Israel from adopting pagan practices that also involved that butchering of animals, practices King Ahab apparently used when he commanded his priest to build an altar "to inquire by" (2 Kings 16:15). This act of "inquiring" on an altar probably refers to what is called "extispicy": examining "the entrails of sacrificial animals, focusing on the inspection of the liver (hepatoscopy), in order to divine the will and intention of the gods"—a heathen practice typical of Ahab, and one which represents "full-fledged syncretism with the pagan religions of the other nations," rather than adherence to sacrificial regulations laid out in the passages above.[1]

But the chopping up and burning of sacrificed animals represents only one aspect of Israel's sacrificial system. Much of Exodus and Leviticus involves the use of blood from these slain beasts, which makes its first appearance—and perhaps its most famous—just as the young nation of Israel was about to escape from slavery and servitude. After inflict-

1. *ESV Study Bible* (Wheaton, IL: Crossway, 2008), 676.

ing numerous plagues on Egypt in hopes of persuading Pharaoh to let Israel go free—none of which worked—God planned a final affliction that would kill off the firstborn male in every Egyptian household; but he would spare the Israelite homes from this plague if they slew a lamb and drained the blood, after which they were to "take a bunch of hyssop and dip it in the blood that is in the basin, and touch the lintel and the two doorposts with the blood" (Ex. 12:22).

Though in this case blood was successfully used for protection, more often it served the purpose of cleansing and consecration for the altar, tabernacle, or temple. All told, the sprinkling, daubing, throwing, or pouring out of sacrificial blood is described more than fifty times in the Old Testament, with Leviticus 4 serving as a typical example: "The anointed priest shall take some of the blood of the bull and bring it into the tent of meeting, and the priest shall dip his finger in the blood and sprinkle part of the blood seven times before the LORD in front of the veil of the sanctuary. And the priest shall put some of the blood on the horns of the altar of fragrant incense, . . . and all the rest of the blood of the bull he shall pour out at the base of the altar of burnt offering" (Lev. 4:5–7).

Often, this blood is dabbed or sprinkled directly onto the priests or the Israelites as a whole. In Exodus, for example, it is thrown against the newly constructed altar and then on the people, serving as "the blood of the covenant that the LORD has made with you" (Ex. 24:6–8); a short time later, the Lord commands that bull's blood be smeared on the garments of Aaron and the priests as well as the tips of their right ears, the thumbs on their right hands, and "the great toes of their right feet" (Ex. 29:20–21). A similar application to the ear, thumb, and toe is prescribed for the cleansing of lepers in Leviticus 14, which also involves a blood-soaked bird bath: one bird is to be slain and another dipped in its blood, which is then sprinkled on the leper seven times (Lev. 14:2–14).

The characteristic bloodshed involved in these rituals must have made for a gruesome scene in some of the later celebrations, when vast numbers of animals were sacrificed at the same time: Nearly 4,000 bulls, rams, and sheep, for example, were slain when King Hezekiah restored temple worship during his reign around 700 B.C.—so many that there weren't enough priests to flay them all, and extra help was needed from the Levite assistants (2 Chron. 29:32–34). Nearly twice that many animals, some 7,700, were sacrificed during the reforms of King Asa (2 Chron. 15:11), and a whopping 142,000 at the dedication of the temple built by Solomon (1 Kings 8:63). The 41,000 sacrificed under King Josiah (2 Chron. 35:7–9) is also impressive. And while it should be noted that this remarkable number includes 33,000 animals donated by the king to help individual families celebrate the Passover, that fact in itself points to the massive numbers of sheep slaughtered annually at this memorial celebration—specifically, one for every family in a nation that, during the reign of King David, contained some 1.3 million men eligible for military service (2 Sam. 24:9).

That's a lot of blood.

But of course, sacrifice is not the only context in which bloodshed appears in the Scriptures. Other noteworthy passages include 2 Kings 3, where the Moabites, preparing to attack Israel, were lured into wholesale slaughter when they mistook water lit by the rising sun for the spilled blood of an already vanquished foe; here, the writer's clever phrase "red as blood" makes a double pun, since the Hebrew words for "red" and "blood" both resemble the word for "Edom"—an ally of Israel, and one of the nations whose blood Moab thought they saw (2 Kings 3:20–24).[2]

Proverbs avers that "pressing the nose produces blood" (Prov. 30:33). Lamentations recalls defeated Israelites who were "so defiled with blood that no one was able to touch their garments" (Lam. 4:14). Ezekiel describes Israel as a helpless newborn "wallowing in your blood" (Exek. 16:6)—with the Hebrew term referring to "the amniotic fluid and blood that her mother had discharged at the time of her birth."[3] Psalm 58:10 predicts that the righteous "will bathe his feet in the blood of the wicked," and Isaiah 63:3 offers a similarly startling image in which the Lord says that because he has trampled his enemies, "their lifeblood spattered on my garments, and stained all my apparel." (The Hebrew word for "lifeblood" here is literally "juice"; there may be echoes of this passage in Revelation 19:13, where the returning Christ is "clothed in a robe dipped in blood.") And Luke

2. Ibid., 650.
3. Daniel I. Block, *The Book of Ezekiel: Chapters 1–24*, New International Commentary on the New Testament (Grand Rapids: Eerdmans, 1997), 480.

mentions a group of Galileans "whose blood Pilate had mingled with their sacrifices" (Luke 13:1). While this latter incident is not found in any other historical source, it seems clear that soldiers under the Roman official Pontius Pilate had slain men who were in the midst of making offerings in the temple, thereby mixing human blood with that of sacrificial beasts.

Two other fascinating occurrences of blood in the New Testament involve episodes near the end of Christ's life. On the night he was arrested, Jesus was praying about his impending death and the cup of God's wrath that he would be required to drink. "And being in agony he prayed more earnestly; and his sweat became like great drops of blood falling down to the ground" (Luke 22:41–44). "Though the word 'like' may indicate that this is to be understood metaphorically, there are both ancient and modern accounts on record of people sweating blood—a condition known as *hematidrosis*, where extreme anguish or physical strain causes one's capillary blood vessels to dilate and burst, mixing sweat and blood."[4] Even if Luke is not describing actual hematidrosis here, it is clear that Christ's sweating was "so profuse that it looked like blood dripping from a wound."[5]

Much later, once Jesus had died—but just before his body was removed from the cross—one Roman soldier "pierced his side with a spear, and at once there came out blood and water" (John 19:34). This may have been done to determine whether Jesus was actually dead, in which case the soldiers wouldn't have to break his legs, an action often performed to hasten death (victims used their legs to support themselves, thereby extending the time required for suffocation, which was the typical means of death in a crucifixion). Numerous medical theories have been advanced as to the nature of this "water," with the only certainty being that it must have been some kind of fluid that had built up during the severe mental and physical anguish experienced by our Lord right before his death.[6]

4. *ESV Study Bible*, 2007.
5. Walter L. Liefeld, *Luke*, in *The Expositor's Bible Commentary*, vol. 8: *Matthew, Mark, Luke*, ed. Frank E. Gaebelein (Grand Rapids: Zondervan-HarperCollins, 1984), 1032.
6. D. A. Carson, *The Gospel according to John*, The Pillar New Testament Commentary (Leicester, UK: Apollos/Inter-Varsity, 1991), 623; William D. Edwards, Wesley J. Gabel, and Floyd E. Hosmer, "On the Physical Death of Jesus Christ," *Journal of the American Medical Association* 255, 11 (March 21, 1986): 1461–62; Leon Morris, *The Gospel according to John*, New International Commentary on the New Testament (Grand Rapids: Eerdmans, 1971), 819.

Many Bible passages take the image of blood to a disturbing new level with references to consumption and intoxication. Numbers describes a lion who has "drunk the blood of the slain" (Num. 23:24); Psalms asks rhetorically whether God himself needs to "drink the blood of goats" (Ps. 50:13); and Revelation describes God's enemies as "drunk with the blood of the saints" (Rev. 17:6). Fittingly, then, Isaiah predicts that those who oppress Israel "shall be drunk with their own blood as with wine" (Isa. 49:26); and Revelation also asserts that while these enemies "have shed the blood of saints and prophets," in return God has "given them blood to drink. It is what they deserve!" (Rev. 16:6).

Indeed most of these bloodthirsty passages—if you'll pardon the pun—involve graphic vengeance on the Lord's opponents. In Deuteronomy, for example, God declares, "I will make my arrows drunk with blood" (Deut. 32:42), and Jeremiah 46:10 similarly asserts, "The sword shall devour and be sated and drink its fill of their blood." Ezekiel 39 uses vivid Levitical language as it tells birds and beasts to prepare for "a great sacrificial feast": "You shall eat the flesh of the mighty, and drink the blood of the princes of the earth—of rams, of lambs, and of he-goats, of bulls, all of them fat beasts. . . . And you shall eat fat till you are filled, and drink blood till you are drunk" (Ezek. 39:17–19).

The language of ritual sacrifice is also used in this startling passage from Isaiah: "The LORD has a sword; it is sated with blood; it is gorged with fat, with the blood of lambs and goats, with the fat of the kidneys of rams. For the LORD has a sacrifice in Bozrah, a great slaughter in the land of Edom. . . . Their land shall drink its fill of blood, and their soil shall be gorged with fat" (Isa. 34:6–7). The final image ties to verse 3, in which "the mountains shall flow with their blood"; the Hebrew word here for "flow" is literally "to dissolve, melt" (the NASB has "drenched")—and thus the prophet here envisions "a new and dreadful soil erosion through the torrential blood of the slain."[7] A similar image—this one addressed to Egypt—occurs in Ezekiel, where, in the words on Iain M. Duguid, "Pharaoh's blood is seen semimythically as watering the land and filling the ravines": "I will drench the

---

7. Alec Motyer, *Isaiah: An Introduction and Commentary*, Tyndale Old Testament Commentaries (Leicester, UK: Inter-Varsity, 1999), 215.

land even to the mountains with your flowing blood, and the ravines will be full of you" (Ezek. 32:6).[8]

This idea of what we might poetically call "a flood of blood" appears elsewhere in the Bible, too. The best-known, of course, is the so-called "plague of blood" with which God afflicted the Egyptians as he was trying to persuade them to free the enslaved people of Israel. The first of ten devastating plagues that descended on Egypt, this occurs in Exodus 7, where God promises to "strike the water that is in the Nile, and it shall turn into blood"—that is, all the water in the land, including "their rivers, their canals, and their ponds, and all their pools of water, . . . even in vessels of wood and in vessels of stone." As a result, "the fish in the Nile died, and the Nile stank, so that the Egyptians could not drink water from the Nile. There was blood throughout all the land of Egypt" (Ex. 7:17–21).

A few writers have suggested that the water did not turn into actual blood, that "any thick red fluid" would serve to resemble blood, perhaps "red clay washed down from Ethiopia" or some "multiplication of red plankton" in the water.[9] However, the traditional Hebrew word for blood—*dam*—is used throughout this passage; and as Peter Enns points out, some sort of natural discoloration would hardly have startled Pharaoh, nor would he have reacted to something he might well have seen before by asking his magicians to do the same thing. Enns also observes that it is likely that not every single drop of water in Egypt was bloodied, since this would have affected the Israelites as well—and furthermore, Pharaoh's magicians did succeed in turning water into blood, implying that there was still some "regular" water lying about somewhere for them to transform. Nonetheless, the filling even of stone and wood vessels (Ex. 7:19) certainly means "there was blood all over the place" in Egypt during this plague.[10]

Scripture also concludes with a sanguinary deluge, when God overthrows his enemies in Revelation 14:19–20: "The angel swung his sickle across the earth and gathered the grape harvest of the earth and threw

---

8. Iain M. Duguid, *Ezekiel*, The NIV Application Commentary (Grand Rapids: Zondervan, 1999), 374.

9. R. Alan Cole, *Exodus: An Introduction and Commentary*, Tyndale Old Testament Commentaries (Leicester, UK: Inter-Varsity, 1973), 90.

10. Peter Enns, *Exodus*, The NIV Application Commentary (Grand Rapids: Zondervan, 2000), 200–202.

it into the great winepress of the wrath of God. And the winepress was trodden outside the city, and blood flowed from the winepress, as high as a horse's bridle, for 1,600 stadia." Roughly 184 miles, this figure may represents the once-famous two-hundred-mile parameter of the Holy Land "from Dan to Beersheba"; but in any case, it is a "monstrous tide of blood."[11] As such, it shows—like so many passages we have discussed in this chapter—that the Word of God reveals little squeamishness or delicacy when dealing with matters of blood and gore.

11. Michael Wilcock, *The Message of Revelation: I Saw Heaven Opened*, The Bible Speaks Today (Leicester, UK: Inter-Varsity, 1975), 136.

11

"Weeping and Gnashing of Teeth"

Beatings, Attacks, and Tortures

THE BIBLE CONTAINS countless killings and murders. Most of these will be examined in chapter 17, but several bear separate examination in this current chapter on physical violence and torture.

To begin once again with regulations on the subject, Old Testament law forbids and punishes unjustified assault of various kinds—with extraordinary specificity:

Whoever strikes a man so that he dies shall be put to death. . . . If a man willfully attacks another to kill him by cunning, you shall take him from my altar, that he may die. Whoever strikes his father or his mother shall be put to death. . . . When men quarrel and one strikes the other with a stone or with his fist and the man does not die but takes to his bed, then if the man rises again and walks outdoors with his staff, he who struck him shall be clear; only he shall pay for the loss of his time, and shall have him thoroughly healed. When a man strikes his slave, male or female, with a rod and the slave dies under his hand, he shall be avenged. . . . When men strive together and hit a pregnant woman, so that her children come out, but there is no harm, the one who hit her shall surely be fined. . . . But if there is harm, then you shall pay life for life, eye for eye, tooth for tooth, hand for hand, foot for foot, burn for burn, wound for wound, stripe for stripe. When a man strikes the eye of his slave, male or female, and destroys it, he shall let the slave go free because of his eye. If he knocks out the tooth of his slave, male or female, he shall let the slave go free because of his tooth. (Ex. 21:12–27)

Assault regulations apply even to animals: an ox must be put to death if it has gored and killed a man or woman; and in addition, if the ox had a reputation for violence but the owner did not take proper precautions, then the owner is to be killed as well—unless, apparently, the victim's family allowed financial restitution instead (Ex. 21:28–31).

Specific personal attacks of this kind are rare in Bible narratives (perhaps these laws were more effective than many of the others we have discussed!); but self-mutilation appears with some explicitness in 1 Kings, when prophets of the pagan storm god Baal were attempting to bring rain. After praying "from morning until noon" and then limping around the altar a while longer, they finally "cut themselves after their custom with swords and lances, until the blood gushed out upon them" (1 Kings 18:26–28). This type of religious self-abuse—an "attempt to manipulate Baal into action"—was well attested in non-Israelite religions at the time, with one ancient text describing men "bathed in their own blood like an ecstatic prophet."[1] Such self-mutilation had been clearly forbidden to God's people in Leviticus 19:28 and Deuteronomy 14:1.

Speaking of assaults on oneself, there is some literal hairpulling in the postexilic books of Ezra and Nehemiah. First, Ezra reacted with horror to news that men of Israel had committed the long-forbidden sin of intermarriage with local non-Jewish women: "As soon as I heard this, I tore my garment and my cloak and pulled hair from my head and beard and sat appalled" (Ezra 9:3). Such hirsute ill-treatment became more widespread later, when Ezra's successor, Nehemiah, was similarly revolted not only by intermarriage but also by the lack of temple offerings, as well as the flouting of Sabbath regulations: "And I confronted them and cursed them and beat some of them and pulled out their hair" (Neh. 13:25).

Some of the most squirm-inducing attacks recounted in the Bible involve broken teeth, which make an unpleasant appearance in four different passages. In Psalm 58, speaking of the wicked against whom

1. Donald J. Wiseman, *1 and 2 Kings: An Introduction and Commentary*, Tyndale Old Testament Commentaries (Leicester, UK: Inter-Varsity, 1993), 169.

he is praying, David asks God to "break the teeth in their mouths" and "tear out the fangs of the young lions" (Ps. 58:6); the final phrase, of course, suggests that this is figurative, as is Job 29:17: "I broke the fangs of the unrighteous and made him drop his prey from his teeth." Job 4:10, however, is perhaps more literal: "the teeth of the young lions are broken." And Psalm 3:7 sounds a bit more definite too: "Save me, O my God! For you strike all my enemies on the cheek; you break the teeth of the wicked."

Besides teeth, other body parts are subject to assault in a number of places. In Judges 1, for example, Israel continues its conquest of the promised land by capturing a local king named Adoni-bezek, then cutting off his thumbs and his big toes. An act that humiliates him while also rendering him unable to ever again wield a weapon in battle, this punishment is especially fitting because, as he himself later admits with some bitterness, "Seventy kings with their thumbs and their big toes cut off used to pick up scraps under my table" (Judg. 1:6–7). In addition to toes and thumbs, the violent removal of eyeballs is referenced in several passages, including Judges 16:21, where Samson's eyes are gouged out, and 1 Samuel 11:2, where a pagan king threatens to do this to everyone in Israel. In 2 Kings, the last Judean king, Zedekiah, suffers this indignity as well—but only after watching the Babylonians slaughter all of his sons (2 Kings 25:7).

All these attacks are sufficiently unnerving; but one passage that appears to contain a vicious assault has probably been misread. This narrative—about the victorious King David and his treatment of vanquished Ammonites—appears in both 2 Samuel and 1 Chronicles. Some older translations, including the NASB, render 2 Samuel 12:31 as it appears in the King James Version: he "put them under saws, and under harrows of iron, and under axes of iron, and made them pass through the brick-kiln." The original Hebrew of the corresponding passage in 1 Chronicles 20:3 says he "sawed them"; but this seems uncharacteristically brutal of Israel's great king, and most modern translations indicate that the torment in this case involved mere hard labor, perhaps even being put to work tearing down their own cities. Thus the ESV puts this passage more clearly, saying that David "set them to labor with saws" and "made them toil at the brick kilns."

Likewise, we would not want too readily to include as "torture" or "attack" the New Testament account of Christ driving merchants and money-changers out of the temple in John 2. Here, Jesus was outraged that the God-ordained place of worship had become instead a sort of common marketplace whose business distracted God's people from the holy purpose at hand. "And making a whip of cords, he drove them all out of the temple, with the sheep and oxen" (John 2:15). As D. A. Carson puts it, "Jesus' physical action was forceful, but not cruel; one does not easily drive out cattle and sheep without *a whip of cords*. Still, his action could not have generated a riotous uproar, or there would have been swift reprisals from the Roman troops."[2]

For a clear version of deliberate and painful flogging, we need look no farther than Judges 8, where the warrior Gideon, angry at the leaders of Succoth for refusing to aid his military campaign, declares, "I will flail your flesh with the thorns of the wilderness and with briers"—a threat he carries out once victory has been achieved (Judg. 8:7, 16). The exact nature of this attack is not clear. It may have involved a whip made from spiky desert plants; alternately, Gideon either dragged the men over thorns, as a threshing sledge was dragged over grain, or perhaps lay them down on top of thorns and drew sledges over them. In any case, the assault was certainly intended to be fatal.[3]

In a similar incident from 1 Kings, young Rehoboam, having recently inherited the throne from Solomon, is asked by his new subjects to "lighten the hard service of your father and his heavy yoke upon us"—to which he foolishly responds, "My father disciplined you with whips, but I will discipline you with scorpions" (1 Kings 12:4, 14). Again, the precise nature of this implement is not clear, but it was probably "a particularly vicious form of whip," perhaps one barbed with nails.[4]

Many of these assaults look painfully like torture, an experience described with some vividness in Hebrews 11: Some Old Testament heroes, it says, "were tortured, refusing to accept release. . . . Others suffered mocking and flogging, and even chains and imprisonment. They were stoned, they were sawn in two, they were killed with the sword" (Heb. 11:35–37). We do not know with certainty whom the writer had

2. D. A. Carson, *The Gospel according to John*, The Pillar New Testament Commentary (Leicester, UK: Apollos/Inter-Varsity, 1991), 179.

3. Daniel I. Block, *Judges, Ruth*, The New American Commentary (Nashville: Broadman, 1999), 290–93; Arthur E. Cundall and Leon Morris, *Judges & Ruth: An Introduction and Commentary* (Leicester, UK: Inter-Varsity, 1968), 116.

4. *ESV Study Bible* (Wheaton, IL: Crossway, 2008), 621; see also Wiseman, *1 and 2 Kings*, 141.

in mind when he described stoning and sawing; extrabiblical tradition indicates that Isaiah and Jeremiah died this way,[5] and the Old Testament records that Jehoiada's son Zechariah was stoned (2 Chron. 24:21), as was the righteous Naboth, who had been framed by King Ahab (1 Kings 21:13). The "torture" referred to in Hebrews almost certainly includes the frequent abuse and persecution of the prophet Jeremiah, who was beaten repeatedly and half buried in mud after bring lowered into an empty cistern (Jer. 20:2; 37:15; 38:6).

According to Jeremiah 20:2, the suffering prophet was also put in stocks, a torturous form of punishment that reappears in 29:26, where the wicked Shemaiah is said to have put various prophets "in the stocks and neck irons." Likewise in 2 Chronicles 16:10, the otherwise decent King Asa was angry over a rebuke from the seer Hanani, so he "put him in the stocks in prison." Figurative references also occur in Job, where the afflicted protagonist twice complains that God has put his "feet in the stocks" (Job 13:27; 33:11).

There is some disagreement over the exact nature of this apparatus, but it is generally agreed that the purpose was restraint and discomfort by "distorting or twisting the body unnaturally." Using a device that could include neck collars (Jer. 29:26) and "blocks into which the feet were inserted," victims were confined at length in a crooked or awkward position that resulted in badly cramped muscles. In the New Testament, Paul and his fellow-worker Silas, unjustly accused of disturbing the peace in Philippi, were also put into stocks, which in that era "may have been made of a wooden beam with five sets of holes for spreading the legs and causing variable degrees of pain."[6] A similarly cruel punishment is mentioned in Lamentations 5:12, where "princes are hung up by their hands." Here, Israelite leaders, suffering at the hands of their conquerors, experience a form of torture, or perhaps even execution by exposure, in which they are "suspended in mid-air with their hands bound together."[7]

All this explanation is necessary because biblical accounts of these often brutal assaults and tortures rarely give specific physical descriptions; indeed, except for the self-flagellating prophets in 1 Kings 18, they do

5. *ESV Study Bible*, 2382.

6. Richard A. Spencer, "Stocks," in *Eerdmans Dictionary of the Bible*, ed. David Noel Freedman (Grand Rapids: Eerdmans, 2000), 1252.

7. R. K. Harrison, *Jeremiah and Lamentations: An Introduction and Commentary*, Tyndale Old Testament Commentaries (Leicester, UK: Inter-Varsity, 1973), 239.

not even mention blood or pain. Nowhere is this restraint more apparent than in the New Testament accounts of flogging, which would include several attacks on Paul and, of course, the scourging of Jesus Christ before he was crucified.

In 2 Corinthians 11:24, the great apostle tells us that on five separate occasions during the course of his ministry, he received the standard Jewish punishment of "forty lashes less one." This was the most severe beating allowed in Scripture, as per regulations in Deuteronomy, where a party found guilty in a dispute must lie down and be beaten with up to 40 lashes, "but not more, lest, if one should go on to beat him with more stripes than these, your brother be degraded in your sight" (Deut. 25:2–3). As Paul's statement indicates, the Jews typically administered only 39 lashes to ensure that the prescribed number was not exceeded by an accidental miscount.[8]

Paul's discussion in 2 Corinthians also explains that he was beaten three times "with rods," a punishment meted out to both Paul and Silas in Acts 16:22: "The crowd joined in attacking them, and the magistrates tore the garments off them and gave orders to beat them with rods." The magistrates in Roman cities were served by attendants, or "lictors," carrying bundles of wooden rods bound together. These bundles, which sometimes had an axe inserted among them, served as symbols of the magistrates' right to inflict corporal and sometimes capital punishment.[9] Such beatings apparently fulfilled Christ's many predictions that his followers would suffer violent persecution at the hands of both religious and political leaders, even to flogging and crucifixion (Matt. 10:17; Mark 13:9). Ironically, Paul himself had been among the first to help fulfill these prophecies when, prior to his conversion, he "imprisoned and beat" several early Christian believers (see Acts 22:19–20; 26:11).

As for the flogging of Christ recounted in all four Gospels, this may well have exceeded 40 lashes, since it was administered not by Jews but rather by Roman authorities, "restricted by nothing but their strength and whim."[10] In this barbaric method of punishment—from the suffer-

8. Ralph P. Martin, *2 Corinthians*, Word Biblical Commentary, vol. 40 (Nashville: Nelson, 1986), 376.

9. *ESV Study Bible*, 2119; F. F. Bruce, *The Book of the Acts*, New International Commentary on the New Testament (Grand Rapids: Eerdmans, 1989), 315.

10. D. A. Carson, *Matthew*, in *The Expositor's Bible Commentary*, vol. 8: *Matthew, Mark, Luke*, ed. Frank E. Gaebelein (Grand Rapids: Zondervan-HarperCollins, 1984), 571.

ing or witnessing of which women were exempt, and which reportedly horrified even the cruel emperor Domitian—the victim was stripped of clothing and tied to an upright post with hands above his head; the back, buttocks, and legs were then exposed, and in most cases two soldiers carried out the beating, one on each side. The actual whip, called a *flagellum*, was made by plaiting pieces of bone or lead into leather thongs, along with, on some occasions, bits of stone, sharp metal, or narrow strips of wood.[11] "Severe flogging not only reduced the flesh to a bloody pulp but could open up the body until the bones were visible and the entrails exposed."[12] "As the Roman soldiers repeatedly struck the victim's back with full force, the iron balls would cause deep contusions, and the leather thongs and sheep bones would cut into the skin and subcutaneous tissues. Then, as the flogging continued, the lacerations would tear into the underlying skeletal muscles and produce quivering ribbons of bleeding flesh."[13] And these soldiers continued their assault "until they were exhausted or their commanding officer called them off."[14] Thus, "it is not surprising that victims of Roman flogging seldom survived."[15]

Christ, of course, did survive this beating to go on to his crucifixion; but as pointed out in a lengthy study published in the *Journal of the American Medical Association*, "the severe scourging, with its intense pain and appreciable blood loss, most probably left Jesus in a preshock state. Moreover, hematidrosis [the sweating of blood discussed on p. 99 above] had rendered his skin particularly tender. The physical and mental abuse meted out by the Jews and the Romans, as well as lack of food, water, and sleep, also contributed to his generally weakened state."[16] All of this explains why he died after such a relatively short time on the cross. (More on this in chap. 13.)

The actual Scripture references for the flogging of Christ are Matthew 27:26; Mark 15:15; Luke 23:16; and John 19:1; but you will

11. James R. Edwards, *The Gospel according to Mark*, Pillar New Testament Commentary (Grand Rapids: Eerdmans, 2002), 464; Walter W. Wessell, *Mark*, in Gaebelein, *Expositor's Bible Commentary*, 775; Carson, *John*, 597; Robert H. Stein, *Mark*, Baker Exegetical Commentary on the New Testament (Grand Rapids: Baker, 2008), 702.

12. Carson, *Matthew*, 571.

13. William D. Edwards, Wesley J. Gabel, and Floyd E. Hosmer, "On the Physical Death of Jesus Christ," *Journal of the American Medical Association* 255, 11 (March 21, 1986): 1457.

14. Carson, *John*, 597.

15. Wessell, *Mark*, 775.

16. Edwards, Gabel, and Hosmer, "Physical Death of Jesus," 1458.

notice that I have not quoted these passages—because there is virtually nothing to quote. Matthew, Mark, and John simply state that Christ was "scourged" or "flogged," with no additional details; and Luke has even less, merely quoting Pilate's intention to "punish" Jesus. As Leon Morris puts it, "Matthew devotes to this horror no more than one word, and he will later do the same with the crucifixion. None of the biblical writers dwells on the dreadful sufferings Jesus endured."[17] And in the words of James R. Edwards, the New Testament "shows no inclination to sensationalize the passion of Jesus by recounting its horrors," but prefers to use "restraint and discretion" by mentioning the matters only briefly.[18]

Two Gospel writers, however, do go on to mention one additional affliction—the "crown of thorns" placed on Jesus' head shortly after he was scourged (Matt. 27:29; John 19:2). This ghastly item was probably twisted together using spikes from the date palm, which could be up to 12 inches in length and would thus "sink into the victim's skull, causing blood to gush out and distorting a person's face."[19] A 1952 article by H. St. J. Hart proposed that the thorns faced outward in the style of "radiate" crowns used for god-kings at that time; but the actual Greek word in both Gospels refers to a different type of headwear donned at festivals and sporting events; thus, "it is simpler to understand the crown here as an implement of torture."[20]

Once again, neither writer provides these details; John is not much more specific when, in the book of Revelation, he outlines the eventual fate of God's enemies, an example of torture that serves as a fitting conclusion for this chapter because it is so widespread and so frighteningly severe. It begins in Revelation 9, which describes "locusts" of such bizarre appearance—gold crowns, human faces, lions' teeth, iron breastplates, noisy wings—that the term probably does not indicate literal insects; but in any case, these horrors are set loose upon all those "who do not have the seal of God on their foreheads. They were allowed to torment them for five months, but not to kill them, and their torment was like

17. Leon Morris, *The Gospel according to Matthew*, Pillar New Testament Commentary (Grand Rapids: Eerdmans, 1992), 708.

18. Edwards, *Mark*, 464.

19. *ESV Study Bible*, 2064.

20. Morris, *Matthew*, 712; the Hart material here is cited in Morris as well and comes from Hart, "The Crown of Thorns in John 19:2–5," *The Journal of Theological Studies* 3, 1 (1952): 66–75.

the torment of a scorpion when it stings someone." As in much of Revelation, the exact nature of this symbolic affliction is unclear, but the resulting anguish is so extreme that those who experience it "will long to die" (Rev. 9:3–10).

More torment rains down in Revelation 16:8–11, where an angel pours out fire from the sun so that the people are "scorched by the fierce heat"; the first and last word in this phrase are closely related in the original Greek, so that a literal reading—"scorched a great scorching"—emphasizes the unrelenting distress.[21] In the following verses, yet another angel unleashes darkness, and the writer observes that "people gnawed their tongues in anguish and cursed the God of heaven for their pain and sores"; but John does not tell us whether the darkness somehow produced these sores or (more likely) the victims still suffer from their earlier scorching.

Revelation goes on to describe the campaign against God's kingdom led by a symbolic beast and his false prophet, and by Satan himself, who uses two nations called Gog and Magog; but just at the very moment when these nations have surrounded God's people, "fire came down from heaven and consumed them, and the devil who had deceived them was thrown into the lake of fire and sulfur where the beast and the false prophet were, and they will be tormented day and night forever and ever" (Rev. 20:7–10).

But of course, they aren't the only ones to suffer this eternal anguish; earlier in the book, all those who worship the beast are condemned to "drink the wine of God's wrath, poured full strength into the cup of his anger," and to be "tormented with fire and sulfur. . . . And the smoke of their torment goes up forever and ever, and they have no rest, day or night" (Rev. 14:9–11).

These last two examples, of course, recall several threatening passages from the Gospels of Matthew, Mark, and Luke. Indeed, it is more than a little ironic that Jesus is often thought of as mild and tolerant when in fact most of what we know about hell—the fire, the terror, the pain, the eternity—comes from the explicit teaching of Christ himself. In Matthew 13:42, for example, Jesus calls hell a "fiery furnace"; Matthew 25:41 has "the eternal fire"; in Mark 9, it is "the unquenchable fire" and

---

21. Leon Morris, *The Book of Revelation: An Introduction and Commentary*, Tyndale New Testament Commentaries (Leicester, UK: Inter-Varsity, 1999), 126.

a place where "their worm does not die and the fire is not quenched" (Mark 9:43–48; see also Matt. 3:12).

Jesus' parable of the rich man and Lazarus makes it clear that those suffering in the afterlife will be conscious, will know who they are, and will remember their earthly lives with a regret for which there is no remedy (Luke 16:19–31). In seven different passages, Jesus describes this "outer darkness" as a place where there is "weeping and gnashing of teeth"—a "proverbial expression of pain and distress" in which the first verb suggests suffering and the second, despair."[22] (See Matt. 8:12; 13:42; 13:50; 22:13; 24:51; 25:30; Luke 13:28.)

In his commentary on Matthew, Leon Morris includes a poignant quote from R. C. Trench that puts the sufferings of hell in perspective while also addressing the anguish of our Savior, which we discussed earlier. Trench writes that the passages about weeping and gnashing of teeth "point to some doom so intolerable that the Son of God came down from heaven and tasted all the bitterness of death that He might deliver us from ever knowing the secrets of anguish, which . . . are shut up in these terrible words."[23]

In this way, Trench suggests that while such passages inspire appropriate dread, they do not elucidate the actual terrors in any detail, for a very good reason: those who trust in Christ will never experience them.

22. The quotation is from Morris, *Matthew*, 196; the note about suffering and despair is from Carson, *Matthew*, 203.

23. R. C. Trench, *Notes on the Parables of Our Lord* (1841), quoted in Morris, *Matthew*, 358.

12

"He Violated Her"

Rape

IN RECENT DECADES, rape has come to be regarded less as a sexual matter and more as a crime of violence. Susan Brownmiller's influential 1975 study *Against Our Will*, for example, places rape "where it truly belongs, within the context of modern criminal violence."[1] While this categorization is now somewhat problematic—especially with the increasing prevalence of date rape, which often involves little or no physical violence—nonetheless, the FBI website still lists rape as a violent crime (the second-worst, right after murder), as does the U. S. Department of Justice, at its *National Criminal Justice Reference Service* site.[2] So I have preserved that distinction here by placing this chapter in the "violence" section of this book rather than the one on "sex"—a location further justified by the association of rape and violence in several Bible passages.

    The Old Testament has only one word that refers specifically to this act—the rare *shagel*. Usually translated "ravish," it is found in only four passages: Deuteronomy 28:30; Isaiah 13:16; Jeremiah 3:2; and Zechariah 14:2. Somewhat more common is *anah*, which literally means "to be bowed down or afflicted." This appears throughout the Old Testament

    1. Susan Brownmiller, *Against Our Will: Men, Women and Rape* (New York: Simon, 1975), 377.
    2. "Violent Crime," *Crime in the United States, 2010*, Federal Bureau of Investigation, U.S. Department of Justice, accessed June 4, 2013, http://www.fbi.gov/about-us/cjis/ucr/crime-in-the-u.s/2010/crime in-the-u.s.-2010/violent-crime. See also, "Violent Crime > Rape and Sexual Assault," National Criminal Justice Reference Service, U. S. Department of Justice, Office of Justice Programs, accessed October 7, 2012, https://www.ncjrs.gov/app/topics/Topic.aspx?topicid=90.

quite often in its ordinary sense; in the handful of verses where it clearly refers to rape, *anah* is often rendered with the verb "violate" (e.g., Deut. 22:24, 29; 2 Sam. 13:12, 14, 22, 32). In many cases, Old Testament writers describe rape using one of the Hebrew idioms for intercourse—such as "lie with" or "know"—with only the context to indicate that the act involves forcible assault.

Exodus 22:16, for example, states that "if a man seduces a virgin who is not betrothed and lies with her, he shall give the bride-price for her and make her his wife." Here we find neither *anah* nor *shagel*, perhaps because the law's focus is not on rape as such. Indeed, while this regulation offered protection for women who had lost their virginity to importunate men and thereby become unmarriageable, the verb *seduce* nonetheless "most likely implies some mutual consent."[3] In any case, this ordinance focuses less on rape than on economic restitution to the father, who faced losing the usual payment received for marrying off a virgin daughter.

Furthermore, this Exodus regulation applies to women "not betrothed"—a stipulation made clearer in Deuteronomy 22:23–29, where intercourse with a betrothed woman is classed principally as adultery rather than rape. In this case, because betrothal was a binding commitment to marriage, the man is sentenced to death because he "violated his neighbor's wife"; and if the act occurred "in the city" and the woman "did not cry for help," this suggests complicity on her part, and both must be put to death—the standard punishment for adultery (Lev. 20:10). However, "if in the open country a man meets a young woman who is betrothed, and the man seizes her and lies with her, then only the man who lay with her shall die." The woman is exonerated because it was out in the country, where presumably she "cried for help and there was no one to rescue her." After tying rape to violence—"for this case is like that of a man attacking and murdering his neighbor"—this passage then reinforces the earlier command in Exodus 22: "If a man meets a virgin who is not betrothed, and seizes her and lies with her, and they are found, then the man who lay with her shall give to the father of the young woman fifty shekels of silver, and she shall be his wife, because he has violated her."

If these passages don't seem to express sufficient outrage over sexual assault, that may be due to the fact that such outrage had already been

3. *ESV Study Bible* (Wheaton, IL: Crossway, 2008), 180.

expressed—namely, in Scripture's first incidence of rape, which predates Exodus and Deuteronomy. Occurring in Genesis 34, the story condemns the assailant and also shows an existing principle that the woman thus victimized was to be honored and cared for by the man, not left destitute and unmarriageable. The victim in this case was Dinah, daughter of the patriarch Jacob; and the man, a Hivite Gentile named Shechem, chose his victim poorly—because she had twelve brothers! After he had "seized her and lay with her and humiliated her," he then requested her as a wife, even offering for her "as great a bride price and gift as you will." Dinah's indignant brothers deceitfully agreed to this arrangement, but their "bride price" was somewhat unusual: they insisted that Shechem and all the other male Hivites first be circumcised; then, after Shechem had agreed and the Hivite men were recovering from this operation, two of Dinah's brothers killed them all (Gen. 34:1–27).

While Jacob expressed alarm over the brothers' treacherous action—"You have brought trouble on me by making me stink to the inhabitants of the land" (v. 30)—the writer vehemently condemns Shechem's treatment of Dinah, saying, "he had done an outrageous thing in Israel by lying with Jacob's daughter, for such a thing must not be done" (v. 7). Indeed, even the narrator's description of the act in verse 2 makes his censure clear; rather than saying "lay with"—a common Old Testament term for intercourse—the actual Hebrew in this text omits the preposition, saying bluntly that "he laid her"; and further, as Gordon J. Wenham points out, the verb "humiliated" (*anah*) is "always used to describe intercourse without marriage"—as in Deuteronomy 22 (above) and 2 Samuel 13 (below). This "duplication of negative terms shows the author's strong disapproval of Shechem's behavior."[4]

Indeed, such disapproval is strongly reaffirmed in the 2 Samuel passage, where David's son Amnon rapes his half sister. Here, the king's firstborn conceives a strong sexual desire for Tamar, who—along with her brother Absalom—was also David's child, but by a different mother. Of course, Leviticus 18:9 forbids sexual relations with a father's daughter, even one brought up in a different home; however, this apparently did not dissuade Amnon, who "was so tormented that he made himself ill because of his sister Tamar, for she was a virgin, and it seemed impossible to Amnon to do anything to her." But with the help of his friend

4. Gordon J. Wenham, *Genesis 16–50*, Word Biblical Commentary, vol. 2 (Dallas: Word, 1994), 311.

Jonadab, he managed to get Tamar alone by first pretending to be ill, then requesting that she bake him some cakes and "bring the food into the chamber, that I may eat from your hand." When she had done so,

> he took hold of her and said to her, "Come, lie with me, my sister." She answered him, "No, my brother, do not violate me, for such a thing is not done in Israel; do not do this outrageous thing. As for me, where could I carry my shame? And as for you, you would be as one of the outrageous fools in Israel. Now therefore, please speak to the king, for he will not withhold me from you." But he would not listen to her, and being stronger than she, he violated her and lay with her.
>
> Then Amnon hated her with very great hatred, so that the hatred with which he hated her was greater than the love with which he had loved her. And Amnon said to her, "Get up! Go!" (2 Sam. 13:11b–15)

And despite her protests, he insisted, "Put this woman out of my presence and bolt the door after her." She then went forth weeping, with a torn robe and ashes on her head, and was found by her brother Absalom, in whose house she thereafter lived "a desolate woman." And after quietly biding his time for two full years, Absalom subsequently murdered his half brother—"because he had violated his sister Tamar" (2 Sam. 13:16–22).

Like the narrative of Shechem and Dinah, this story is carefully constructed to heap maximum condemnation on Amnon's despicable actions. Several commentators have observed that the Hebrew word for "cakes" in verse 6—*lebibah*—is similar to the term for "heart"—*lebab*—thus "implying something like 'heart-shapes'"; so Amnon seems to be fomenting a romantic atmosphere, yet his actual treatment of Tamar in the chamber is described in strongly negative language. The phrase "he took hold of her" uses "a strong verb meaning 'overpowered'"—one found in 1 Samuel 17:50 when David "prevailed" over Goliath.[5] Once again, despite the ESV translation of verse 14, the original Hebrew omits "with," saying bluntly that Amnon "laid her." And of course there is the phraseology of Tamar herself—"such a thing is not done in Israel"—which clearly echoes Genesis 34:7. In addition, these two rape narratives both use the Hebrew *nebalah*, translated in each case as "outrageous thing"; it is related to *nabal*, meaning "foolish" or "senseless," a word Tamar plays

---

5. Joyce G. Baldwin, *1 and 2 Samuel: An Introduction and Commentary*, Tyndale Old Testament Commentaries (Leicester, UK: Inter-Varsity, 1988), 248.

on in her following statement about "fools" (*nabal*), and one that had served earlier as the appropriate name for Abigail's doltish husband (1 Sam. 25).

Amnon's actions after raping Tamar are even more indicative of his sin and stupidity. If the earlier statement that "he made himself ill" over Tamar was not enough to suggest that his longing was mere unvarnished lust, then his reaction after the rape certainly is. At least in Shechem's case, "his soul was drawn to Dinah" after the deed, and he "spoke tenderly to her" (Gen. 34:3); but here the narrator uses a form of the word "hate" four times in one sentence (2 Sam. 13:15), suggesting that Amnon's infatuation was just that—mere physical desire followed swiftly by repulsion, rejection, and unfathomable cruelty once his lust had been sated. Peter J. Leithart points out how Amnon's horrific attitude is revealed in verse 17, where the phrase "put this woman out" does not use the normal Hebrew term for a female (*ishshah*) but rather *zeh*, which literally means "this, here"; and thus Amnon's command is better rendered "put this thing out of my presence."[6] And this despite the fact that she was both his sister and a princess, the daughter of King David!

As we have seen, earlier regulations in Exodus and Deuteronomy would have required that Amnon marry this unbetrothed woman he had violated; it goes without saying that he completely ignored these laws. Yet commentator A. A. Anderson points out that even if an incestuous marriage could have been arranged, Amnon's treatment of Tamar showed that he would not have accepted it; rather, he demonstrated an "unmistakable intention to humiliate both Tamar and Absalom, more or less implying that she was not fit to be married even by a rapist."[7]

Though Amnon was likely unaware of it, his lustful request for Tamar to "lie with me" echoes an earlier episode in which the wife of an Egyptian official named Potiphar tried repeatedly to seduce the righteous young Jew Joseph. Having already importuned him "day after day," she finally got him alone in the house and "caught him by his garment, saying, 'Lie with me.' But he left his garment in her hand and fled and got out of the house" (Gen. 39:10–12). This assault on Joseph's virtue did not succeed—but we might deem the incident "near-rape" due to the unrelenting nature of the woman's insistence; in addition, "the main items

6. Peter J. Leithart, *A Son to Me: An Exposition of 1 and 2 Samuel* (Moscow, ID: Canon, 2003), 234.
7. A. A. Anderson, *2 Samuel*, Word Biblical Commentary, vol. 11 (Word: Waco, TX, 1989), 175.

of attire in patriarchal times were mid-calf shorts and a tunic"—a sort of long T-shirt—so that pulling off either of these "against the wearer's will must have involved surprise and violence."[8] The entire incident suggests that even in Bible times, men were not alone in getting aggressive with their sexual desires. Nor is this the only such episode in Scripture.

There is similar aggression in Proverbs 7, where a lustful adulteress "seizes" a wayward youth while her husband is away, insisting that he come to her chamber so they can take their fill of love "till morning" (Prov. 7:13–18). Commentator Bruce K. Waltke cites evidence that in this context, "seize" can more precisely mean "rape" or "violate" (it is used of viciously grabbing genitals in Deut. 25:11). Indeed, the woman's "approach of grabbing and kissing him and her brazen, seductive speech are the female counterpart of male rape. The male overpowers the female through brute force; the female, through seduction."[9] In this case, the woman's attempt is more successful, for "all at once he follows her, as an ox goes to the slaughter, or as a stag is caught fast till an arrow pierces its liver" (Prov. 7:22–23). The phraseology once again links this sort of assault to violence.

Besides the fact that women are sometimes the aggressors in Scripture, another surprising aspect of rape in the Bible is the number of times it occurs as a consequence—that is, as part of a whole array of afflictions unleashed as a result of sin and disobedience. In Isaiah 47:3, for example, the prophet declares to the wicked kingdom of Babylon, "Your nakedness shall be uncovered"; here, ravishment is suggested by the notion of "uncovered nakedness," a common Hebrew idiom for illicit sex, found in such passages as Leviticus 18 and 20. This idea is clearer in Isaiah 13:16, which also addresses Babylon: "Their houses will be plundered and their wives ravished." Nahum 3:5 makes a similar suggestion about the fate of Nineveh: God "will lift up your skirts over your face" and "make nations look at your nakedness." Most of these rape-as-consequence passages, however, refer to Israel itself.

Indeed, in Deuteronomy 28, the people of God are warned that such things will surely follow disobedience. Along with various other curses including pestilence, drought, blindness, and famine, men in Israel will

8. Wenham, *Genesis 16–50*, 376.
9. Bruce K. Waltke, *The Book of Proverbs: Chapters 1–15*, New International Commentary on the Old Testament (Grand Rapids: Eerdmans, 2004), 376.

be doomed to "betroth a wife, but another man shall ravish her" (Deut. 28:30). Similar threats are found as Jerusalem is much later facing exile in Jeremiah 13:22–26: "Your skirts are lifted up and you suffer violence. . . . I myself will lift up your skirts over your face, and your shame will be seen." (See also Zech. 14:2.) The book of Lamentations, written after the nation had suffered brutal treatment at the hands of Babylon, makes it clear that these threats had become a reality: "Women are raped in Zion, young women in the towns of Judah" (Lam. 5:11).

The most extensive of these texts occurs in Ezekiel 16, which addresses a symbolic young woman who represents the nation of Israel in her infidelity to the Lord. Condemning this figurative adulteress for "whorings with your lovers," the Lord declares that those very lovers will turn on her: "I will gather them against you from every side and will uncover your nakedness to them, that they may see all your nakedness. And I will judge you . . . and bring upon you the blood of wrath and jealousy. . . . They shall strip you of your clothes and take your beautiful jewels and leave you naked and bare. They shall bring up a crowd against you, and they shall stone you and cut you to pieces with their swords" (Ezek. 16:36–40). Once again, the passage uses idioms for intercourse while also linking rape to violence. Given the presence again of the sexual idiom "uncover nakedness," this brutal passage may warrant Brian Godawa's description: "God even goes so far as to pictorialize his punishment of Israel in the shockingly graphic terms of gang rape."[10] In any case, there is no question about gang rape and brutal violence in Judges 19, probably the most blood-curdling passage in all of Scripture.

In a lengthy narrative that often echoes Genesis 19, a Levite traveling with his concubine plans to spend the night in the town square at an Israelite village called Gibeah; but an old man coming in from the fields insists on hosting the Levite in his home instead. Then, "as they were making their hearts merry, behold, the men of the city, worthless fellows, surrounded the house, beating on the door. And they said to the old man, the master of the house, 'Bring out the man who came into your house, that we may know him.'" Clearly tying his narrative to Genesis, the writer uses the Hebrew idiom "to know," also found in Genesis 19:5, where it likewise means sexual intercourse (see pp. 43–44, 86). Of

10. Brian Godawa, *Hollywood Worldviews: Watching Films with Wisdom and Discernment* (Downers Grove, IL: InterVarsity, 2002), 198.

course, the host objects to such a proposal, calling it a "vile thing." And just as Lot had offered his own virgin daughters in Genesis 19, the old man here makes a counterproposal:

> "Behold, here are my virgin daughter and his concubine. . . . Violate them and do with them what seems good to you, but against this man do not do this outrageous thing." But the men would not listen to him. So the man seized his concubine and made her go out to them. And they knew her and abused her all night until the morning. . . . And as morning appeared, the woman came and fell down at the door of the man's house where her master was, until it was light.
>
> And her master rose up in the morning, and when he opened the doors of the house and went out to go on his way, behold, there was his concubine lying at the door of the house, with her hands on the threshold. He said to her, "Get up, let us be going." But there was no answer. Then he put her on the donkey, and the man rose up and went away to his home. And when he entered his house, he took a knife, and taking hold of his concubine he divided her, limb by limb, into twelve pieces, and sent her throughout all the territory of Israel. (Judg. 19:14–29)

Typing out the whole story here, I have to agree with Michael Wilcock, who writes that this incident "beggars the imagination"[11]—though the narrator describes it without much graphic detail, even using the mild idiom "know" instead of *anah*, *shagel*, or some other strong term more suited to the actual events. Yet while he does not give us the gory specifics of gang rape, the writer repeatedly emphasizes its length—"all night until the morning"—causing one commentary to observe that "if ever a human being endured a night of utter horror it was the Levite's concubine on that night, which must have seemed as interminable as eternity and as dark as the pit itself."[12]

Indeed, rather than focusing on the rape itself, much of the material in Judges 19 serves to indict the cruelty of the men responsible—and I am not referring principally to the rapists, though they are vilified in no uncertain terms. Commentators Cundall and Morris observe that

11. Michael Wilcock, *The Message of Judges: Grace Abounding*, The Bible Speaks Today (Leicester, UK: Inter-Varsity, 1992), 168.

12. Arthur E. Cundall and Leon Morris, *Judges and Ruth: An Introduction and Commentary*, Tyndale Old Testament Commentaries (Leicester, UK: Inter-Varsity, 1968), 197–98.

since the offenders were apparently not punished—nor were their actions repudiated in Gibeah—the event must have involved a majority of local men, perhaps even some town leaders.[13] To make matters worse, "it was not just that the rowdies of Gibeah got together after nightfall for an orgy, that they came out on to the streets to enjoy it openly, that it was going to involve not only rape but also male rape, and that it did in fact lead to the death of the girl. All that was incredible enough. It was that all this was apparently expected, as part of the regular night-life of the town. And not among Jebusites or Canaanites, but among the people of God!"[14]

As this quote suggests, the incident in Judges 19 is especially vile because it involves four simultaneous sins—homosexuality, adultery, rape, and murder (never mind the flouting of basic hospitality). And it is not only the men of Gibeah who come in for condemnation. Yes, the old man showed laudable foresight by urging the Levite away from the open square; but then he had the audacity to preserve his own honor as host by offering another man's consort for rape and abuse. Yet the Levite didn't seem to mind, for he himself "seized" her—a word often used in violent contexts (1 Sam. 17:35; 2 Sam. 2:16; Jer. 6:24)—and thrust her out "like one tosses a scrap of meat to dogs," with "a callous disregard for the one he professed to love, or, perhaps more pertinently, with a greater concern for his own skin."[15]

His actions the next morning were, if anything, even worse. He opened the door to go on his way, apparently not even remembering his concubine until he saw her lying there "with her hands on the threshold"—a phrase that suggests "she had been too weak to open the door or even to knock."[16] The writer spares us details, but her physical condition must have been visibly apparent; nonetheless, the Levite, rather than helping her in any way, simply commanded her to get up, then threw her on his donkey and rode off.

The Levite's later description of this event says "they violated my concubine, and she is dead" (Judg. 20:6), wording that suggests her death may not have occurred at their hands, but only later, perhaps because the Levite did nothing to help her in the morning. Daniel I. Block advances the

13. Ibid., 196–97.

14. Wilcock, *The Message of Judges*, 169.

15. The two quotes are taken, respectively, from Daniel I. Block, *Judges, Ruth*, The New American Commentary (Nashville: Broadman, 1999), 539, and Cundall and Morris, *Judges and Ruth*, 197–98.

16. Block, *Judges, Ruth*, 541.

possibility that she was still alive even after the Levite arrived home, and that he himself murdered her in a fit of rage. In any case, "he desacralizes her body, treating her as if it were an animal carcass." Not surprisingly, Block then concludes that this incident is "among the most grotesque and sickening in the book, if not in the entire Scriptures," a story of "unrestrained animal lust and human depravity."[17] Cundall and Morris agree, observing, "This foul deed was considered to be the outstanding atrocity since the time of the Exodus,"[18] a point clearly demonstrated in Hosea, where these horrors have become a proverbial byword for wickedness: "They have deeply corrupted themselves as in the days of Gibeah" (Hos. 9:9); and, "From the days of Gibeah, you have sinned, O Israel" (Hos. 10:9).

We have observed many times in this book that biblical narrators often make no editorial comment on the depraved acts they describe. In the story of Lot sleeping with his own daughters; in the brutal flogging of Christ; in the tale of young Esther sacrificing her virginity to a pagan king along with countless other women in the "harem"—neither in these three texts nor in many others do the narrators condemn the immorality of the action or include any characters who call them into question. Of course, this is not to suggest that the writers condone any of the acts they are describing—only, perhaps, that it is not necessary to express a personal opinion every single time some atrocity is presented. It is worth noting, however, that all three major episodes of rape in the Bible provide abundant condemnation of the deed.

As we have seen, the rapes of both Dinah and Tamar are accompanied by a statement that "such a thing is not done in Israel" (2 Sam. 13:12; see also Gen. 34:7). The writer of Judges makes a similar claim in the final verse of chapter 19: "And all who saw it said, 'Such a thing has never happened or been seen from the day that the people of Israel came up out of the land of Egypt until this day.'" (Of course, it is possible that the writer here is describing the Levite's butchery as well as the horrific rape of his concubine.) Likewise in Judges 19, the old man describes the attempted rape with the same word Tamar will later use to Amnon: "outrageous"—literally, "act of folly or disgrace."

Taken together, these unusually strong denunciations make rape one of the most vigorously condemned sins in all of Scripture.

17. Ibid., 532, 542.
18. Cundall and Morris, *Judges and Ruth*, 198–99.

13

"Wallowing in His Blood"

Dismemberment and Other Disgusting Deaths

THE PREVIOUS CHAPTER on rape concluded with the ghastly passage from Judges 19, in which a rape victim also suffered dismemberment, perhaps while she was still alive. In that text, the ESV says her husband "divided her, limb by limb, into twelve pieces" (Judg. 19:29); but the actual Hebrew is somewhat more specific: he divided his concubine "according to her bones"—prompting writer Daniel I. Block to assert that "even in death there is no respect for this woman. Seized for the second time, she becomes a sacrificial victim of male violence."[1] Block employs the language of sacrifice because the Hebrew word "divide" here is the same verb used of ritual dissection in the priestly regulations from Leviticus (Lev. 1:6, 12, 17; 8:20; see also Ex. 29:17; 1 Kings 18:23).

As one might guess, this is not the only instance of dismemberment in Scripture. The sacrificial language reminds us that many, many animals were divided up or chopped into pieces; not only those used in the temple and tabernacle (for instance, birds torn open by their wings, Lev. 1:17), but also the heifer, goat, and ram cut in half by Abram (Genesis 15) and the oxen cut up by Saul in 1 Samuel 11 (pieces of these were—like the concubine's body in Judges 19—sent throughout all Israel).

But of course dismemberment is also carried out on humans, and usually in passages where there is little question that the victim was still

1. Daniel I. Block, *Judges, Ruth*, The New American Commentary (Nashville: Broadman, 1999), 546.

alive at the time. In 1 Samuel 15:33, for example, the Amalekite king Agag was chopped up by Samuel himself. But while this narrative describes an actual event with blunt specifics ("Samuel hacked Agag to pieces before the LORD"), most of these instances involve a future *threat* of being cut to pieces: in Daniel, for instance, the Babylonian king Nebuchadnezzar twice threatens that those not obeying his commands will be "torn limb from limb" (Dan. 2:5; 3:29); and in Deuteronomy 32:26, the Lord threatens his people with the same possibility if they are disobedient. In Ezekiel, this divine threat becomes a promise for those who have committed spiritual infidelity with heathen gods; Israel's so-called pagan "lovers" will turn and "cut you to pieces with their swords" (Ezek. 16:40), or at the very least, "cut off your nose and your ears" (Ezek. 23:25). Likewise, the unfaithful steward in Jesus' New Testament parable will be cut "in pieces" for being drunk and abusive rather than preparing for "the coming of the Son of Man" (Matt. 24:36–51; see also Ps. 50:22).

The Ezekiel 23 passage is accompanied by additional details of mutilation, for God says that the woman portrayed here—a symbolic depiction of God's adulterous people—will gnaw shards of pottery and tear out her own breasts (Ezek. 23:34), thereby uprooting "the bodily members that led her into sin in the first place."[2] This language is echoed in the book of Hosea, where the Lord again promises judgment on his people: "I will tear open their breast, and there I will devour them like a lion, as a wild beast would rip them open" (Hos. 13:8).

In these passages, specific body parts are in view—the breasts, and perhaps also in Hosea the heart (being inside the opened chest cavity). Elsewhere, it is the head that gets removed. Indeed, decapitation occurs in several Bible stories, including 1 Samuel 17:51, where David crowns his victory over Goliath by cutting off the giant's head as he lies slain upon the ground. Later in the same book, Philistines come upon the corpse of King Saul and cut his head off as well (1 Sam. 31:9). A few chapters hence, Saul's son Ish-bosheth is killed and then beheaded by two of his officers, who bring the head to King David, thinking they have done the king a favor by disposing of this rival ruler; but David "commanded his young men, and they killed them and cut off their hands and feet and hanged them" (2 Sam. 4:7–12).

2. Iain M. Duguid, *Ezekiel*, The NIV Application Commentary (Grand Rapids: Zondervan, 1999), 304.

In all these cases—which are described frankly but without the lurid detail that might indicate how tough it is to chop off someone's head with a sword—the victim is already dead when beheaded. That may not have been the case with the seventy sons of King Ahab slain in 2 Kings 10; here, the moment Jehu commanded the men of Samaria to do this, "they took the king's sons and slaughtered them, seventy persons, and put their heads in baskets and sent them to him at Jezreel"—after which Jehu had the heads piled "in two heaps at the entrance of the gate until the morning" (2 Kings 10:1–8).

It seems likely that John the Baptist was still alive at the time of his decapitation as well. Arguably the most famous beheading in Scripture, this event is recorded in three of the four Gospels—specifically, Matthew 14, Mark 6, and Luke 9. As we saw in chapter 9 above, John had been imprisoned by Herod, a Roman official overseeing parts of Palestine, for having angered Herod by preaching against the ruler's marriage to Herodias, the ex-wife of Herod's own brother. Apparently John had provoked Herodias as well, for when her daughter pleased the king with an appealing dance at a banquet, he offered her virtually anything she asked for; the young dancer was prevailed upon by her mother to request the head of John the Baptist on a platter. "And immediately the king sent an executioner with orders to bring John's head. He went and beheaded him in the prison and brought his head on a platter and gave it to the girl, and the girl gave it to her mother" (Mark 6:17–29). The detail of the "platter" suggests that this depraved spectacle had overtones of being yet one more "dish" that Herod served to his guests, though it does not appear to have disturbed the diners. Commentator R. T. France calls it "an unedifying story, told with a bald realism which conveys the atmosphere of a licentious oriental court."[3]

Now that we have covered dismemberment and decapitation in the Bible, let's move on to a third and fourth "D" in this chapter: disgusting deaths—of which there are so many, and in such variety, that the organization of subsequent material here may seem somewhat scattershot.

An early instance involves Israelites intermarrying with local pagans in the time following the exodus from Egypt. After "the people began to whore with the daughters of Moab"—even to the point of worshiping

---

3. R. T. France, *The Gospel according to Matthew: An Introduction and Commentary*, Tyndale New Testament Commentaries (Leicester, UK: Inter-Varsity, 1985), 234.

Moabite gods—God commanded Moses to kill all those who had thus defiled both themselves and the nation. Just after the Israelite leader had instructed his judges to carry out this order, "behold, one of the people of Israel came and brought a Midianite woman to his family, in the sight of Moses and in the sight of the whole congregation of the people of Israel, while they were weeping. . . . When Phinehas the son of Eleazar, son of Aaron the priest, saw it, he rose and left the congregation and took a spear in his hand and went after the man of Israel into the chamber and pierced both of them, the man of Israel and the woman through her belly" (Num. 25:1–8). This seems like a fairly ordinary killing, but some commentators feel that the wording, with the two apparently killed simultaneously—"and the woman through her belly"—suggests that Phinehas slew them in the very act of sexual intercourse.[4]

Another pagan woman killed in grisly fashion was Jezebel, daughter of a pagan king and wife of the Old Testament monarch Ahab, who himself also died a memorable death. Presiding over the northern kingdom for about two decades in the ninth century B.C., Ahab was among the worst in a long line of Israelite rulers who consistently flouted God's laws, but in this case, the corrupt national leader was led on by his pagan wife; for "there was none who sold himself to do what was evil in the sight of the LORD like Ahab, whom Jezebel his wife incited." This incitement included urging Ahab to frame and execute the innocent Naboth so the king could seize his vineyard. As a result, the prophet Elijah told the wicked ruler, "In the place where dogs licked up the blood of Naboth shall dogs lick your own blood"; and as for Jezebel, "the LORD also said, 'The dogs shall eat Jezebel within the walls of Jezreel'" (1 Kings 21:19, 23, 25). (Elijah's prophecies here also include the annihilation of Ahab's line, realized in the decapitation of seventy sons discussed above.)

Sure enough, in the very next chapter, during a battle with the Syrians, an arrow struck Ahab "between the scale armor and the breastplate." Having been taken out of the fray, "the king was propped up in his chariot facing the Syrians, until at evening he died. And the blood of the wound flowed into the bottom of the chariot," which was later washed out "by the pool of Samaria, and the dogs licked up his blood, and the prostitutes washed themselves in it" (1 Kings 22:34–38). This ignominious end fulfills the prophecy twice, for Scripture establishes a

4. See, for example, *ESV Study Bible* (Wheaton, IL: Crossway, 2008), 307.

connection between dogs and prostitutes, using the phrase "wages of a dog" to describe a whore's payment in Deuteronomy 23:18.

This pool of Samaria, however, was *not* located where Naboth had died; rather, that part of the prophecy—focused on Naboth's dwelling-place in Jezreel—was likely fulfilled by another gory death, described with some detail in 2 Kings 9: Here, God had commanded the future king Jehu to wipe out Ahab's line, a task he began by assassinating the current monarch, Ahab's son Jehoram. Having pursued Jehoram at length, "Jehu drew his bow with his full strength, and shot Jehoram between the shoulders, so that the arrow pierced his heart, and he sank in his chariot. Jehu said to Bidkar his aide, '. . . the LORD made this pronouncement against him: "As surely as I saw yesterday the blood of Naboth and the blood of his sons—declares the LORD—I will repay you on this plot of ground." Now therefore take him up and throw him on the plot of ground, in accordance with the word of the LORD'" (2 Kings 9:24–26).

Completing his task with this episode's most explicit killing, Jehu then proceeded to the gate of Jezreel, where Jezebel—apparently certain she still possessed the charms that had worked on Ahab—"painted her eyes and adorned her head and looked out of the window." Looking up, Jehu asked of the men with her, "Who is on my side?" And when a few indicated assent, "He said, 'Throw her down.' So they threw her down. And some of her blood spattered on the wall and on the horses, and they trampled on her." Shockingly, the resolute Jehu then went inside and had dinner, after which he instructed some of his men, "'See now to this cursed woman and bury her, for she is a king's daughter.' But when they went to bury her, they found no more of her than the skull and the feet and the palms of her hands." Jehu concluded, "This is the word of the LORD, which he spoke by his servant Elijah the Tishbite: 'In the territory of Jezreel the dogs shall eat the flesh of Jezebel, and the corpse of Jezebel shall be as dung on the face of the field'" (2 Kings 9:30–37). Peter J. Leithart points out that the pagan queen's death is described in sacrificial terms, since the Hebrew verb for "spattered" in this passage is the same one used for sprinkling the altar and mercy seat in such earlier passages as Leviticus 4, 14, and 16. He further compares Jehu's meal to the "supper of the lamb" after the "great prostitute" has been slain in Revelation 19 (see vv. 2, 9, and 17).[5]

---

5. Peter J. Leithart, *1 and 2 Kings*, Brazos Theological Commentary on the Bible (Grand Rapids: Brazos, 2006), 221.

Another interrelated series of gory murders involves Joab, the skilled military general who served as commander of the army under King David in 2 Samuel. These killings began when Joab and his two brothers, Asahel and Abishai, were suppressing forces of the rebel king Ish-bosheth, which were in turn led by another skilled commander, Abner. Asahel vigorously pursued Abner, who repeatedly urged Asahel to turn back, "but he refused to turn aside. Therefore Abner struck him in the stomach with the butt of his spear, so that the spear came out at his back. And he fell there and died where he was" (2 Sam. 2:18–23). It is possible that Abner simply stopped, causing the hurtling pursuer to impale himself on the back of the spear, but the wording suggests an active thrust on Abner's part. It is also possible that Abner used the butt of his weapon in hope of less injury—but again, that is hard to accept, given the severity of the wound. A. A. Anderson feels rather that Abner killed Asahel with the blunter instrument as "proof of his superiority."[6]

In any case, Joab was so incensed by Abner's act that even after Abner had made peace with David—pledging his entire support for the new king—nonetheless, Joab treacherously slew David's new ally: he "took him aside into the midst of the gate to speak with him privately, and there he struck him in the stomach, so that he died, for the blood of Asahel his brother" (2 Sam. 3:17–27). Note that Joab was careful to stab his victim in the same place where Asahel had been wounded by Abner's spear.

Some time later, another rebellion was under way, with David's son Absalom seeking to seize the kingdom from his own father. In the resulting warfare, Absalom, riding a donkey, somehow got "his head caught fast" as he passed beneath a large oak tree; though the text doesn't say so, most readers agree that Absalom's famously luxuriant hair—stressed in 2 Samuel 14:26—got tangled in the branches. In any case, "he was suspended between heaven and earth, while the mule that was under him went on." Since David had asked Joab to "deal gently for my sake with the young man Absalom," one soldier hesitated to take advantage of the situation, reminding Joab of the king's request. In a passage of bracing bluntness, however, Joab told the reluctant soldier, "'I will not

6. A. A. Anderson, *2 Samuel*, Word Biblical Commentary, vol. 11 (Waco, TX: Word, 1989), 45; see also Joyce G. Baldwin, *1 and 2 Samuel: An Introduction and Commentary*, Tyndale Old Testament Commentaries (Leicester, UK: Inter-Varsity, 1988), 186.

waste time like this with you.' And he took three javelins in his hand and thrust them into the heart of Absalom while he was still alive in the oak. And ten young men, Joab's armor-bearers, surrounded Absalom and struck him and killed him" (2 Sam. 18:5–15).

This rebellion having been put down, Joab was then demoted—probably for having disregarded the king's wishes regarding Absalom; he was replaced as commander of the army by Amasa, who had, ironically, served under Absalom in the recent insurrection. During yet another rebellion by a "worthless man" named Sheba, Joab and Amasa met—resulting in the grisliest of these four killings: "Now Joab was wearing a soldier's garment, and over it was a belt with a sword in its sheath fastened on his thigh, and as he went forward it fell out. And Joab said to Amasa, 'Is it well with you, my brother?' And Joab took Amasa by the beard with his right hand to kiss him. But Amasa did not observe the sword that was in Joab's hand. So Joab struck him with it in the stomach and spilled his entrails to the ground without striking a second blow, and he died." Joab and Abishai then called for help in pursuing Sheba, but were hampered because "Amasa lay wallowing in his blood in the highway. And anyone who came by, seeing him, stopped." So one of Joab's men "carried Amasa out of the highway into the field and threw a garment over him" (2 Sam. 20:1–12).

Three points are worth emphasizing in this narrative. First, Joab may have dropped his sword deliberately, so as to have it in hand without calling undue attention to the act of drawing it out. Second, he purposely refused to strike Amasa a second time, probably to prolong his suffering. And third, there's little doubt why the corpse had to be removed, as the victim had been disemboweled and was thus "wallowing" in a good deal more than just blood.

Though it is possible to understand Joab's actions in the case of Absalom—who might well have succeeded in displacing his father—nonetheless, the homicidal commander could probably have used a refresher on some Old Testament laws against murder and manslaughter. Perhaps the most applicable would be Exodus 21:14: "If a man willfully attacks another to kill him by cunning, you shall take him from my altar, that he may die." This passage keys on premeditation, as does Deuteronomy 19:11–12, which decrees the death penalty for anyone who "hates his neighbor and lies in wait for him and attacks him and strikes him fatally so that he dies."

Of course, these are only two of the many Old Testament regulations about killing, so perhaps this might be an appropriate spot to discuss some others as well. The very first such prohibition was delivered directly to Noah after the flood—"Whoever sheds the blood of man, by man shall his blood be shed" (Gen. 9:6)—but surely the best known is the sixth commandment, "You shall not murder," found in both Exodus 20:13 and Deuteronomy 5:17. According to the *ESV Study Bible*, the verb used in these two passages covers "the unlawful or immoral killing of another human being (the specific meaning of the English word 'murder')"; it also includes "causing the death of another human being through careless or negligent behavior."

Several passages provide "cities of refuge" to which a man may flee if the killing was accidental, "as when someone goes into the forest with his neighbor to cut wood, and his hand swings the axe to cut down a tree, and the head slips from the handle and strikes his neighbor so that he dies" (Deut. 19:4–10; see also Ex. 21:13; Num. 35:9–15, 22–29). But probably the most specific laws involving murder are found in Numbers 35, which names various possible implements that indicate premeditation—"an iron object," "a stone tool," or "a wooden tool that could cause death"; also included here are scenarios in which the assailant "pushed him out of hatred or hurled something at him, lying in wait, so that he died, or in enmity struck him down with his hand, so that he died." In every case here, the perpetrator is labeled "a murderer," and "the murderer shall be put to death" (Num. 35:16–21).

This list of ad hoc murder methods seems to anticipate the book of Judges, which has a clear motif of "improvised weapons," including Samson's jawbone (Judg. 15:15), Shamgar's oxgoad (Judg. 3:31), Gideon's clay jars (Judg. 7:16–21) and three hundred fox-tail torches (Judg. 15:4–5). Without wishing to get into rights and wrongs—that is, without trying to apply earlier regulations on homicide to the complexities of each case—let's look more closely at three of these unusual killings in Judges, starting with the death of Abimelech in chapter 9.

Abimelech was a son of Gideon who, having slain seventy of his own brothers, "ruled over Israel three years" (Judg. 9:22), at which point the people of Shechem rebelled against him. After several skirmishes and many deaths, Abimelech attacked the Shechemite city of Thebez, where the people had taken refuge in "a strong tower." While the army was besieging this tower, "a certain woman threw an upper millstone on Abimelech's head and crushed his skull. Then he called quickly to the young man his armor-bearer and said to him, 'Draw your sword and kill me, lest they say of me, "A woman killed him."' And his young man thrust him through, and he died" (Judg. 9:50–54). Commentators Cundall and Morris tell us that grinding with millstones was not normally done atop a tower or roof; and since these upper stones were two or three inches thick and eighteen inches across, this woman's maneuver must have been both deliberate and desperate, as she would have had to haul a weighty stone up all those stairs.[7] It goes without saying that the unnamed Shechemite appears to have been a fairly good shot with her makeshift weapon as well.

Jael's tent peg is another improvised weapon found in Judges. Chapters 4 and 5 describe Israel's fight against the oppressive Canaanites, in particular the pursuit of the army commander Sisera, who ran away after his troops were routed in a battle at Mount Tabor. He seemed to have found refuge in the tent of a Kenite woman named Jael, who "opened a skin of milk and gave him a drink and covered him." Sisera then asked that she stand at the tent door to turn away anyone seeking him; but instead, she "took a tent peg, and took a hammer in her hand. Then she went softly to him and drove the tent peg into his temple until it went down into the ground while he was lying fast asleep from weariness. So he died" (Judg. 4:17–22).

While this prose account is presented with "brutal detail," the writer elaborates on it with "bloodthirsty relish" and "savage pleasure"[8] in the celebratory poem that comprises the following chapter: "He asked for water and she gave him milk; she brought him curds in a noble's bowl. She sent her hand to the tent peg and her right hand to the workmen's mallet; she struck Sisera; she crushed his head; she shattered and pierced his temple. Between her feet he sank, he fell, he lay still; between her feet he sank, he fell; where he sank, there he fell—dead" (Judg. 5:25–27).

One wonders how Jael managed this difficult feat without awakening Sisera the minute she started, but the narrator does tell us that

---

7. Arthur E. Cundall and Leon Morris, *Judges and Ruth: An Introduction and Commentary*, Tyndale Old Testament Commentaries (Leicester, UK: Inter-Varsity, 1968), 136.

8. The three phrases are taken, in the order presented in my text, from Block, *Judges, Ruth*, 207 and 240, and Michael Wilcock, *The Message of Judges: Grace Abounding*, The Bible Speaks today (Leicester, UK: Inter-Varsity, 1992), 66.

he was worn out from his battle and flight; and note too that instead of the water he asked for (Judg. 4:19), she gave him milk, a known soporific. Coming from a woman—one of a tribe that was allied with Canaan, not Israel—this is an almost motherly act, giving Sisera every reason to sleep like a baby. Furthermore, her dexterity with peg and mallet is explained by the fact that putting up and taking down tents was the work of women at that time; and her attack was hardly tentative, since the peg went all the way through his skull and into the ground underneath. In any case, Jael's actions "broke every accepted standard of hospitality. Every detail is dealt with with relish, and finer feelings vanished in the savage delight occasioned by Sisera's death."[9] Commentators use terms like "savage" and "brutal" because, among other things, chapter 5 employs four different verbs to recount the attack: "struck," "crushed," "shattered," and "pierced."

Ehud's killing of Eglon in Judges 3, accomplished with a sword, may not seem to belong with other passages about makeshift weapons, but note that Ehud had to make the weapon himself (Judg. 3:16); and it is worth observing here that all these unusual implements may have been necessitated by a policy among conquering nations to remove all possible weapons from subdued peoples as the Philistines had done in 1 Samuel 13:19–22. (This policy is also suggested in Judges 5:8: "Was shield or spear to be seen among forty thousand in Israel?")

In any case, Ehud was a left-handed man who fashioned himself an eighteen-inch sword with two edges, "and he bound it on his right thigh under his clothes." He then went to pay tribute to the leader of those oppressing Israel at the time, King Eglon, "a very fat man." Having come into Eglon's presence, Ehud said—probably with some irony—"I have a secret message for you, O king." So Eglon sent all his attendants out, "and Ehud came to him as he was sitting alone in his cool roof chamber. And Ehud said, 'I have a message from God for you.' And he arose from his seat. And Ehud reached with his left hand, took the sword from his right thigh, and thrust it into his belly. And the hilt also went in after the blade, and the fat closed over the blade, for he did not pull the sword out of his belly; and the dung came out." Ehud then fled, securing the door behind him, and when Eglon's servants saw the room locked, they thought, "Surely he is relieving himself in the closet

9. Cundall and Morris, *Judges and Ruth*, 89, 100.

of the cool chamber"—and their ensuing wait prevented discovery of the death until it was too late to capture Ehud (Judg. 3:15–24).

This is undoubtedly among the most revolting passages in all of Scripture, the more so because it is described in such lurid detail. Yet there remain some questions about what actually happened when Eglon was stabbed. Certainly Ehud's use of his left hand and right leg made the attack more unexpected; further, the Hebrew word for "thrust" is the same one used for Jael's attack in Judges 4:21, which shows why Ehud's weapon went in so far. And surely the sword's relatively small size, together with the king's noted corpulence, helps explain why Ehud chose not to pull the sword back out once it had disappeared into the king's fat belly.

But what is meant by "the dung came out"?

The word used for "dung" appears only here in Scripture and has no clear etymology. Some infer that Eglon's intestines were pierced, releasing fecal matter; but linguistic work by Cundall and Morris suggests that the downward movement of the dagger caused it to emerge from the king's anus (the ASV has "it came out behind"). Daniel I. Block, on the other hand, sees it this way: "When Eglon fell to the ground and expired, his bowels relaxed and discharged their contents." But whatever happened, it is quite clear that excrement emerged into the open air, since Eglon's attendants could smell it and thus assumed he was "relieving himself" (in the original Hebrew, this is the idiomatic "covering his feet"). As Cundall and Morris put it, "Such sensational details have a habit of impressing themselves indelibly upon the human memory." Block sums it up more graphically: "The irony and humor of the situation would not have escaped the early Israelite leaders. All that remained of Eglon, the fattened calf, the mighty ruler of Moab, was a corpse and a pile of feces."[10]

From deaths described in unusual detail, we move to deaths described with very little—namely, executions by the ancient method known as stoning. Mentioned dozens of times in both the Old and New Testaments, this process is specifically prescribed as a punishment for sin in at least ten passages (Ex. 19:3; Lev. 24:14; Deut. 13:10; etc.), though it is probably implied in the many other laws requiring death, since it was the standard Jewish method of execution even in the time of Christ

10. Ibid., 77–78; Block, *Judges, Ruth*, 168.

and the apostles. Some of the sins requiring the death penalty include adultery and such pagan practices as divination, necromancy, and child sacrifice (Deut. 22:22–24; Lev. 20:2, 27).

In addition to numerous references in the law, stoning is either threatened or actually carried out in more than two dozen other passages (Ex. 17:4; 1 Kings 21:13; Ezek. 16:40; Matt. 21:35; Heb. 11:37; etc.). It sometimes constitutes formal judgment rendered for sin. For example, in Leviticus 24:10–23 an Israelite woman's son is stoned for blasphemy, and in Numbers 15:32–36 a man is stoned for gathering sticks on the Sabbath. At other times, it was the result of mob violence, as when "all Israel" stoned to death a taskmaster sent to them by King Rehoboam (1 Kings 12:18), or when the apostle Paul was stoned—though not fatally—by an angry crowd in Acts 14:19. Mob violence may also have been involved with the well-known stoning of the New Testament martyr Stephen, where no judicial sentence is mentioned by the narrator (Acts 7:54–59).

Yet despite these numerous references, the Bible writers never describe the actual process of stoning with any specificity, except perhaps that the severity of the act is reflected in the oft-used phrase "stoned him with stones," employing the traditional Hebrew practice of repetition to intensify an expression (e.g., "vanity of vanities," "Lord of lords," "holy, holy, holy"). Some facts can be reconstructed by looking carefully at a few individual verses. For example, we know that in the case of formal trials, witnesses to the sin involved were to cast the first stones, followed by the rest of the congregation (Deut. 17:7; see also Deut. 13:9). Exodus 19:13—"no hand shall touch him, but he shall be stoned"—further suggests that this particular method of execution prevented the ceremonial uncleanness that would have resulted from touching a dead body (see Num. 19:11); this may be why Exodus 19:13 also offers the option of shooting the culprit with an arrow. (Together with the plenitude of rocks in Palestine, this concept of uncleanness probably accounts for the standard use of stoning in executions.)[11] And in Ezekiel 16:39–40, the victim is stripped before being stoned, though this passage does not necessarily serve as a representative example.

Fortunately, specific details of the actual stoning process appear in the Mishnah, a collection of Jewish writings compiled around A.D. 200.

---

11. R. Alan Cole, *Exodus: An Introduction and Commentary*, Tyndale Old Testament Commentaries (Leicester, UK: Inter-Varsity, 1973), 147.

According to this source, the victim was indeed stripped (though not completely) and then pushed into a declivity from a height of about ten feet—preferably by one of the witnesses. If this did not kill him, a second witness was to hurl a large stone down onto his head or chest. And if this also failed to cause death—or perhaps even if it did—the rest of the people would pelt the body with stones. The final verses of Deuteronomy 21 also make provision for taking the corpse of a stoning victim and hanging it on a tree afterward; "this was probably done to increase their punishment by depriving them of burial and leaving them as food for beasts of prey."[12] It is not clear how often hanging was utilized after stoning—perhaps only for the most heinous crimes (it would certainly have resulted in uncleanness for those involved). However, even when the victim had been hanged, the corpse was to be taken down before sunset: "You shall bury him the same day, for a hanged man is cursed by God." This passage is later applied to Christ in Galatians 3:13.

As it happens, hanging is another method of execution used in the Bible, though it generally does not bear much resemblance to the noose-and-scaffold methodology later employed so often in Europe and the United States. One of the few clear instances of this occurs in the New Testament, namely, the suicide of Judas described in Matthew and Acts. These two accounts are sometimes regarded as contradictory, since Matthew tells us that "he went and hanged himself" (Matt. 27:5), while the fairly graphic story in Acts says that "falling headlong he burst open in the middle and all his bowels gushed out" (Acts 1:18). Most commentators resolve this difference quite simply: some time after the hanging, the rope broke, dumping Judas's corpse onto the ground, where it ruptured and disgorged his entrails. This explanation is all the more likely because the Greek phrase "falling headlong" can also mean "swelling up,"[13] creating a picture of decomposition and disembowelment that is truly disgusting.

Hanging occurs a handful of times in the Old Testament, starting with Genesis, where one of Joseph's fellow prisoners, a baker, was hanged

---

12. W. Corswant, *A Dictionary of Life in Bible Times*, trans. Arthur Heathcote (New York: Oxford University Press, 1960), 261. See also Dennis Gaertner, "Stoning," in *Eerdmans Dictionary of the Bible*, ed. David Noel Freedman (Grand Rapids: Eerdmans, 2000), 1253.

13. *ESV Study Bible*, 2082; I. Howard Marshall, *The Acts of the Apostles: An Introduction and Commentary*, Tyndale Old Testament Commentaries (Leicester, UK: Inter-Varsity, 1980), 65; Leon Morris, *The Gospel according to Matthew*, Pillar New Testament Commentary (Grand Rapids: Eerdmans, 1992), 695.

by Pharaoh (Gen. 40:19–22). In 2 Samuel 21:6, seven sons of King Saul were hanged in recompense for their father's treatment of the Gibeonites. Certainly the best-known Old Testament examples occur in Esther, where enemies of King Ahasuerus were "hanged on the gallows" (Est. 2:23); later, Ahasuerus's official, Haman, suffered the same fate, along with his ten sons (Est. 7:10; 9:14). In place of the suggestive "gallows" in these passages from Esther, the ESV offers an alternate translation—"suspended on a stake"—because the actual Hebrew word is "tree." According to the *New Geneva Study Bible*, "this refers to impalement on wooden stakes, a Persian and Assyrian form of execution."[14] Regarding Numbers 25:4, where idolatrous Israelite leaders were hanged "in the sun before the LORD," the *ESV Study Bible* says, "This most likely refers to the ancient Near Eastern practice of impaling dead bodies on a stick after heinous crimes, as a form of disgrace (rather than burying the bodies)." This description may well cover most of the Old Testament hangings; in Joshua 10:26, for instance, five pagan kings were clearly killed before being hanged: "Joshua struck them and put them to death, and he hanged them on five trees. And they hung on the trees until evening." Such was probably the case with Joshua's treatment of the king of Ai as well, for he was likewise "hanged . . . on a tree until evening" (Josh. 8:29).

Significantly, this also appears to be the method of execution threatened by King Darius in the book of Ezra. Having issued a decree that supported the rebuilding of Israel's temple, the Babylonian ruler added, "If anyone alters this edict, a beam shall be pulled out of his house, and he shall be impaled on it" (Ezra 6:11). There is some question about the actual methodology here, for the final clause in Hebrew is literally, "and lifted up he shall be smitten upon it." To some, this suggests public flogging or perhaps even crucifixion, with the latter notion supported by the fact that, according to the historian Herodotus, Darius had already used this method on three thousand Babylonians. This information is provided by commentator Derek Kidner, who adds that the literal Hebrew of Ezra 6:11 may also figure in Christ's statement from John 12:32, "When I am lifted up."[15] In fact, it seems likely that New Testament writers

14. *New Geneva Study Bible: Bringing the Light of the Reformation to Scripture* (Nashville: Nelson, 1995), 590.

15. Derek Kidner, *Ezra and Nehemiah: An Introduction and Commentary*, Tyndale Old Testament Commentaries (Leicester, UK: Inter-Varsity, 1979), 57–58.

considered crucifixion to be a type of hanging, as is clearly implied in Galatians 3:13, which applies Deuteronomy 21:23 to Christ: "Cursed is everyone who is hanged on a tree."

Yet if crucifixion is to be classed as "hanging," it is surely the cruelest and most painful type, for unlike the Old Testament cases above, here the victim was hanged alive. Indeed, by any standard, the killing of Christ is among the most painful and torturous deaths recorded in all of Scripture. "In the ancient world," writes D. A. Carson, "this most terrible of punishments is always associated with shame and horror. It was so brutal that no Roman citizen could be crucified without the sanction of the Emperor"; indeed, as Leon Morris points out, "ancient writers regarded it as the most shameful of deaths, and they refused to dwell on it."[16]

A good deal more is said about it nowadays, however. Indeed, in a 1986 issue of the *Journal of the American Medical Association*, physicians William D. Edwards, Wesley J. Gabel, and Floyd E. Hosmer published an illustrated nine-page article titled "On the Physical Death of Jesus Christ." Much of the following description is taken from their painstakingly researched piece, which references the accounts in Matthew 27, Mark 15, Luke 23, and John 19.

As we saw earlier, Jesus was first severely flogged, a brutal process that would have left his back in shreds (see pp. 108–9). Victims of crucifixion were usually naked, though Mark 15:20 tells us that the Roman soldiers, after mocking Christ with a pseudo-royal robe, "stripped him of the purple cloak and put his own clothes on him." So Jesus may have been allowed a garment during the ordeal, perhaps in deference to Jewish sensibilities.[17] Yet since he had been scourged with a whip that likely included bits of bone and metal, the mock robe "had probably stuck to the clots of blood and serum in the wounds," and thus its removal would have "caused excruciating pain, just as when a bandage is carelessly removed." As the soldiers then led Jesus out to crucifixion, there is no account of the whipping that was customarily applied during the journey to the stake, probably because Jesus was "too weak to survive

16. D. A. Carson, *The Gospel according to John*, Pillar New Testament Commentary (Leicester, UK: Apollos/Inter-Varsity, 1991), 610; Morris, *Matthew*, 708.

17. Robert H. Stein, *Mark*, Baker Exegetical Commentary on the New Testament (Grand Rapids: Baker, 2008), 712.

an additional beating."[18] For this same reason, he was apparently not required to carry the large wooden "patibulum," which was also typical in Roman crucifixions.

Matthew, Mark, and Luke tell us that a passerby was drafted to carry this large wooden bar; since John's account has Christ "bearing his own cross" (John 19:17), it is usually assumed that Jesus set out with the patibulum but "collapsed on the way, whereupon Simon of Cyrene was pressed into service."[19] A large crossbar to which Christ's hands would eventually be nailed, this piece of wood weighed somewhere between 75 and 125 pounds; "it was placed across the nape of the victim's neck and balanced along both shoulders. Usually, the outstretched arms were then tied to the crossbar."[20] "One can hardly imagine the pain caused by the rough heavy beam pressing into the lacerated skin and muscles of Jesus' shoulders."[21]

After a journey of about six hundred yards, the procession reached "the Place of the Skull" outside Jerusalem's city walls; "the criminal was then thrown to the ground on his back, with his arms outstretched along the patibulum. The hands would be nailed or tied to the crossbar, but nailing apparently was preferred by the Romans." From archeological evidence in the form of crucified remains, we know that these nails were tapered wrought-iron spikes about six inches long, with a square shaft one centimeter across. These would have been driven through the wrists rather than the palms, since "the ligaments and bones of the wrist can support the weight of a body hanging from them, but the palms cannot." The driven nails would have crushed or severed the wrists' large median nerve, causing "excruciating bolts of fiery pain in both arms."[22]

Once the patibulum had been raised and attached to the upright wooden stipe—one of several that always stood ready outside the city—the victim's feet were then attached to the post as well; once again, archeological evidence indicates that the Romans preferred nails for this process. The left foot was pressed back against the right, and with both

18. Walter W. Wessell, *Mark*, in *The Expositor's Bible Commentary*, vol. 8: *Matthew, Mark, Luke*, ed. Frank E. Gaebelein (Grand Rapids: Zondervan HarperCollins, 1984), 777.

19. *ESV Study Bible*, 2065.

20. William D. Edwards, Wesley J. Gabel, and Floyd E. Hosmer, "On the Physical Death of Jesus Christ," *Journal of the American Medical Association* 255, 11 (March 21, 1986): 1459.

21. Wessell, *Mark*, 778.

22. Edwards, Gabel, and Hosmer, "Physical Death of Jesus," 1459–60.

feet pointing downward, another nail was driven through the arches, leaving the knees somewhat flexed.[23] As with the wrists, various nerves were likely damaged in this process, although, with the exception of flogging, crucifixion itself was "a relatively bloodless procedure," since no major arteries were severed. By pushing against the nail in his feet, the victim could take some weight off his arms; and he was further aided in these efforts by straddling a wooden block about halfway down the post, but this had been placed there only to prolong the crucifixion process.[24] In the words of Leon Morris, this "sedile"—or seat—would "prevent flesh tearing from the nails" and was thus "designed to increase the agony, not relieve it."[25]

And after this: the interminable wait for death.

"The length of survival generally ranged from three or four hours to three or four days and appears to have been inversely related to the severity of the scourging.... Not uncommonly, insects would light upon or burrow into the open wounds or the eyes, ears, and nose of the victim, and birds of prey would tear at these sites."[26] These grueling hours would probably be marked by the victim's repeated efforts to push upward with his legs in order to take weight off the arms and make breathing easier; yet the pain caused by pressure on the nailed feet would scarcely afford relief. Furthermore, the arms would eventually fatigue, causing "great waves of cramps" and "knotting them in deep, relentless, throbbing pain."[27]

The primary physical effect of crucifixion, however, was "a marked interference with normal respiration.... The weight of the body, pulling down on the outstretched arms and shoulders, would tend to fix the intercostal muscles in an inhalation state and thereby hinder passive exhalation." With the cramping, the exertion on wounded feet, and the repeated scraping of a torn-open back against the wooden stipe as the body moved up and down, "each respiratory effort would become agonizing and tiring and lead eventually to asphyxia." Among other things,

23. Wessell, *Mark*, 779; the detail of permanent stipes outside the city is from Edwards, Gabel, and Hosmer, "Physical Death of Jesus," 1459.

24. Edwards, Gabel, and Hosmer, "Physical Death of Jesus," 1461.

25. Leon Morris, *The Gospel according to John*, New International Commentary on the New Testament (Grand Rapids: Eerdmans, 1971), 805.

26. Edwards, Gabel, and Hosmer, "Physical Death of Jesus," 1459–60.

27. Wessell, *Mark*, 779.

this slow suffocation would have made Jesus' seven short speeches from the cross particularly difficult and painful.[28]

The actual cause of death was "multifactorial and varied somewhat in each case," a combination of dehydration, congestive heart failure (from fluid building up in the lungs), and possible brain damage caused by reduced blood circulation; but the main factors were shock and asphyxiation.[29] If the victim were slow in dying, his legs would be broken with an iron mallet so that he could no longer lift himself, thus hastening suffocation. But "Jesus had been so brutally beaten that when the soldiers came to him to see whether they would have to break his legs, he was dead already,"[30] as indicated in John 19:32–33.

Quoting Albert Reville's *Jesus of Nazareth*, Leon Morris's commentary on John sums up this appalling event:

> Nothing could be more horrible than the sight of this living body, breathing, seeing, hearing, still able to feel, and yet reduced to the state of a corpse by forced immobility and absolute helplessness. We cannot even say that the crucified person writhed in agony, for it was impossible for him to move. Stripped of his clothing, unable even to brush away the flies which fell upon his wounded flesh, already lacerated by the preliminary scourging . . . the cross represented miserable humanity reduced to the last degree of impotence, suffering and degradation. The penalty of crucifixion combined all that the most ardent tormentor could desire: torture, the pillory, degradation, and certain death, distilled slowly drop by drop. It was an ideal form of torture.[31]

And yet—to describe all the horrors recounted in the paragraphs above, the Gospel writers have only one phrase: "They crucified him" (Mark 15:24; Luke 23:33; John 19:18; see also Matt. 27:31).

Many commentators have remarked on the brevity with which these events are described in Scripture, using phrases such as "terse," "eloquently understated," "utter objectivity," "extreme reserve and economy of language." "None of them portrays the physical agony of the crucifixion in the shocking details that might have been given. The stark facts are

---

28. Edwards, Gabel, and Hosmer, "Physical Death of Jesus," 1461–62.
29. Ibid., 1461; see also Morris, *Matthew*, 709.
30. Wessell, *Mark*, 780; see also Carson, *John*, 622.
31. Albert Reville, *Jesus of Nazareth* (1897), quoted in Morris, *John*, 805–6.

there but are presented with sober restraint."[32] James R. Edwards adds that this conciseness helps avoid sensationalism and sentimentality, while Norval Geldenhuys wisely observes that "the physical agony which Jesus had to endure was but the faintest reflection of the spiritual suffering He had to undergo. . . . For this reason, the Gospels give practically no details on His physical suffering, so that the reader's attention should not be concentrated upon outward things and thus overlook the deepest essence of His suffering."[33]

What Geldenhuys refers to here—"the deepest essence of His suffering"—is neither the physical nor the idiomatic "hell" Christ endured on the cross, but rather the agony of actual and complete separation from the Father he loved with all his being. Because "he himself bore our sins in his body on the tree" (1 Peter 2:24), because the Lord had "laid on him the iniquity of us all," he was therefore "smitten by God, and afflicted" (Isa. 53:4–6); that is, God turned aside from him as the most sinfully obscene being who had ever lived on earth. And thus, Christ endured the *true* hell that awaits all sinners, "away from the presence of the Lord" (2 Thess. 1:9). This—rejection, abandonment, the prospect of facing the "cup" of God's wrath all alone—is what caused Christ to sweat blood beforehand (Luke 22:42–44); and it is what caused him to cry out on the cross, "My God, my God, why have you forsaken me?" (Matt. 27:46; Mark 15:34).

This indeed is and should be the focus when we consider what Christ endured on our behalf; yet it is perhaps helpful to remember also that he did endure this unimaginable desolation—a torment far worse than any physical pain—even in the midst of horrific bodily anguish; and that at the height of this suffering, he still called out to the God who was—for him alone—no longer there.

---

32. The first two phrases are from Stein, *Mark*, 711; the other three quotes, in the order presented in my text, are from James R. Edwards, *The Gospel according to Mark*, Pillar New Testament Commentary (Grand Rapids: Eerdmans, 2002), 469; R. Alan Cole, *The Gospel according to Mark: An Introduction and Commentary*, Tyndale New Testament Commentaries (Leicester, UK: Inter-Varsity, 1999), 314; and Walter L. Liefeld, *Luke*, in *The Expositor's Bible Commentary*, vol. 8: *Matthew, Mark, Luke*, ed. Frank E. Gaebelein (Grand Rapids: Zondervan-HarperCollins, 1984), 1042.

33. Edwards, *Mark*, 469; Norval Geldenhuys, *Commentary on the Gospel of Luke* (Grand Rapids: Eerdmans, 1988), 608.

14

"The Smoke of a Furnace"

Death by Fire

FIRE HAS SOMETIMES been regarded as one of the worst ways to die, since the vital organs would be consumed only after the victim had already endured excruciating agony as the skin and muscles burned first. However, in most cases of death by fire, the actual cause of death is inhalation of carbon monoxide or other toxins produced by combustion, with the burning of the body and its organs occurring after the victim has already died.[1]

But as with stoning, hanging, and many other deaths in the Bible, the writers do not provide these sorts of details on the victims' experiences. Indeed, since most scriptural accounts of death by fire are quite brief, this chapter will simply proceed through the Bible from beginning to end, examining the instances as they appear one by one. Among other things, this organizational method enables us to begin with one of Scripture's most familiar incinerations, namely, the destruction of Sodom and Gomorrah in Genesis 19.

This entire story is described and discussed more fully in chapter 9 above; we are concerned here only with the end, where Abraham's nephew, Lot—along with his wife and two daughters—fled from Sodom after angels had warned that "the LORD is about to destroy the city. . . . Escape for your life. Do not look back or stop anywhere

1. Valerie J. Rao, "Forensic Pathology of Thermal Injuries," *Medscape Reference: Drugs, Diseases, and Procedures*, accessed April 6, 2011, http://emedicine.medscape.com/article/1975728-overview.

in the valley." Once Lot had reached a nearby place of safety, "the LORD rained on Sodom and Gomorrah sulfur and fire from the LORD out of heaven. And he overthrew those cities, and all the valley, and all the inhabitants of the cities, and what grew on the ground. But Lot's wife, behind him, looked back, and she became a pillar of salt." The next morning, when Abraham looked down to where the cities had been, "behold, the smoke of the land went up like the smoke of a furnace" (Gen. 19:14–28).

Deuteronomy 29:23 makes it clear that this conflagration included not only Sodom and Gomorrah but also two of the other "cities of the plain" mentioned in Genesis 14:2 (the fifth city, Zoar, was apparently spared; see Gen. 19:22). These five cities were located in the low-lying region of the Dead Sea, an area that even today remains abundant in petroleum, bitumen, asphalt, and sulfur; "but what combination of natural or supernatural agents destroyed the towns remains speculative."[2] Some writers feel that an earthquake was involved, with gases, sulfur, and bitumen spewing into the air and then igniting in the lightning that frequently accompanies an earthquake.[3] Indeed, it is even possible that an earthquake may have set off some of the chemical deposits in the Dead Sea itself—the potash, magnesium, calcium chlorides, and bromide that give the sea "its buoyancy and its fatal effects on fish."[4]

The word "sulfur" in this story—translated "brimstone" in other versions—is the Hebrew *gophrith*, which appears in several other Old Testament passages, notably Ezekiel 38:21–22, where the Lord threatens another rain of "fire and sulfur" on the evil kingdom of Gog. In an exegesis of the Ezekiel passage, Daniel I. Block defines this chemical as "a yellow crystalline substance that ignites readily in air, giving off suffocating fumes. Since it is often found in regions of volcanic activity, Ezekiel may have envisioned a volcanic eruption, with the hot lava gushing forth and igniting anything combustible in its path."[5]

2. Gordon J. Wenham, *Genesis 16–50*, Word Biblical Commentary, vol. 2 (Dallas: Word, 1994), 59.

3. Bruce K. Waltke and Cathi J. Fredricks, *Genesis: A Commentary* (Grand Rapids: Zondervan, 2001), 279.

4. A. R. Millard, "Dead Sea," in *The New Bible Dictionary*, 2nd ed., ed. J. D. Douglas (Leicester, UK: Inter-Varsity, 1982), 271.

5. Daniel I. Block, *The Book of Ezekiel: Chapters 25–48*, New International Commentary on the Old Testament (Grand Rapids: Eerdmans, 1998), 359.

In any case, in the story of Sodom, it appears that molten substances, falling from the sky like rain, hurtled down onto the hesitating wife of Lot, encasing her in what later solidified into a "pillar of salt." The useful *New Bible Dictionary* tells us that even today, at the southwest corner of the Dead Sea, a hill of salt is "eroded into strange forms, including pillars which are known as 'Lot's wife' by local Arabs."[6]

The next fiery deaths in Scripture involve Aaron's sons Nadab and Abihu, who made an incense offering that violated sacrificial regulations—that is, they offered what they wanted to, rather than what God had prescribed; as a result, "fire came out from before the LORD and consumed them, and they died before the LORD" (Lev. 10:1–2). Similarly, in Numbers 16:35, when more than 250 men of Korah claimed priestly prerogatives that God had not given them, "fire came out from the LORD and consumed the 250 men offering the incense."

These passages suggest that after the great flood in Genesis 6–8—following the Lord's promise not to destroy the earth again by water (Gen. 9:11)—God often preferred fire for punishment and destruction. We see this again in Deuteronomy, with the following command regarding any pagan city that tried to draw Israel into its own polytheistic worship: "You shall gather all its spoil into the midst of its open square and burn the city and all its spoil with fire, as a whole burnt offering to the Lord your God" (Deut. 13:12–16).

Though not technically a pagan, an Israelite named Achan was among the first to suffer this sort of fiery wrath in the conquest of the Promised Land. In confiscating some of the spoil from the doomed city of Jericho, Achan had violated God's specific command that such goods were either to be destroyed or brought into "the treasury of the LORD" (Josh. 6:17–19). For this presumption, Achan and his family were burned with fire and stoned with stones (Josh. 7:25). The book of Joshua also recounts the wholesale burning of Jericho, Ai, and Hazor; in each case, most of the citizens had been slain by the sword beforehand, but when the fighting men of Ai were lured out of their city and it was then set ablaze, some of the women and children left behind were likely killed in the conflagration (Josh. 6:24; 8:14–25; 11:11).

6. Millard, "Dead Sea," 271.

There are many other clearer cases of being burned alive in Scripture. In Judges, during the civil war between Gideon's son Abimelech and the people of Shechem, Abimelech's men forced a great number of enemies into a local temple called El-berith, whereupon they hewed down brushwood and set it in bundles against the structure; "and they set the stronghold on fire over them, so that all the people of the Tower of Shechem also died, about 1,000 men and women" (Judg. 9:46–49). Farther along in Judges, a prolonged conflict between Samson and some Philistines led at one point to the wife of Samson being burned alive, along with her father (Judg. 15:6).

Much later, Israel's King Zimri, seeing that his seven-day reign was coming to an end, "went into the citadel of the king's house and burned the king's house over him with fire and died" (1 Kings 16:18). Subsequently, King Ahaziah of Israel became ill and, wanting to know whether he would recover, sent fifty soldiers and a captain to the prophet Elijah. Since Elijah had already told Ahaziah that he would not recover (because the king had first inquired of the pagan god Baal-zebub instead of the Lord), this appears to have been an attempt to capture and subdue the troublesome prophet.[7] So when the captain said to Elijah, "O man of God, the king says, 'Come down,'" Elijah answered, "If I am a man of God, let fire come down from heaven and consume you and your fifty." At which point, "fire came down from heaven and consumed him and his fifty"—an event repeated virtually word for word when a second set of fifty men came to seize Elijah (2 Kings 1:2–12).

And of course, even folks unfamiliar with the Bible probably know something of Shadrach, Meshach, and Abednego in the book of Daniel. The Babylonian king Nebuchadnezzar attempted to have these three Israelites burned alive because they would not bow down and worship a massive golden statue. Indeed, the wicked king was so incensed by their refusal that "he ordered the furnace heated seven times more than it was usually heated." When the three men then "fell bound into the burning fiery furnace," God intervened to save them, and thus Nebuchadnezzar's attempt failed—but not before the men carrying Shadrach, Meshach, and Abednego had all been incinerated by the inferno (Dan. 3:8–27).

7. *ESV Study Bible* (Wheaton, IL: Crossway, 2008), 646.

And finally, in keeping with the judgment and destruction theme of so many conflagrations in Scripture, the New Testament relies heavily on fire imagery to convey the horrors of eternal punishment. In Matthew, Christ calls hell a "fiery furnace" and an "eternal fire" (Matt. 13:42–50; 25:41); the latter concept is sustained in Mark and Luke, where he uses the word "unquenchable" to describe the blaze (Mark 9:43–48; Luke 3:17). As we already established in chapter 11, this idea is picked up with considerably more detail in Revelation, describing first the utter destruction of God's enemies on earth and then their eternal destiny in flaming torment.

Revelation, for instance, depicts God's judgment as "hail and fire, mixed with blood," which are "thrown upon the earth. And a third of the earth was burned up, and a third of the trees were burned up, and all green grass was burned up." After this, "a great mountain, burning with fire, was thrown into the sea, and a third of the sea became blood. A third of the living creatures in the sea died, and a third of the ships were destroyed" (Rev. 8:7–9). Of course, much of Revelation is symbolic, as indicated by this passage's complex imagery involving hail, fire, and blood, so we are probably not talking about literal burning, but likely something harder to describe. This nonliteral but nonetheless grave use of fire imagery continues in the graphic language of Revelation 11:5, which describes two witnesses who will prophecy in the end times: "and if anyone would harm them, fire pours from their mouth and consumes their foes."

As Revelation builds to its triumphant climax where God's opponents are defeated once and for all, these fiery fates are directed at such demonic figures as "the great prostitute" and "Babylon the great," who will both be "burned up with fire" (Rev. 18:8; see also 17:16). As for the symbolic sinful cities of Gog and Magog, just as they are about to attack God's saints, the writer watches as "fire came down from heaven and consumed them, and the devil who had deceived them was thrown into the lake of fire and sulfur where the beast and the false prophet were" (Rev. 20:7–10). Finally, even Death and Hades are "thrown into the lake of fire. . . . And if anyone's name was not found written in the book of life, he was thrown into the lake of fire. . . . But as for the cowardly, the faithless, the detestable, as for murderers, the sexually immoral, sorcerers, idolaters, and all liars, their portion will be in the lake that burns with fire and sulfur, which is the second death" (Rev. 20:14–15; 21:8).

As with the earlier blood and hail, the imagery of both lake and fire in these later passages—with such incorporeal figures as death and hell being thrown in—suggests that we are not dealing with literal, physical pictures, but rather that the writer is struggling to express something much more complex, and much worse, than mere death by fire; perhaps it is something that cannot really be expressed in words at all, but which is at least presaged and hinted at by all those who had died fiery deaths earlier in Scripture. In this case, however, "they will be tormented day and night forever and ever" (Rev. 20:10).

15

"And Sons Shall Eat Their Fathers"

Cannibalism

I ONCE HEARD the story of a skeptic who came to believe the truth of God's Word because of its pervasive and profound portrayal of human depravity. No mere human document, he admitted, could possibly depict its own race as so consistently and hopelessly degenerate. And nowhere is this corruption more apparent than in the material covered in this chapter and the next, the more so because these sins—cannibalism and butchering children—sometimes occur together, with children being eaten by their own parents; and furthermore, most of the time these twin horrors are perpetrated by members of God's covenant people!

Perhaps we can ease into the grisly subject of cannibalism with a few passages where the feast seems to be figurative, rather than literal. Indeed, the sometimes metaphorical nature of eating flesh and blood was apparently not clear to many first-century Jews, who were troubled by Christ's insistence that he was "living bread," that this bread was his "flesh," and that those who wanted eternal life would have to eat it. "The Jews then disputed among themselves, saying, 'How can this man give us his flesh to eat?' So Jesus said to them, 'Truly, truly, I say to you, unless you eat the flesh of the Son of Man and drink his blood, you have no life in you. Whoever feeds on my flesh and drinks my blood has eternal life. . . . For my flesh is true food, and my blood is true drink. Whoever feeds on my flesh and drinks my blood abides in me, and I in him'" (John 6:51–56).

Isaiah offers an earlier example where feeding on human flesh seems largely figurative. The passage decrees this future curse on the disobedient people of Israel: "They slice meat on the right, but are still hungry, and they devour on the left, but are not satisfied; each devours the flesh of his own arm, Manasseh devours Ephraim, and Ephraim devours Manasseh; together they are against Judah" (Isa. 9:20–21).

A subtler but fascinating instance occurs later, when the righteous Shadrach, Meshach, and Abednego are slandered before Babylon's King Nebuchadnezzar; here the phrase "maliciously accused" is, in the literal Hebrew, "ate the pieces of the Jews" (Dan. 3:8). Shortly thereafter, in Daniel 6:12–13, scandalmongers similarly accuse Daniel of disloyalty to the king; while the cannibalistic idiom is not used to describe their hatred in this early part of chapter 6, it does show up in verse 24, where the language comments ironically (and in this case quite literally) on those who accused—or "ate the pieces of"—Daniel: They were "cast into the den of lions—they, their children, and their wives. And before they reached the bottom of the den, the lions overpowered them and broke all their bones in pieces."

As in the case of Daniel's accusers, several other Old Testament passages also use cannibalism as a metaphor demonstrating oppression of fellow humans. In Psalm 27:2, for example, David complains of those who "eat up my flesh"; and in Psalm 14:4, God describes "evildoers who eat up my people as they eat bread." Likewise, Proverbs 30:14 inveighs against "those whose teeth are swords, whose fangs are knives, to devour the poor from off the earth, the needy from among mankind."

Undoubtedly the longest, sternest, and most graphic of these cannibalism-as-oppression passages is found in Micah. Here, the Lord excoriates those "who tear the skin from off my people and their flesh from off their bones, who eat the flesh of my people, and flay their skin from off them, and break their bones in pieces and chop them up like meat in a pot, like flesh in a cauldron" (Mic. 3:2–3). It might be unwise to overstress the figurative nature of this language, because Micah is saying of these wealthy rulers and prophets that "in effect the rich food on their banqueting tables came directly from the flesh of God's people." The language uses a combination of "flesh" (*sheer*, "inward meat") and "meat" (*basar*, "outward flesh"), and this "underscores the total consumption of the Lord's people."[1] "In the most gruesome figure, showing their brutality and their venality, Micah portrays them as tearing the skin off their victims, tearing their flesh off their bones, and eating their flesh, leaving only the unpalatable skin and bones. But as if that were not bad enough, they break even the bones in pieces, chop up the flesh, and throw it into the cooking pots before eating it. . . . No other prophet spoke so crudely as Micah. Our vitriolic prophet does not back off from his macabre figure. He repeats it again and again, detail by detail."[2]

All this is gruesome enough; as suggested earlier, however, several Old Testament passages cite cannibalism that is not merely figurative but actual, physical—and often quite graphic. In Isaiah 49:26, for example, God pledges to rescue Israel from her oppressors, for he will make these nations "eat their own flesh, and they shall be drunk with their own blood as with wine." Edward J. Young posits that either these people have been maddened to the point of consuming their own bodies, or perhaps the idiomatic "flesh and blood" suggests, as it would in modern English, that they will eat their own relatives.[3]

Sadly, this latter supposition is the actual case in every other Old Testament reference to cannibalism. Jeremiah 19:9, for example, levies these curses not on pagan oppressors but on God's very own people: "I will make them eat the flesh of their sons and their daughters, and everyone shall eat the flesh of his neighbor" (see also Lev. 26:29). A short time later, the prophet Ezekiel had a similar warning for the nation of Judah: "Because of all your abominations I will do with you what I have never yet done, and the like of which I will never do again. Therefore fathers shall eat their sons in your midst, and sons shall eat their fathers" (Ezek. 5:9–10).

Both Ezekiel and Jeremiah brought God's message to the southern nation of Judah just before it fell to Babylon in 586 B.C. The short book of Lamentations, written after this catastrophe, suggests that the dire predictions of both prophets were indeed fulfilled. As the writer laments all the terrible ills that befell God's people under Babylonian assault, he asks,

---

1. Bruce K. Waltke, *Micah*, in *The Minor Prophets: An Exegetical and Expository Commentary*, vol. 2: *Obadiah, Jonah, Micah, Nahum, and Habakkuk*, ed. Thomas Edward McComiskey (Grand Rapids: Baker, 1993), 658.

2. Bruce K. Waltke, *A Commentary on Micah* (Grand Rapids: Eerdmans, 2007), 156.

3. Edward J. Young, *The Book of Isaiah: The English Text, with Introduction, Exposition, and Notes*, vol. 3, *Chapters 40–66* (Grand Rapids: Eerdmans, 1972), 293.

"Should women eat the fruit of their womb, the children of their tender care?" (Lam. 2:20); later, he baldly asserts, "The hands of compassionate women have boiled their own children; they became their food" (Lam. 4:10).

Regarding the verse in Ezekiel 5 (above), Daniel I. Block observes that many passages in the Old Testament deal with cannibalism, "but the horror of Ezekiel's description supersedes them all."[4] Much as I prize Dr. Block's insightful work, I would personally give the top-horror spot not to Ezekiel, but to a pair of passages in Deuteronomy and 2 Kings.

Most commentators agree that all the literal passages above, even the short one from Isaiah, refer to cannibalism necessitated by siege conditions—that is, a city has been surrounded by an attacking army, so that incoming food is cut off for an extended time; the resulting widespread starvation is such that, in 2 Kings 6:25 for example, valuable animals are slaughtered for food, with even their barely edible heads selling for exorbitant prices. Such siege conditions are also the background for Deuteronomy 28:53–57, a gut-wrenching passage that warns about what will happen if Israel forgets her covenant with God:

> You shall eat the fruit of your womb, the flesh of your sons and daughters, whom the LORD your God has given you. . . . The man who is the most tender and refined among you will begrudge food to his brother, to the wife he embraces, and to the last of the children whom he has left, so that he will not give to any of them any of the flesh of his children whom he is eating, because he has nothing else left. . . . The most tender and refined woman among you, who would not venture to set the sole of her foot on the ground because she is so delicate and tender, will begrudge to the husband she embraces, to her son and to her daughter, her afterbirth that comes out from between her feet and her children whom she bears, because lacking everything she will eat them secretly, in the siege and in the distress.

An earlier phrase here says that the enemies doing the besieging will "eat the offspring of your cattle and the fruit of your ground"; and thus,

> a vivid contrast is drawn between the natural appetites of the invaders (51) and the unnatural lust of the Israelites under siege who eat their

---

4. Daniel I. Block, *The Book of Ezekiel: Chapters 1–24*, New International Commentary on the Old Testament (Grand Rapids: Eerdmans, 1997), 204.

children (53) and in whom every vestige of mercy and tenderness seems to have been cast aside. The picture in these verses is blood-curdling in the extreme. There are few more degrading pictures in the Bible than that of a mother who, even during a siege, ought to have put away the after-birth of her child and to have cherished her new-born baby, but in her desperate need eats both, secretly denying to her own husband any share in the ghastly meal.[5]

Some of these grisly predictions seem to have been realized in 2 Kings 6, when Ben-hadad of Syria besieged the northern kingdom of Israel, also known as Samaria. As King Jehoram passed along a city wall, a woman cried out to him for help. When he asked what the problem was, she replied: "This woman said to me, 'Give your son, that we may eat him today, and we will eat my son tomorrow.' So we boiled my son and ate him. And on the next day I said to her, 'Give your son, that we may eat him.' But she has hidden her son" (2 Kings 6:26–29).

Talk about bloodcurdling.

In a passage that applies to many of the others we've discussed, Peter J. Leithart calls this "cannibalism of the future. The woman's story is chilling, her request more so. She does not present a case against her murderous friend, but instead asks the king to approve yet another murder of yet another child. She is Israel herself, the mother who devours her own children and boils her kids in mother's milk (Deut. 14:21)."[6]

But when it comes to children being deliberately murdered in Scripture, this horrific passage is only the beginning.

5. J. A. Thompson, *Deuteronomy: An Introduction and Commentary*, Tyndale Old Testament Commentaries (Leicester, UK:Inter-Varsity, 1974), 276.

6. Peter J. Leithart, *1 and 2 Kings*, Brazos Theological Commentary on the Bible (Grand Rapids: Brazos, 2006), 208.

16

"This Abomination"

Murdering Children

THANKS TO FREQUENT holiday readings of New Testament texts about the birth of Christ, the best-known instance of killing children in the Bible is probably Herod's "slaughter of the innocents" in Matthew 2.

Informed by the wise men that a new "king of the Jews" had been born, Herod—that is, Herod the Great, or Herod I, appointed by Rome to rule Israel and Judah—could not stomach the thought of a rival; so "he sent and killed all the male children in Bethlehem and in all that region who were two years old or under" (Matt. 2:16). Commentator R. T. France posits that this may indicate as few as twenty deaths, given a Bethlehem population of between three hundred and one thousand. However, Matthew's text adds, "and in all that region," suggesting that the number was considerably higher; as Leon Morris puts it, Herod wasn't taking any chances.[1]

This attempt to quash a perceived threat by killing children may remind some readers of Exodus 1. Here, Egypt's Pharaoh sought to weaken his Israelite slave population—and thus forestall possible rebellion—by ordering Hebrew midwives to kill every male Hebrew newborn. When the women managed to sidestep this ghastly mandate, Pharaoh then decreed, "Every son that is born to the Hebrews you shall cast into the

---

1. R. T. France, *The Gospel according to Matthew: An Introduction and Commentary*, Tyndale New Testamtent Commentaries (Leicester, UK: Inter-Varsity, 1985), 86; Leon Morris, *The Gospel according to Matthew*, Pillar New Testament Commentary (Grand Rapids: Eerdmans, 1992), 45.

Nile" (Ex. 1:15–22). The narrator does not tell us just how thoroughly this order was carried out, though the reality of the threat is clear from subsequent actions of Moses' mother, who, when she could no longer hide her three-month-old son, put him in a basket on the Nile, where he was somewhat ironically saved by Pharaoh's daughter (Ex. 2:1–6).

These narratives are probably the most familiar in our current chapter, and certainly the Herod story does give some sense of the profound grief involved ("weeping and loud lamentation," mothers who "refused to be comforted"); but many other passages about killing children are considerably more horrific.

Take, for example, 2 Kings 15:16, where the renegade Israelite king Menahem attacked the city of Tiphsah and "ripped open all the women in it who were pregnant"; the exact same phraseology appears again in Amos 1:13, where the Ammonites are cursed for having slain expectant mothers along with their unborn children. In Nahum 3:10, infants of Nineveh are "dashed in pieces at the head of every street," while Isaiah uses similar language against Babylon: "Their infants will be dashed in pieces before their eyes; their houses will be plundered and their wives ravished" (Isa. 13:16). As in this instance, several similar passages combine mothers and children in the slaughter. Hosea recalls an earlier battle in which "mothers were dashed in pieces with their children" (Hos. 10:14), and he then prophesies the same fate for Samaria: "Their little ones shall be dashed in pieces, and their pregnant women ripped open" (Hos. 13:16; see also 2 Kings 8:12).

But it gets worse.

These passages all involve warfare and—except for the wicked Menahem—the horrors are not perpetrated by Israel or Judah. Yet Scripture contains at least twenty references to parents voluntarily sacrificing their own offspring, usually by means of a burnt offering. And most of these acts occur in Israel itself. This despite the fact that no less than four separate passages in the Pentateuch specifically forbid child sacrifice, with Deuteronomy 18:10 serving as a representative example: "There shall not be found among you anyone who burns his son or his daughter as an offering" (see also Deut. 12:31; Lev. 18:21; 20:2–5).

Nevertheless, several hundred years later, in the southern kingdom of Judah,, the wicked King Ahaz "burned his son as an offering" (2 Kings 16:3); so did his grandson, the similarly wicked King Manasseh

(2 Kings 21:6). Plenty of others had apparently been doing this as well, and often to victims both male and female: 2 Kings 17:17 condemns Israel because, among other things, "they burned their sons and their daughters as offerings." Later we find Judah's righteous King Josiah destroying a site in "the Valley of the Son of Hinnom" where sons and daughters had been burned as offerings to the pagan god Molech (2 Kings 23:10).

Later prophetic writings show that the practice was indeed widespread, with Jeremiah 32:35 giving some indication of how violently God himself condemned such deeds: "They built the high places of Baal in the Valley of the Son of Hinnom, to offer up their sons and daughters to Molech, though I did not command them, nor did it enter into my mind, that they should do this abomination" (for additional instances, see Jer. 7:31; 19:5; Ps. 106:37–38; Isa. 57:5; Ezek. 16:20–21; 20:31; 23:37–39).

In many of these passages—such as those describing Ahaz and Manasseh—the Hebrew literally says "made them pass through fire," causing some scholars to wonder whether this may have been a dedicatory rite that somehow involved fire but was not necessarily fatal, one that might simply have committed or set apart children to a pagan god such as Baal or Molech.[2] However, the passages in Jeremiah 7 and 19 both use the simple Hebrew verb that means "burn"; and in his commentary on Ezekiel, Daniel I. Block indicates that the phrase "pass through fire" means "to submerge it completely in flames, causing it to be consumed." Indeed, most commentators are now sure that these references all involve the literal death of children as an offering to pagan gods.[3]

Once again, the Bible writers do not describe the actual method of such sacrifices in any detail, leaving open the question of whether the children were burned alive. In examining the Ezekiel passages, John B. Taylor opines that the process involved "first slaying the child and then

2. See, for example, Donald J. Wiseman, *1 and 2 Kings: An Introduction and Commentary*, Tyndale Old Testament Commentaries (Leicester, UK: Inter-Varsity, 1993), 260–61.

3. Daniel I. Block, *The Book of Ezekiel: Chapters 1–24*, New International Commentary on the Old Testament (Grand Rapids: Eerdmans, 1997), 490. See also Peter J. Leithart, *1 and 2 Kings*, Brazos Theological Commenaty on the Bible (Grand Rapids: Brazos, 2006), 246; Martin J. Selman, *2 Chronicles: A Commentary*, Tyndale Old Testament Commentaries (Leicester, UK: Inter-Varsity, 1994), 520; Michael Wilcock, *The Message of Chronicles: One Church, One Faith, One Lord*, The Bible Speaks Today (Leicester, UK: Inter-Varsity: 1987), 257.

burning its body"[4]—a theory supported by the phraseology in Psalm 106:37–38: "They sacrificed their sons and their daughters to the demons; they poured out innocent blood, the blood of their sons and daughters, whom they sacrificed to the idols of Canaan, and the land was polluted with blood." If these children were also burned, as elsewhere, it seems clear that they had been slain first. Isaiah 57:5 offers further clarity on the matter, using the word "slaughter," a term found often in the priestly regulations from Leviticus and Exodus, where it refers to animals being first butchered and then burned as offerings (see, e.g., Ex. 29:11; Lev. 9:12; 14:19).

The exact purpose of such pagan sacrifices remains uncertain, though Raymond B. Dillard points out that the context of Deuteronomy 18:10 (above) suggests divination. Alec Motyer avers that the children were in fact burned alive "as a charm against death, propitiating the gods of the underworld." The *ESV Study Bible*, also insisting that victims were burned alive, goes on to give further details as well: "Child sacrifice was known from Canaanite/Phoenician contexts. The offering of children, especially firstborn, to the gods was seen as a means of manipulating deities to grant fertility to the offerer. Archaeological excavations at Carthage, a Phoenician colony founded in the eighth century B.C., include the charred remains of thousands of child sacrifices."[5]

The preceding paragraphs cover several passages all at once, due to their brevity and similarity; however, three references to child sacrifice are more complex and require individual treatment: the rebuilding of Jericho in 1 Kings; the action of the Moabite ruler named Mesha in 2 Kings; and Jephthah's treatment of his daughter in Judges.

Regarding Jericho, when Joshua led Israel on its conquest of the Promised Land in the book that bears his name, one of the nation's first victories involved this Canaanite city. The stronghold having been vanquished, razed, and thoroughly burned, Joshua then declared that anyone attempting to rebuild the city would do so at the cost of his firstborn and his youngest son (Josh. 6:26). Nonetheless, some centuries later, in the time of Israel's King Ahab, an otherwise unknown figure named

---

4. John B. Taylor, *Ezekiel: An Introduction and Commentary*, Tyndale Old Testament Commentaries (Leicester, UK: Inter-Varsity, 1969), 138.

5. Raymond B. Dillard, *2 Chronicles*, Word Biblical Commentary, vol. 15 (Waco, TX: Word, 1987), 221; Alec Motyer, *Isaiah: An Introduction and Commentary*, Tyndale Old Testament Commentaries (Leicester, UK: Inter-Varsity, 1999), 355; *ESV Study Bible* (Wheaton, IL: Crossway, 2008), 1388.

Hiel did indeed rebuild the city: "He laid its foundation at the cost of Abiram his firstborn, and set up its gates at the cost of his youngest son Segub" (1 Kings 16:34). Since "child sacrifice was a prominent feature among polytheistic Canaanite religions of the day," it is possible that Hiel deliberately made an offering of his children in order to secure the blessing of pagan divinities on his rebuilt city.[6] However, such acts of "foundation sacrifice" were rare in ancient times, and Hiel's children may with equal likelihood have died simply through an act of divine judgment that fulfilled Joshua's curse.[7]

The brief story of child sacrifice in 2 Kings 3 is also somewhat unclear. Here, the Moabite king Mesha had rebelled against Israel's King Jehoram, to whom he was paying a massive annual tribute. Jehoram convinced the kings of Judah and Edom to join him in suppressing Moab, and when Mesha saw the battle going badly for his side, "he took his oldest son who was to reign in his place and offered him for a burnt offering on the wall. And there came great wrath against Israel. And they withdrew" (2 Kings 3:27).

The question here, of course, is whose anger caused Jehoram's forces to abandon their campaign.

Donald J. Wiseman notes that "the human sacrifice of the crown-prince publicly on the walls of the capital was a rare practice . . . used to appease the national god Chemosh 'who was angry with his land'"—the last phrase having been inscribed by Mesha himself on a famed archeological artifact called the Moabite Stone.[8] But Mesha's words cannot stand as the final explanation; no writer of Old Testament Scripture would have ascribed victory to the mollification of a non-existent pagan god.

By contrast, the *ESV Study Bible* points out that the Hebrew word used here for "wrath"—*qatsaph*—shows up in two subsequent passages referring to human anger: 2 Kings 5:11 and 13:19; and thus, the *ESV* posits that "Mesha's troops respond to his desperate act with an anger that carries them to victory against the odds." But the language of 2 Kings 3 clearly implies that the opposing troops withdrew, rather than being vanquished by angry Moabites. Wiseman suggests that if the verse does

---

6. *ESV Study Bible*, 632.
7. Wiseman, *1 and 2 Kings*, 163.
8. Ibid., 201–2.

indeed refer to human wrath, it may indicate horror and dismay on the part of Israel, causing them to leave the battlefield.[9]

But Peter J. Leithart insists that *qatsaph* is most often used of God's wrath (Num. 16:46; 2 Chron. 32:26; Ps. 38:1; Isa. 60:10; etc.; see especially 1 Chron. 27:24, "wrath came upon Israel"). And thus, the anger was indeed that of Jehovah—yet we can hardly envision God accepting a ritual sacrifice which he had repeatedly and unequivocally declared abhorrent. Rather, Leithart posits that God was angry because he had earlier commanded Israel not to attack Moab (Deut. 2:9), and not to destroy trees in their military campaigns (Deut. 20:19–20), an act they did in fact perpetrate in this case (2 Kings 3:25). Thus, "Yahweh's 'great wrath' burns against Israel because they conduct their war in flagrant disregard of his laws."[10] The unsanctioned alliance with heathen Edom may have factored into God's displeasure as well; perhaps God was angry because the various sins of Israel had forced Mesha into such a desperate position.

And finally, there's Jephthah, an Old Testament name often associated with child sacrifice—though again, there is some question about what actually happened in this instance. Here is a summary of what the writer of Judges tells us in chapter 11: Having headed up a renegade gang of marauders, Jephthah was asked to help fend off an impending invasion of Gilead by the nearby Ammonites. Before consenting, he arranged a deal whereby victory would secure him a continuing place of leadership as judge in Israel, so Jephthah was naturally anxious to succeed against Ammon. Thus, he took a vow to the Lord, swearing, "If you will give the Ammonites into my hand, then whatever comes out from the doors of my house to meet me when I return in peace from the Ammonites shall be the LORD's, and I will offer it up for a burnt offering" (Judg. 11:30–31).

After Jephthah had defeated his foes in this campaign, he returned home to be greeted on arrival by his daughter, an only child. Though deeply saddened, Jephthah felt that he could not take back his vow, and his daughter agreed; but she did make one stipulation: "Leave me alone two months, that I may go up and down on the mountains and weep for my virginity"(Judg. 11:37). Once this grieving process was complete,

9. *ESV Study Bible*, 651; Wiseman, *1 and 2 Kings*, 202.
10. Leithart, *1 and 2 Kings*, 180.

Israel's new judge "did with her according to his vow that he had made. She had never known a man, and it became a custom in Israel that the daughters of Israel went year by year to lament the daughter of Jephthah the Gileadite four days in the year" (Judg. 11:39–40).

Some writers have attempted to soften the horror of this account by suggesting that Jephthah intended nothing more than an animal sacrifice; but most commentators agree that verse 31 should be rendered *"whoever* comes out" and "I will offer *him*," rather than "whatever" and "it."[11] In any case, if animal sacrifice was all Jephthah intended, then he would not have regarded the vow as binding in the case of a human being. So apparently the ambitious general returned to his home "no doubt expecting that the fulfillment of his vow would involve no more than the sacrifice of one of his many household servants."[12]

Failing the animal-sacrifice interpretation, other readers have tried to tone down the passage by arguing that Jephthah did not actually kill his daughter, but rather sentenced her to perpetual virginity, perhaps in some sort of special service to the Lord. Such an act would indeed have been tragic for both parties, the more so since she was his only child, and thus permanent chastity would guarantee an end to Jephthah's line. Naturally, the principal argument against this milder reading is quite simple: that is plainly *not* what Jephthah actually vowed. Arthur M. Cundall and Leon Morris explain:

> All the earlier commentators and historians accepted that Jephthah actually offered up his daughter as a burnt-offering. It was not until the Middle Ages that well-meaning but misguided attempts were made to soften down the plain meaning of the text. The susceptibilities of enlightened minds may well be shocked at such an action, . . . but the attempt to commute the sentence of death to one of perpetual virginity cannot be sustained. The final reference to the virginity of Jephthah's daughter is added to point to the tragedy of the affair. . . . The plain statement, that he *did with her according to his vow which he had vowed*, must be allowed to stand. The desolation of Jephthah (35), the two-month reprieve (37, 38), and

11. Arthur E. Cundall and Leon Morris, *Judges and Ruth: An Introduction and Commentary*, Tyndale Old Testament Commentaries (Leicester, UK: Inter-Varsity, 1968), 146; *ESV Study Bible*, 459; J. Rea, "Jephthah," in *The New Bible Dictionary*, 2nd ed., ed. J. D. Douglas (Leicester, UK: Inter-Varsity, 1982), 558.

12. Cundall and Morris, *Judges and Ruth*, 147.

the institution of a four-day feast would hardly be likely if nothing more was involved than perpetual virginity.[13]

Hebrew grammar allows the italicized statement above to occupy only a handful of words in the original text; and thus, "the narrator describes with five simple words in Hebrew the abhorrent and unspeakable notion that an Israelite sacrificed his child to Yahweh as a whole burnt offering."[14]

And lest we conclude that God somehow accepted this sacrifice when he granted success to the misguided general: it is certainly true that the narrator makes no moral judgment on these events, but he probably felt no need to, given the numerous injunctions against such actions clearly set down in the law of Moses (see above).

As Matthew Henry puts it, Jephthah "did ill to make so rash a vow, and worse to perform it."[15]

13. Ibid., 148.

14. Daniel I. Block, *Judges, Ruth,* The New American Commentary (Nashville: Broadman, 1999), 375.

15. *Matthew Henry's Commentary on the Whole Bible,* vol. 2 (McLean, VA: MacDonald Publishing, n.d.), 198.

17

"120,000 in One Day"

Mass Killings and Assassinations

AMONG MY COPIOUS NOTES for this book, the section on "mass killings" is by far the largest. All told, it encompasses more than seventy significant passages, each of which depicts many people—often thousands—being put to death at the same time. Indeed, looking only at texts where an actual number is given, the total amounts to somewhere near two million—but that figure would swell immeasurably if we added the dozens of cities wiped out in Joshua's conquest, the Great Flood in Genesis 6–7, and verses in Revelation predicting the death of countless populations.

Naturally, this mass of passages creates something of an organizational nightmare; so as in previous chapters, we'll look first at some of the legislation, though that hardly constitutes an easy start. In the case of widespread slayings, several key regulations do not involve prohibitions; on the contrary, Israelites are sometimes directly commanded to kill en masse. We are talking, of course, about the Old Testament "ban," which instructed Israel to completely exterminate local cities and peoples as they moved into the Promised Land.

Deuteronomy 7:1–2 puts it this way: "When the LORD your God brings you into the land that you are entering to take possession of it, and clears away many nations before you, . . . and when the LORD your God gives them over to you, and you defeat them, then you must devote them to complete destruction." A later passage specifies exactly what is meant by this: "You shall save alive nothing that breathes" (Deut. 20:16). In both cases, an ESV footnote explains that the conquered peoples are to be "set apart as an offering to the Lord (for destruction)." In a later note, the *ESV Study Bible* adds, "This practice, known also as 'imposing the ban,' denotes setting aside something as the Lord's share. Usually such a ban meant that all living things—men, women, children, and livestock—were to be killed."[1]

During the conquest under Joshua, this "ban" was imposed a number of times, perhaps most clearly in the defeat of Jericho, where—after the Lord had miraculously felled the city walls—"they devoted all in the city to destruction, both men and women, young and old, oxen, sheep, and donkeys, with the edge of the sword" (Josh. 6:21). Interestingly, in a few cases, this "complete destruction" seems to have been carried out even before Moses outlined it in Deuteronomy; the language of the ban first appears in Numbers 21:1–3, where—having vanquished Canaanites under the king of Arad—Israel "devoted them and their cities to destruction. So the name of the place was called Hormah"—which means "destruction." A few verses later, Israel defeated both the Amorites and Bashan, victories later described in Deuteronomy with the language of the ban: "We captured all his cities at that time and devoted to destruction every city, men, women, and children. We left no survivors" (Deut. 2:34; see also 3:6).

Once the terms of the ban had been clearly laid out in Deuteronomy, the Israelite army lost no time obliterating dozens of cities, starting with Jericho and then followed quickly by Ai, whose inhabitants were pursued until "all of them to the very last had fallen by the edge of the sword. And all who fell that day, both men and women, were 12,000, all the people of Ai" (Josh. 8:24–25). In swift succession, Joshua 10 and 11 recount the conquest of dozens of local kings and cities, most of which were dealt with according to the ban, as the narrator indicates in a mid-point summary: Joshua, the writer tells us, "left none remaining, but devoted to destruction all that breathed, just as the LORD God of Israel commanded" (Josh. 10:40).

In the midst of all this, however, an interesting note appears in Joshua 11; here, even though Joshua is repeatedly praised because "he left nothing undone of all that the LORD had commanded Moses," we find

1. *ESV Study Bible* (Wheaton, IL: Crossway, 2008), 515.

that in several places, the Israelites retained as plunder "all the spoil of these cities and the livestock" (Josh. 11:14–15). Some scholars have noted, therefore, that the injunction to leave "nothing that breathes" was not always taken to include animals,[2] as in the case of Ai, where God specifically told Joshua and his troops that they could keep the goods and the livestock for themselves (Josh. 8:2).

This is an important detail, for while today's sensitive culture recoils from commands to wipe out every living thing, these exceptions suggest that the mandate for complete destruction was not always fully carried out; in our profound discomfort with "the ban," we do well not to jump to conclusions about how thoroughly it was applied in every case.

We must note, for example, that according to Deuteronomy 7 and 20, the ban applies only to cities within the Promised Land—that is, the cities of "the Hittites, the Girgashites, the Amorites, the Canaanites, the Perizzites, the Hivites, and the Jebusites" (Deut. 7:1; see also 20:16–17). Other cities—"all the cities that are very far from you"—must first be offered the chance to surrender: "When you draw near to a city to fight against it, offer terms of peace to it. And if it responds to you peaceably and it opens to you, then all the people who are found in it shall do forced labor for you and shall serve you" (Deut. 20:10–15). Since this passage is directly followed by the command to "save alive nothing that breathes" in nearer cities, it is possible that those cities within the Promised Land may also have been offered the chance to surrender. The *ESV Study Bible* advances this possibility based partly on the fact that Israelite troops sometimes did spare lives of Promised Land inhabitants who helped out or surrendered: Rahab of Jericho (Josh. 6:22–25), a man and his family in Bethel (Judg. 1:24–26), and all the inhabitants of Gibeon (Josh. 9:26–27).[3]

In other words, the ban was not thoroughly executed in every single situation; sometimes the spoil and livestock were spared, and sometimes individuals as well. Commentator J. A. Thompson remarks that during the conquest, there were evident "differences in practice in regard to the treatment of peoples defeated in war." In general, the carrying out of the ban

2. See, for example, J. G. McConville, *Deuteronomy*, Apollos Old Testament Commentary (Nottingham, UK: Apollos/InterVarsity, 2002), 321.
3. *ESV Study Bible*, 360.

was not invariable, although theoretically it was always likely to be carried out. In later centuries Israel laid siege to towns outside the boundaries of the promised land (e.g., 2 Sa. 12:26ff.; 2 Ki. 3:25f.). In some cases it is specifically stated that the occupants were spared but were put to work as slaves (e.g., 2 Sa. 12:31). This may have happened, at least in part, in every such case. However, the cities within the bounds of the promised land were a greater danger both to Israel's political freedom and to her religious independence, so that there was more reason to apply the practice of sacred dedication.[4]

In others words, we don't know how thoroughly the ban was instituted throughout Israel's history. Nonetheless, it seems to have been applied quite methodically in many cases, particularly those described in Joshua 6, 10, and 11. Many modern readers are deeply disturbed by this. Such deliberate and systematic slaughter seems contrary to the New Testament ethic of love for neighbors, and even to the sixth commandment forbidding murder.

To some degree, this knotty issue is beyond the scope of this book, requiring a much longer and more complex elaboration than we have room for here. But perhaps a few thoughts are in order.

In its introduction to Joshua, the *ESV Study Bible* lays out a terse and persuasive defense of "the ban," insisting that such commands were given to Moses directly by God and were intended solely for the unique nation-state of Israel—and thus, "no people today have any right to use them as a warrant to support injustice."

Indeed, Israel's "unique mission" to serve God alone—to represent his uncompromising holiness and to preserve the Messianic line—was constantly threatened by the polytheism of nearby pagan peoples. Even with "the ban" in place, God's people continually caved in to idol worship, ritual prostitution, and child sacrifice, among other sins practiced by surrounding nations; in fact, as suggested in Judges 1–3, the apostasy that plagued Israel throughout its history must have been due in some part to the fact that in many places within the Promised Land, Israel never did complete the conquest by defeating and driving out the local pagans (see esp. Judg. 1:18–36). Since they could not manage holiness even with the ban in place, just imagine how swiftly Israel's religious identity

---

4. J. A. Thompson, *Deuteronomy: An Introduction and Commentary*, Tyndale Old Testament Commentaries (Leicester, UK: Inter-Varsity, 1974), 222–23.

would have vanished if the people had allowed not just some but *all* of the heathen Canaanites to remain within their own lands.

Along these lines, it is worth noting also that the ban is not some sort of "ethnic cleansing," since Deuteronomy 13 and 17:2–7 (among other passages) decree the death penalty even for Israelites who fall into pagan practice. (Though rarely carried out in the degraded atmosphere of Israel's ongoing national idolatry, the death sentence was executed by Phinehas in Numbers 25:7–8; by Elijah on 450 Jewish prophets of Baal in 1 Kings 18:40; and by Jehu on untold numbers of idol worshipers in 2 Kings 10:18–27.)

Furthermore, as we have already noted, "even though the laws about destroying the Canaanites are stated in an uncompromising and unconditional way (in keeping with the rhetoric of ancient Near Eastern conquest accounts, which allows for this kind of unqualified statement), the way Israel applied those laws apparently made room for some of the Canaanites to surrender and survive. . . . This means that the appearance of implacability in these laws is just that, an appearance, and there is an implied allowance for exceptions."[5]

But the most important consideration in defending the ban is God's sovereign right to adjudicate land, life, death, and judgment as he sees fit—for "The earth is the LORD's, and all it contains, the world, and those who dwell in it" (Ps. 24:1 NASB). If it is true that God "works all things according to the counsel of his will" (Eph. 1:11), then the decree of extermination pronounced in "the ban" is essentially no different from any number of God-appointed natural catastrophes—for example, earthquakes, volcanoes, tsunamis, and hurricanes, or a flood like the one in Genesis 6–7.

Indeed, that flood—in which God "blotted out every living thing that was on the face of the ground" (Gen. 7:23)—is a chilling picture of the final judgment; that is, as the first mass killing in Scripture, it is simply a presage of the last. And in that final judgment, God will render to all human beings "according to what they had done. . . . And if anyone's name was not found written in the book of life, he was thrown into the lake of fire" (Rev. 20:13–15). Those who have a serious problem with the "complete destruction" passages in Deuteronomy and Joshua have a problem not so much with the ban itself as with God's right to judge;

5. Material in the three preceding paragraphs is taken from the *ESV Study Bible*, 390–91.

for the killing of idolatrous Canaanites is simply a judgment for their pagan practices—and hardly the most drastic one in Scripture.

Take, for example, Revelation 9:15–18, where a third of mankind is summarily wiped out. Or the "plague of death" directed at Egypt under the leadership of Moses, when "the LORD struck down all the firstborn in the land of Egypt, from the firstborn of Pharaoh who sat on his throne to the firstborn of the captive who was in the dungeon. . . . And there was a great cry in Egypt, for there was not a house where someone was not dead" (Ex. 12:29–30). And let's not forget catastrophic military defeats—again, clearly ordained by a sovereign God—such as that of King Sennacherib, in which "the angel of the LORD went out and struck down 185,000 in the camp of the Assyrians" (2 Kings 19:35); or Judah's one-day loss of 120,000 men while fighting King Pekah of Israel (2 Chron. 28:6); or Israel's earlier loss of half a million men in a single battle with Judah's King Abijah (2 Chron. 13:17).

Raymond B. Dillard is one of many scholars who feel that such numbers seem unusually high; he points out, for example, that U.S. fatalities in World War II—the deadliest military conflict in history—totaled about 400,000 for the entire war, with a similar number for Britain and about half that many for France.[6] Since we still have quite a few additional passages to examine in this chapter—many of which list very large death tolls—this might be a good time to note an ongoing difficulty with the numbering system in the Old Testament.

This complicated issue, nicely summarized in the *ESV Study Bible*'s introduction to the book of Numbers, focuses on the Hebrew word *eleph*. That key term is translated as "thousand" in a vast array of Old Testament passages; but it can also mean "clan," "division," "family," or "tribe," as in Micah 5:2, Joshua 22:21, and Numbers 10:4, among others. So it could be a figure simply for a group, or perhaps for an especially large group that does not mean literally or exactly one thousand—as in Ecclesiastes 6:6, where a man could rhetorically live "a thousand years twice over" (see also Mic. 6:7; Deut. 32:30; Job 9:3). To muddy matters further, *eleph* bears a strong resemblance to the Hebrew *alluph*, meaning "chief" or "clan," as used repeatedly in Genesis 36 and in Zechariah 12:5–6, for example.

---

6. Raymond B. Dillard, *2 Chronicles*, Word Biblical Commentary, vol. 15 (Waco, TX: Word, 1987), 106–7; see also "World War II casualties," *Wikipedia*, accessed January 6, 2013, http://en.wikipedia.org/wiki/World_War_II_casualties.

Thus, the many casualty figures listed throughout the Old Testament could refer to *groups* of soldiers. In other words, a recording of 120,000 deaths may mean that 120 divisions suffered some casualties within their ranks; or that 120 military *leaders* were killed. Alternately, these specific figures may incorporate some complex numbering system that is no longer known to us; or as suggested earlier, they may simply represent some very large but indeterminate amount.[7]

As an additional consideration, the Hebrew word used in many of these massacres—*nakah*—does not always denote death. It can mean "wound" or simply "strike," and is sometimes used of hitting an inanimate object (Ex. 7:17; 8:16; 17:6). Furthermore, other verbs such as *naphal* ("fall") and *chalal* ("pierce" or "wound") are sometimes used, as with the half-a-million passage in 2 Chronicles 13:17, which has all three terms, or Judges 8:10, which says simply "fallen" and could mean that not all of the casualties were fatal.[8]

In any case, most commentators agree that there is no easy answer to questions surrounding Hebrew numbers, especially in warfare; and we do not solve the problem simply by redefining the use of "thousand," for that creates difficulties with many other mathematical figures in the Old Testament.[9] Thus, throughout this chapter, it is well to keep in mind that in these numerical military reports, we may be seeing more than meets the eye—or less.

One of the earliest "big-number" passages involves the rebellion of Korah, Dathan, and Abiram in Numbers 16. Here, several priestly families objected to the special leadership prerogatives God had granted to Moses and Aaron. As the quarrel grew more heated, God indicated his strong displeasure, and Moses told the rest of the people to move back; then, while the rebels stood by their tents—together with "their wives, their sons, and their little ones"—"the ground under them split apart.

7. Material in the two preceding paragraphs has been carefully assembled from the following: Joyce G. Baldwin, *1 and 2 Samuel: An Introduction and Commentary*, Tyndale Old Testament Commentaries (Leicester, UK: Inter-Varsity, 1988), 68–69; Dillard, *2 Chronicles* 106–7, 222; *ESV Study Bible*, 261; R. Laird Harris, Gleason L. Archer Jr., and Bruce K. Waltke, *Theological Wordbook of the Old Testament* (Chicago: Moody, 1980), 48; Martin J. Selman, *2 Chronicles: A Commentary*, Tyndale Old Testament Commentaries (Leicester, UK: Inter-Varsity, 1994), 479; and Donald J. Wiseman, *1 and 2 Kings: An Introduction and Commentary*, Tyndale Old Testament Commentaries (Leicester, UK: Inter-Varsity, 1993), 178.

8. Harris, Archer, and Waltke, *Theological Wordbook*, 578.

9. Dillard, *2 Chronicles*, 222; see also *ESV Study Bible*, 261.

And the earth opened its mouth and swallowed them up, with their households and all the people who belonged to Korah. . . . But on the next day all the congregation of the people of Israel grumbled against Moses and against Aaron, saying, 'You have killed the people of the LORD.'" The result of this further insurrection was a plague from God, killing another 14,700 (Num. 16:23–49).

Several other deadly plagues were unleashed on Israel during her history, most of them for similar rebellious complaints. Numbers 21:7 tells of "fiery serpents" that killed great numbers of people; these serpents were probably snakes whose bite produced a lethal, burning inflammation.[10] Numbers 11:31–33 recounts a plague that killed a similarly large number in Israel, with Numbers 25:9 listing another 24,000 felled by pestilence as a punishment for intermarriage and polytheistic worship with surrounding pagans. Together with the 70,000 later slain when David instituted a census (2 Sam. 24:15), that is an unimaginable number of Israelites killed by divinely ordained disease. To this already astronomical figure, we might well add Sennacherib's 185,000 troops in 2 Kings 19:35; slain quite suddenly and without much specific detail, they are thought to have been wiped out by some sort of disease, perhaps bacillary dysentery.[11]

Along with Numbers, Judges also offers several intriguing accounts of widespread death. Using a clever strategy of loud noise and bright light, for example, Gideon and his tiny army felled some 120,000 Midianites (Judg. 8:10); this is a remarkable number however you reckon it, considering that a short time earlier, Israel had already decimated Midian, killing all adult men and "every male among the little ones" (Num. 31:7–17). In chapter 13, we discussed the motif of "makeshift weapons" that runs through Judges; and thus, along with Gideon's trumpets, torches, and smashed jars, we find an earlier judge, Shamgar, using an oxgoad, an instrument with an eight- or ten-foot handle and a point tipped with metal; "when freshly sharpened it would have many of the qualities of a spear."[12] Using this handy implement, Shamgar killed 600 Philistines, not a particularly large number among the others in this chapter, but

10. Gordon J. Wenham, *Numbers: An Introduction and Commentary* (Leicester, UK: Inter-Varsity, 1981), 157.

11. Wiseman, *1 and 2 Kings*, 284.

12. Arthur E. Cundall and Leon Morris, *Judges and Ruth: An Introduction and Commentary*, Tyndale Old Testament Commentaries (Leicester, UK: Inter-Varsity, 1968), 81.

impressive for one man wielding an agricultural tool (Judg. 3:31). Other individual warriors elsewhere in Scripture are described as having slain as many as 800 men at one time (2 Sam. 23:8; 1 Chron. 11:11).

A good deal more remarkable was Samson, who single-handedly slew more than two thousand men with even more unlikely weapons. One such victory prompted Samson to compose this self-explanatory poem:

> With the jawbone of a donkey,
>   heaps upon heaps,
> with the jawbone of a donkey
>   have I stuck down a thousand men. (Judg. 15:16)

Commentator C. F. Burney notes that the Hebrew word for "donkey" in this poem literally means "red-colored animal"; positing wordplay involving the resultant pile of Philistine corpses, Burney retranslates Samson's ditty as follows: "With the red ass's jawbone I have reddened them bright red." His remarks are quoted by Cundall and Morris, who add that "such a coarse illustration is typical of Samson."[13]

In two separate piques of rage involving a woman he loved, Samson had earlier slain thirty Philistines (Judg. 14:19) and then again an unspecified number whom he struck "hip and thigh with a great blow" (Judg. 15:8). "Hip and thigh" appears to be an obscure Hebrew idiom, perhaps indicating that Samson "left his enemies in a tangled jumble of legs and thighs."[14] Much later, after Delilah had conspired to get him captured and imprisoned by the Philistines, Samson managed to push over two pillars supporting a house full of men and women, some of whom were also on the roof; "and the house fell upon the lords and upon all the people who were in it. So the dead whom he killed at his death were more than those whom he had killed during his life" (Judg. 16:27–30).

Judges also recounts 10,000 Moabite deaths (Judg. 3:29), the sacking of twenty cities under Jephthah (Judg. 11:33), and a civil war that killed 42,000 men of Ephraim (Judg. 12:6); but perhaps the most shocking figures in this blood-soaked historical book involve an even more devastating civil war in chapters 20 and 21. Here, eleven tribes of Israel rallied against Benjamin because the twelfth tribe had refused to yield

13. Ibid., 172.
14. *ESV Study Bible*, 464.

the culprits after a horrific gang rape in the Benjamite city of Gibeah (see chap. 12 above for details on this incident). When all was said and done, more than 90,000 men of Israel and Benjamin fell in this conflict; the line of Benjamin lay on the verge of extinction, the more so because all Israel had taken a vow not to give their daughters in marriage to this tribe. When Israel realized that there were no Jewish women to marry the few remaining Benjamite men, they compounded the bloodshed of this long conflict by wiping out the town of Jabesh-gilead—which had not joined them in the battle against Benjamin—leaving only four hundred virgins, who were then seized for Benjamite marriage.

The narrator of Judges concludes this section—and indeed, his entire book—with the terse but telling remark that during these times, "everyone did what was right in his own eyes" (Judg. 21:25); yet his earlier accounts of the conflict with Benjamin evince ironic disapproval as well. At one point, for instance, the men of Benjamin look back to see their entire city going up in flames (Judg. 20:40), a verse in which the Hebrew word *kalil*, or "whole," echoes the "whole burnt offering" language of the ban in Deuteronomy 13:16.[15] Significantly, Israel's order for the slaughter at Jabesh-gilead is couched even more pointedly in the language of the ban: "Go and strike the inhabitants of Jabesh-gilead with the edge of the sword; also the women and the little ones. . . . Every male and every woman that has lain with a male you shall devote to destruction" (Judg. 21:10–11). Here, the severest form of the ban is instituted not against a pagan nation, as in the earlier conquest, but against a city of fellow Israelites.

The most tragic part of this disheartening episode is that it is only the first in a seemingly endless series of internal conflicts that killed thousands if not millions of Jews during the ensuing centuries of Israel's history. To be sure, there were many deaths among external conflicts with declared enemies: King David killed more than 80,000 Edomites and Syrians (2 Sam. 8:5–13; 10:18); Ahab—with some help from a timely wall collapse—slew 127,000 enemies of Israel in one battle (1 Kings 20:29–30); more than 75,000 Persians died at Esther's behest (Est. 9:12–16); in two smaller episodes, David conducted a series of skirmishes against various enemies, leaving "neither man nor woman alive" (1 Sam. 27:9)—and after defeating Moab in 2 Samuel 8:2, he made them lie down on the ground

---

15. Daniel I. Block, *Judges, Ruth*, The New American Commentary (Nashville: Broadman, 1999), 566.

in rows: "two lines he measured to be put to death, and one full line to be spared." Yet most of the remaining examples in this grim chapter do not involve conflict between Israel and some oppressive outside power; rather, the vast majority occurred during hostilities among God's chosen people—though in some cases, the slaughter was divinely commanded, in an effort to purge the nation of wicked rulers who led them into idol worship and other pagan sins.

Perhaps the lowest point in the long power struggle between Israel's first king, Saul, and his successor, David, involved the priestly town of Nob. As David was fleeing from Saul in 1 Samuel 21, he was helped by Ahimelech at Nob, where the priest loyally fed David and his men, also handing over the famed sword of Goliath that had been stored there. Observing all this was an Edomite named Doeg, the chief of Saul's herds-men, who reported the incident to his king. Outraged by the alleged disloyalty of Ahimelech, Saul commanded his men to kill him and the other priests of Nob; when the men proved unwilling to obey such a blatantly wicked order, Doeg stepped up "and struck down the priests, and he killed on that day eighty-five persons who wore the linen ephod. And Nob, the city of the priests, he put to the sword; both man and woman, child and infant, ox, donkey and sheep, he put to the sword" (1 Sam. 22:18–19). Once again, the writer's language invokes the ban, here instituted in its most extreme form—the extermination of everything that breathes.

Yet in this case, as commentator Joyce G. Baldwin observes, the wrong is highlighted by a contrast with Saul's earlier treatment of Amalek. Because that hateful pagan nation had harassed Israel during the exodus, God ordered Saul to "go and strike Amalek and devote to destruction all that they have." Yet Saul wound up sparing the Amalekite king, along with the best of the livestock—in spite of God's specific command to "kill both man and woman, child and infant, ox and sheep, camel and donkey" (1 Sam. 15:1–9). There is little doubt that the writer's distinctly parallel language regarding Doeg echoes this earlier disobedience that cost Saul his kingship; unwilling to carry out the ban against a pagan enemy as commanded by God himself, Saul had no compunction about unleashing it on fellow Israelites, even to the point of wiping out an entire city of priests.[16]

16. Baldwin, *1 and 2 Samuel*, 141.

A similarly thorough approach was taken during a series of dire assassinations marking the blood-soaked history of northern Israel after it split from Judah and Jerusalem. For example, Israel's early King Nadab, the son of King Jeroboam, was killed and supplanted by Baasha, who then "killed all the house of Jeroboam. He left to the house of Jeroboam not one that breathed, until he had destroyed it" (1 Kings 15:27–29). Baasha's successor, his son Elah, was then assassinated by Zimri, who immediately upon assuming the throne, "struck down all the house of Baasha. He did not leave him a single male of his relatives or his friends" (1 Kings 16:9–11).

Such wholesale slaughter of enemies was a common practice at that time, partly "to avoid any focus for reprisals or a blood feud after a coup"; at the same time, in these instances it "may be related to the thoroughness of divine punishment," and as a way "to prevent the deliberate spread of sin,"[17] since in the case of both Jeroboam and Baasha, God had clearly decreed that their houses would be thoroughly wiped out (see 1 Kings 15:29 and 16:3–4).

Such was also the case with the ungodly line of Ahab, one of the most depraved among Israel's many vicious kings. The story is recounted in 2 Kings 9 and 10. Anointing a man named Jehu as the new ruler of Israel, God declared that he would use Jehu to "cut off from Ahab every male, bond or free, in Israel. And I will make the house of Ahab like the house of Jeroboam the son of Nebat, and like the house of Baasha the son of Ahijah" (2 Kings 9:6–9). Ahab himself was already dead at this point, so Jehu carried out his mission by killing Ahab's son, King Jehoram of Israel, and at the same time slaying King Ahaziah of Judah, a grandson of Ahab through his mother, who had married into the line of Judean kings (2 Kings 9:14–27).

Ahab's infamous wife, Jezebel, was still alive at this time, and Jehu had her killed as well (2 Kings 9:30–37; see chap. 13 above for more detail on this grisly incident). Besides Jehoram of Israel, Ahab also left behind some seventy other sons; Jehu had them wiped out too, in this case commanding that their heads be cut off in the city where they lived. These heads were then sent to Jehu in baskets and piled at the city gate (2 Kings 10:1–8), apparently a customary action in the ancient Near East as a warning against further rebellion. Jehu then proceeded to polish off the line of King Ahaziah in Judah, for he "slaughtered . . . forty-two

17. Wiseman, *1 and 2 Kings*, 158.

persons, and he spared none of them"; but he may have exceeded his warrant when he slew even nonrelatives of the hated King Ahab, including "all his great men and his close friends and his priests, until he left him none remaining" (2 Kings 10:11–14).[18]

Yet Jehu still wasn't done. In what may have been an application of the earlier death sentence decreed against idolatrous practices (see Deut. 13 and 17:2–7), Jehu deceitfully declared a mass religious service in honor of the pagan god Baal, calling forth Baal's servants and prophets from throughout all Israel; and indeed, so many gathered that "the house of Baal was filled from one end to the other." After carefully ascertaining that there were no true servants of the Lord among these idol worshipers, Jehu had them all killed, giving a macabre meaning to an earlier statement in which he declared, "I have a great sacrifice to offer to Baal." In an especially pungent note, the narrator concludes this episode by noting that Jehu then destroyed the house as well, "and made it a latrine to this day" (2 Kings 10:18–27; see also p. 211).

While Jehu was undeniably thorough in executing his divine mission, I have sometimes wondered whether he was right in carrying it over even to Ahab's relatives in Judah, for in doing so, he came frighteningly close to snuffing out the line of Davidic kings that would eventually lead to the world's Messiah. Judah's King Ahaziah, you see, was the son of Athaliah, herself a daughter of Ahab and Jezebel. Still alive when her son was assassinated, the queen mother swiftly turned and slew "all the royal family"—presumably her own sons and grandsons. This abomination then placed her on the throne, making her the only female monarch in all the history of Israel and Judah. Fortunately for the line of David, one of Ahaziah's sisters managed to grab a young male nephew, Joash, "and stole him away from among the king's sons who were being put to death"; and with the later help of some loyal soldiers and the chief priest Jehoiada, Joash took the throne, and the wicked Athaliah was put to death (2 Kings 11:1–16).

While we're on the subject of assassinations, we might note that after a good start, Joash later conspired against Jehoiada's son, Zechariah, and had him stoned to death; and Joash himself was thereafter killed by his own servants as he lay wounded after a battle (2 Chron. 24:20–26). Joash's son, Amaziah, then assumed the throne, but was likewise assassinated

18. Ibid., 226.

by unnamed conspirators (2 Chron. 25:25–27). A few generations later, King Amon of Judah—father of the better-known Josiah—was killed by his own servants, though in this case the conspirators were subsequently executed as well (2 Chron. 33:24–25). The Bible also mentions the assassination of Assyria's King Sennacherib by his own sons during pagan worship (2 Kings 19:37) and of Ben-hadad of Syria by his messenger Hazael; this latter death apparently occurred by suffocation: Ben-hadad was ill, and Hazael simply "took the bed cloth and dipped it in water and spread it over his face, till he died" (2 Kings 8:7–15).

But the most ghastly series of assassinations occurred in the northern kingdom of Israel, which saw a swift succession of six kings in just over thirty years. The last of Jehu's line, King Zechariah, had his six-month reign brought to an end when he was killed by Shallum, who was in turn slain by Menahem one month later. Menahem died of natural causes after managing to retain the throne for a decade; he was followed by his son, Pekahiah, who was assassinated two years later by Pekah, himself killed after twenty years by Israel's final king, Hoshea. Though the precise chronology in this period is "full of difficulties,"[19] nonetheless the narrator plunges through this bloody six-king period in less than one chapter (see 2 Kings 15:8–31).

The reader may have noted that the various narrators in all these mass killings and assassinations rarely go into detail, though the deaths of 500,000 Israelites (2 Chron. 13:17) at the hands of Judah is described with the term "great force" (Hebrew, *makkah*), which is usually reserved for the defeat of pagan enemies. (It is translated as "a great blow" in Josh. 10:10 and 10:20, as well as in 1 Sam. 19:8 and 23:5.)[20] One other mass death not covered above—an account in which troops under King Amaziah slew 20,000 men of Edom—does provide a picturesque detail: "The men of Judah captured another 10,000 alive and took them to the top of a rock and threw them down from the top of the rock, and they were all dashed to pieces" (2 Chron. 25:12).

Most of the time, however, the narrator is content to state simply that those killed were "devoted to destruction," put to the "edge of the sword," or "struck down." J. A. Thompson points out that the expression

19. Peter J. Leithart, *1 and 2 Kings*, Brazos Theological Commentary on the Bible (Grand Rapids: Brazos, 2006), 243.
20. Selman, *2 Chronicles*, 383.

"to the sword" in the ban regulations of Deuteronomy 20:13 is literally "to the mouth of the sword," adding that "ancient swords discovered in excavations often have the blade emerging from the haft as the tongue of a wild beast whose head forms a feature at the end of the handle. Thus the expression suggests that the sword was inserted up to the hilt."[21]

As for "struck down," this is the Hebrew word *nakah*, literally meaning "smite"; in various forms, it occurs in Scripture well over four hundred times. Here are a few of the English words used for *nakah* in the NASB, a telling summary of how the Old Testament deals with murder, mayhem, and military conquest: attack, beat down, destroy, inflict, kill, overthrow, ruin, shoot, slap, slaughter, slay, smash, smite, strike, thrust, wound.

21. Thompson, *Deuteronomy*, 222.

PART 3

"Any Unclean Thing"—
Other Blunt or Unsavory Material

18

"Unclean until the Evening"

Menstruation, Semen, and Other "Discharges"

MOST OF US probably do not think of menses, semen, and sexually transmitted disease as falling into the same category; but the extensive regulations in Leviticus 15 treat them together under the heading of "discharges," all of which result in ceremonial uncleanness. Following Scripture's lead, we'll examine these topics in the current chapter, though the material here is not restricted to Levitical regulations, as many other passages deal with these various "discharges"; nor will I use the same order as Leviticus 15, preferring instead to start with the clearest and simplest of these: menstruation.

As we've seen in many other texts dealing with indelicate matters, the Bible does not have a specific word that denotes this subject and nothing else. Occasional euphemisms occur, such as "the fountain of her blood" in Leviticus 20:18 and "the way of women" in Genesis 31:35; even in Leviticus 20:18, the ESV phrase "during her menstrual period" translates a word that literally means "sick, faint, or unwell." In most passages about menstruation—Leviticus 15 and a few others—the phrase "menstrual impurity" renders the Hebrew word *niddah* (simply, "impurity, filthiness"). Throughout Scripture, the use of this word is colored by the early passages about menses, but it can also be translated as "unclean," "filthy thing," or "abhorrent," as in, for example, Lamentations 1:17 and Ezekiel 7:19–20.[1]

---

1. Robert L. Thomas, ed., *The New American Standard Exhaustive Concordance of the Whole Bible* (Nashville: Holman, 1981), 1559; R. Laird Harris, Gleason L. Archer Jr., and Bruce K. Waltke, *Theological Wordbook of the Old Testament* (Chicago: Moody, 1980), 556.

It is interesting that Scripture devotes so much frank attention to this subject, yet never employs a word that names it with explicit exclusivity.

Most people familiar with the Old Testament know that Jewish ceremonial law forbade sexual intercourse during a woman's monthly period. This instruction is carefully repeated three separate times; but the general regulations concerning various aspects of menstruation actually occupy much more space.

Here is the relevant material from Leviticus:

> When a woman has a discharge, and the discharge in her body is blood, she shall be in her menstrual impurity for seven days, and whoever touches her shall be unclean until the evening. And everything on which she lies during her menstrual impurity shall be unclean. Everything also on which she sits shall be unclean. And whoever touches her bed shall wash his clothes and bathe himself in water and be unclean until the evening. And whoever touches anything on which she sits shall wash his clothes and bathe himself in water and be unclean until the evening. Whether it is the bed or anything on which she sits, when he touches it he shall be unclean until the evening. And if any man lies with her and her menstrual impurity comes upon him, he shall be unclean for seven days, and every bed on which he lies shall be unclean. (Lev. 15:19–24)

Before reacting with indignation at what seems to be an off-putting label for a perfectly natural monthly condition, we do well to remember a few important factors, not the least of which is that menstruation in ancient times, with none of the countless hygiene products now available, was probably a somewhat messier affair than it is today. Indeed, given the greater inconvenience of monthly periods in those days, these regulations may have provided a regular interlude of rest for busy young wives.[2] And in any case, as Gordon J. Wenham points out, monthly periods were much less common in ancient Israel due to early marriage, late weaning, and large families; indeed, these rules in Leviticus 15 would have applied largely to unmarried teens—and thus, the threat of ritual uncleanness would serve to dissuade men from premarital sex.[3]

2. R. K. Harrison, *Leviticus: An Introduction and Commentary*, Tyndale Old Testament Commentaries (Leicester, UK: Inter-Varsity, 1980), 164.
3. Gordon J. Wenham, *The Book of Leviticus*, New International Commentary on the Old Testament (Grand Rapids: Eerdmans, 1979), 223–24.

As to the reason why menstruation is "unclean," the *ESV Study Bible* points out that, in general, the ceremonial regulations throughout Leviticus locate uncleanness in proximity with anything that smacks of death, while the opposite idea, holiness, can be seen broadly as associated with life. The *New Geneva Study Bible* then observes that Leviticus 15 deals with "loss of life fluids" such as blood or semen; through the resulting reminder of death, such matters are therefore "incompatible with the presence of God, who is perfect life."[4]

Slightly more problematic in Leviticus 15 are the seven days of uncleanness that result from intercourse during menses; this seems to contradict the sterner law in Leviticus 20:18, which decrees that those involved be summarily cast out: "If a man lies with a woman during her menstrual period and uncovers her nakedness, he has made naked her fountain, and she has uncovered the fountain of her blood. Both of them shall be cut off from among their people." Since other similar prohibitions are also strongly worded—see Leviticus 18:19 and Ezekiel 18:6—the milder consequence in Leviticus 15:24 can probably be explained by the wording in that verse: if her menstrual impurity "comes upon him." In other words, rather than a brazen flouting of the law as in other passages, the sin here may be inadvertent: either the man did not know she was menstruating, or—perhaps more likely—the period actually began during intercourse.[5]

After these rather detailed regulations, Scripture brings up the subject of menstruation in only a handful of verses, most of which are tastefully discreet in dealing with the matter. Probably the subtlest of these is found in Isaiah 64, a passage so low-key that many Christians who know it well still have no idea that it refers to menses: "We have all become like one who is unclean, and all our righteous deeds are like a polluted garment"—or, in the more familiar King James wording, all our righteousness is "filthy rags" (Isa. 64:6). The Hebrew phrase translated as "polluted garment" and "filthy rags" is literally "a garment of times," or "a garment of menstruation."[6] This admittedly surprising reading is supported by the first half of the verse, which clearly posits that it is not

4. *ESV Study Bible* (Wheaton, IL: Crossway, 2008), 212; *New Geneva Study Bible: Bringing the Light of the Reformation to Scripture* (Nashville: Nelson, 1995), 172.

5. *ESV Study Bible*, 237; Wenham, *Leviticus*, 220.

6. The two phrases are from, respectively, Alec Motyer, *Isaiah: An Introduction and Commentary*, Tyndale Old Testament Commentaries (Leicester, UK: Inter-Varsity, 1999), 391, and

dealing with typical dirt but rather with something traditionally regarded as "unclean"—the same Hebrew word found in countless Levitical regulations like those discussed above. In this case, it is a shockingly effective way to convey the worthlessness of human achievements in respect to God's transcendent holiness.

Ezekiel is somewhat more overt. Chapter 18 offers the portrait of an ideal man who, among his many other virtues, does not "approach a woman in her time of menstrual impurity" (Ezek. 18:6). Note the euphemistic "approach" in this laudatory verse, which is replaced by a different verb in chapter 22. Here, in the midst of a lengthy list of national sins, the men of Israel are reproved because "they violate women who are unclean in their menstrual impurity" (Ezek. 22:10). The more strident "violate" in this text is a Hebrew word that elsewhere frequently refers to rape (Deut. 22:24, 29; 2 Sam. 13:12, 14, 22); in this way, Ezekiel 22 highlights "the abusiveness of the men's actions."[7]

Another euphemism is found in our final passage on menstruation—the story of Rachel stealing from her father in Genesis 31. In this brief episode, Jacob was leaving the home of his father-in-law, Laban, after working there for fourteen years in a deal that yielded him not one but two wives—Laban's daughters, Leah and Rachel. For reasons not stated, Rachel decided to steal her father's "household gods," probably a set of small figurines representing the pagan deities worshiped in that apparently heathen household.[8] Laban set off in pursuit and, upon reaching Jacob's camp, searched all over for the idols, even in Rachel's tent. "Now Rachel had taken the household gods and put them in the camel's saddle and sat on them. Laban felt all about the tent, but did not find them. And she said to her father, 'Let not my lord be angry that I cannot rise before you, for the way of women is upon me.' So he searched but did not find the household gods" (Gen. 31:19, 33–35).

Commentators find in this passage a sardonic attitude toward these worthless pagan deities, with the narrator taking "malicious pleasure at the deadly fun made of the *terafim*: they are only to be 'saved' by a menstruation. This means that they are as unclean as

---

Edward J. Young, *The Book of Isaiah: The English Text, with Introduction, Exposition, and Notes,* vol. 3, *Chapters 40–66* (Grand Rapids: Eerdmans, 1969), 497.

7. Daniel I. Block, *The Book of Ezekiel: Chapters 1–24*, New International Commentary on the Old Testament (Grand Rapids: Eerdmans, 1997), 710.

8. *ESV Study Bible*, 104.

can be"; it also suggests that "the gods were equivalent to a sanitary napkin."⁹

This is a minor passage, but I chose it to conclude our section on menses because it seems both frank and tasteful, with the author making a sly joke on a subject many of us tend to avoid. Yet if a woman's monthly period is something we don't discuss much in Christian circles, semen is probably even less so; and though Scripture hardly shies away from this uncomfortable topic, we will see that its actual language tends to express a similar reticence and delicacy.

We noted in chapter 6, for example, that sexual intercourse accompanied by "an emission of semen" results in ceremonial uncleanness for both the man and woman until evening (Lev. 15:18). Looking more thoroughly at this passage, we find that any such discharge has a similar effect: "If a man has an emission of semen, he shall bathe his whole body in water and be unclean until the evening. And every garment and every skin on which the semen comes shall be washed with water and be unclean until the evening" (Lev. 15:16–17). The second sentence clearly indicates that this regulation refers to ejaculation outside of intercourse, as in Deuteronomy 23:10–11, which contains instructions for purifying any man who "becomes unclean because of a nocturnal emission."

The actual language in these passages is markedly indirect. While modern English employs such distinct nouns as "sperm," "semen," and "ejaculate"—words that cannot really mean anything else—Leviticus's "seminal emission" is constructed of two more general Hebrew words, the first having to do with "lying down" and the second a broad term for "sowing," also translated as "descendants," "family," "offspring," or "seed." Gordon J. Wenham suggests that the phrase is best translated as "an outpouring of seed,"¹⁰ while a marginal note in the NASB tells us that "emission of semen" in Leviticus 15:16 is literally "man's, goes out from him." And the passage in Deuteronomy 23 is even more elliptical. The actual Hebrew rendered "nocturnal emission" in verse 10 comes from the root "encounter, meet, befall" and means simply "chance, accident"; as commentator J. G. McConville observes, the Hebrew literally says the

---

9. The two comments are taken, respectively, from Gordon J. Wenham, *Genesis 16–50*, Word Biblical Commentary, vol. 2 (Dallas: Word, 1994), 276, and Bruce K. Waltke and Cathi J. Fredricks, *Genesis: A Commentary* (Grand Rapids: Zondervan, 2001), 430.

10. Wenham, *Leviticus*, 219.

man becomes unclean because of "something that happens"[11]—with the meaning inferred from the subsequent instructions for cleansing, which closely parallel those about semen in Leviticus 15.

Such reticence also characterizes the key narrative passage on ejaculation: Genesis 38, the famous story of Onan and his sister-in-law, Tamar. Here, due to a somewhat obscure tradition, Onan was expected to marry and beget children with his brother's widow as a way of carrying on the deceased sibling's bloodline (see Deut. 25:5–10). However, for reasons not entirely clear, the young man refused, possibly feeling that these surrogate children might be more blessed than his own: "Onan knew that the offspring would not be his. So whenever he went in to his brother's wife he would waste the semen on the ground" (Gen. 38:9).

An early tradition viewed this action as masturbatory, a reading once so common that it gave us the English word "onanism," a well-known synonym for masturbation. But it is clear from the wording here that Onan was actually engaging in the Bible's one and only example of *coitus interruptus*. And it is likewise clear that he did it several times, as indicated by the ESV and NIV's use of "whenever."[12] More significantly, the usual terms for "seminal emission" are nowhere present in this verse; the original Hebrew actually omits the noun entirely, reading literally "spilled on the ground." It's a frank passage, but the writer is apparently trying to keep the gross-out factor at a minimum.

Two texts in Ezekiel 23, however, show considerably less delicacy. In that chapter, cited so often throughout this book, Ezekiel condemns the spiritual adultery of God's faithless people by depicting the northern kingdom of Samaria as a sluttish woman named Oholah. Among other things, the prophet tells us that her lovers "poured out their whoring lust upon her" in verse 8, where Daniel I. Block insists that "the reference must be to ejaculation." Verse 20 is even less equivocal, comparing the "members" of these lovers to "those of donkeys," and adding that their "issue was like that of horses." As we saw in chapter 2, the Hebrew term here rendered "issue" derives from a root meaning "to pour, gush

---

11. J. G. McConville, *Deuteronomy*, Apollos Old Testament Commentary (Nottingham, UK: Apollos/InterVarsity, 2002), 346.

12. See also Derek Kidner, *Genesis: An Introduction and Commentary*, Tyndale Old Testament Commentary (Leicester, UK: Inter-Varsity, 1967), 180.

forth" or "a flood of rain, downpour."[13] Thus, this shocking passage is indeed describing the copious ejaculate of the whorish woman's lovers, which comes streaming out from their oversized organs like that of a donkey or horse.

Getting back to Leviticus 15, that passage actually opens and closes with lengthy regulations on other male and female discharges that do not seem to involve semen or menstruation. Indeed, the strictures on male discharges are by far the most extensive and specific in this chapter: "When any man has a discharge from his body, his discharge is unclean. . . . Whether his body runs with his discharge, or his body is blocked up by his discharge, it is his uncleanness." The following nine verses then lay out what persons and objects are contaminated by this man's uncleanness: anything he sits on or lies on or touches, including saddles and vessels of clay or wood; anyone who touches his bed or sits where he sat; anyone who touches his body, or anything that was "under him," or the discharge itself; and even "if the one with the discharge spits on someone who is clean," that person is to be considered unclean as well (Lev. 15:2–12).

The nature of the fluid or discharge in this passage is somewhat unclear. "As early as the Septuagint the complaint in question has been identified as gonorrhea, and most commentators accept this diagnosis. But apart from the fact that an abnormal discharge from the male organ is being described, few specific details are given here." The word for "discharge" is literally "flow," a noun that appears in Scripture only in this chapter; the related verb "to flow" is rare, though it does show up in the common Old Testament phrase "flowing with milk and honey." The word "runs" in verse 3 suggests "slimy juice," connected to the Hebrew for "saliva," as in 1 Samuel 21:13–14 (the term is used for juice from fruit in Job 6:6). "It may block (lit. 'cause to seal') the male organ, presumably because it is thick and coagulates."[14]

Earlier in this chapter, we posited that menstrual blood was "unclean" because of its symbolic association with death. R. K. Harrison makes a similar connection in the case of this discharge: "Most probably the reason why discharges were defiling was that they contained dead

13. Block, *Ezekiel 1–24*, 737, 742; the final definition of "issue" here is from Thomas, *NASB Concordance*, 1515.

14. Wenham, *Leviticus*, 218; see also Harrison, *Leviticus*, 160.

matter within themselves. This, as is now known, includes white blood cells that have succumbed in the attempt to halt the spread of the infection, as well as actual necrosed tissue on many occasions."[15] This may likewise be the case with seminal fluid, which contains living organisms that also will die upon ejaculation.

So, we have looked at scriptural dealings with menstrual fluid, seminal emission, and gonorrheal discharge; now we turn our attention back to blood again, for Leviticus 15 closes with a lengthy section on any woman who has "a discharge of blood for many days, not at the time of her menstrual impurity, or if she has a discharge beyond the time of her impurity." Once again, in such cases "she shall be unclean," along with "every bed on which she lies" and "everything on which she sits," as well as "whoever touches these things" (Lev. 15:25–27). This ailment clearly involves nonmenstrual bleeding from the vagina, but no more is said about its specific nature. It may be worth noting, however, that these regulations become especially pertinent in the well-known New Testament story of the woman "who had had a discharge of blood for twelve years" and who was healed when she pushed through a crowd to touch Jesus Christ (Mark 5:25–34; see also Matt. 9:20–22; Luke 8:43–48).

R. T. France notes that this woman's ailment was "a menstrual disorder," while D. A. Carson observes that it was probably "chronic bleeding from the womb."[16] Due to the Old Testament laws discussed above, this woman was not only anemic, unmarriageable, hopeless, and broke (for she "had spent all that she had" on doctors), but also ceremonially unclean. In fact, her condition was so woeful that in verses 29 and 34, Mark describes it with the Greek word *mastix*. Meaning "whip" or "scourge," this is a graphic term that "can refer to the lashes received in criminal punishment,"[17] as in Acts 22:24 and Hebrews 11:36. The *ESV Study Bible* points out that by touching Jesus, the woman would technically have made him ceremonially unclean, according to Levitical law; "but Jesus is

15. Harrison, *Leviticus*, 161.

16. R. T. France, *The Gospel according to Matthew: An Introduction and Commentary*, Tyndale New Testament Commentaries (Leicester, UK: Inter-Varsity, 1985), 170; D. A. Carson, *Matthew*, in *The Expositor's Bible Commentary*, vol. 8: *Matthew, Mark, Luke*, ed. Frank E. Gaebelein (Grand Rapids: Zondervan-HarperCollins, 1984), 230.

17. Robert H. Stein, *Mark*, Baker Exegetical Commentary on the New Testament (Grand Rapids: Baker, 2008), 164, 269.

greater than any purity laws, for he makes her clean by his power instead of becoming unclean himself."[18]

Christ's encounter with this helpless woman makes an especially fitting conclusion to our current chapter, for it reminds us that, as the Westminster Confession of Faith puts it, all these ceremonial laws about uncleanness and purification "are now abrogated, under the new testament."[19] In the words of the *New Bible Dictionary*, "Christ repealed all the levitical regulations on unclean animals and practices (Mt. 15:1–20 and Mk. 7:6–23). . . . It is emphasized in Heb. 9:13f that the only pollution that matters *religiously* is that of the conscience, from which the sacrifice of Christ, offered in the spiritual realm, alone can cleanse."[20]

All this of course applies not only to the uncleanness of "discharges" but also to such "unclean" ailments as leprosy—and to Christ's interaction with those so afflicted; but a lengthy discussion of such diseases requires us to begin a separate chapter.

---

18. *ESV Study Bible*, 1902.

19. *The Confession of Faith and Catechisms with Proof Texts* (Willow Grove, PA: OPC Christian Education Committee, 2005), 85–86.

20. C. L. Feinberg, "Clean and Unclean," in *The New Bible Dictionary*, 2nd ed., ed. J. D. Douglas (Leicester, UK: Inter-Varsity, 1982), 216.

19

"Wasting Disease and Fever"

Bowels, Boils, Tumors, and Leprosy

AS WE SAW IN CHAPTER 17, plagues are fairly common in the Bible, but the writers rarely give us much information about the specific type of disease involved. Though we already discussed several illnesses in that earlier chapter, this current section focuses on passages where the nature of the maladies, their symptoms and effects, are described or at least apparent from the text, so that we can once again see just how the Bible deals with this sort of graphic material.

Let us begin with the little-known but chilling death of Judah's King Jehoram in 2 Chronicles 21. Because of Jehoram's many sins—not the least of which was marrying the daughter of Israel's notorious King Ahab—God pronounced the following curse on the king through Elijah: "You yourself will have a severe sickness with a disease of your bowels, until your bowels come out because of the disease, day by day." The narrator then drives this home by repeating it even more forcefully, for after Jehoram's wife, sons, and possessions were carried away during an enemy attack, "the LORD struck him in his bowels with an incurable disease. In the course of time, at the end of two years, his bowels came out because of the disease, and he died in great agony" (2 Chron. 21:14–19).

Translation difficulties make it hard to discern the precise chronology in this episode,[1] but the ESV's careful wording suggests a lengthy

---

1. Raymond B. Dillard, *2 Chronicles*, Word Biblical Commentary, vol. 15 (Waco, TX: Word, 1987), 169.

ailment, with bowels prolapsing at the very end. Even with this in mind, however, it has proven tough to pinpoint the condition plaguing Jehoram. Various conjectures have been made, with the most likely being chronic dysentery, which, "when very severe and prolonged, occasionally may be complicated by prolapse of the rectum or more of the large intestine."[2] In any case, it was clearly a torturous way to die. Together with Amasa, who "spilled his entrails to the ground" after being stabbed by Joab, and Judas, who "burst open in the middle and all his bowels gushed out," we have a trio of truly horrific Bible scenes about disembowelment of one kind or another (2 Sam. 20:10; Acts 1:18; see pp. 129, 135).

Ailments involving the nether end of the digestive tract may also be involved in 1 Samuel 5 and 6. Here, enemy Philistines had captured the ark of God from Israel and set it up in a pagan temple in their own land. As the meeting-place between Yahweh and Israel, and a symbol of God's divine presence with his people, the ark did not belong in such a locale, and the Lord eventually induced its return by afflicting local Philistines with terror, panic, and a series of mysterious tumors. Philistine religious leaders urged that the ark be returned with a "guilt offering" of "five golden tumors and five golden mice"—that is, "images of your tumors and images of your mice that ravage the land" (1 Sam. 6:4–5). The final phrases here suggest that an infestation of rodents had also occurred, and that perhaps the "tumors" here were associated with the bubonic plague so famously transmitted by verminous creatures.

This well-known pestilence "causes painful swellings of the lymph nodes, or buboes, in the armpits and groin." That description is from Joyce G. Baldwin, one of several scholars who remain unconvinced that bubonic plague is indeed the actual affliction described in this passage. For one thing, if untreated, the bubonic plague kills more than half of its victims, yet actual death is never mentioned in the detailed accounts of tumors, terror, and "deathly panic" with which God here afflicted Philistia (see 1 Sam. 5:6–12). Furthermore, as Baldwin points out, occurrences of this disease are not attested in the Middle East until many centuries after this period.[3] And finally, the Hebrew word for "tumors"

2. D. H. Trapnell, "Health, Disease and Healing," in *The New Bible Dictionary*, 2nd ed., ed. J. D. Douglas (Leicester, UK: Inter-Varsity, 1982), 460. See also Martin J. Selman, *2 Chronicles: A Commentary*, Tyndale Old Testament Commentaries (Leicester, UK: Inter-Varsity, 1994), 437.

3. Joyce G. Baldwin, *1 and 2 Samuel: An Introduction and Commentary*, Tyndale Old Testament Commentaries (Leicester, UK: Inter-Varsity, 1988), 74.

in this passage is a standard term related to the verb "swell"; however, the writer uses a different word in 1 Samuel 6:11 and 17. Suggesting sores that resulted from dysentery, this rare word—*techor*—derives from roots meaning "to eject" and "to strain at stool."[4] Thus, *The Concise Hebrew and Aramaic Lexicon of the Old Testament* suggests that the Philistines' ailment may have been "boils or abscesses at the anus."[5] This is why some translations use the word "hemorrhoids" instead of tumors: the KJV, for example, has "emerods in their secret parts" (1 Sam. 5:9), while the Wycliffe Bible somewhat comically describes the idols as "likenesses of their arses" (1 Sam. 6:11). If this was the case, the affliction may have been particularly humiliating to its sufferers, the more so if they made "golden hemorrhoids" and sent them to Israel along with the ark!

Boils or abscesses make a few other appearances in Scripture, perhaps most notably in the so-called "plague of boils" unleashed on Egypt in Exodus. Here, following precise instructions from the Lord, Moses and Aaron "took soot from the kiln and stood before Pharaoh. And Moses threw it in the air, and it became boils breaking out in sores on man and beast" (Ex. 9:10). The NIV renders "boils breaking out" as "festering boils," while John I. Durham calls them "inflamed swellings breaking into septic sores." Noting that the use of "soot" suggests black spots covering the skin, R. Alan Cole calls them "inflamed areas," using "a term common in the medical sections of the law of Moses (Lev. 13:18). This then breaks out in various 'heads' or 'open sores.' . . . Another possible meaning is areas of infected 'prickly-heat,' an eruptive skin rash common to all tropical countries."[6] In any case, this plague of boils is probably in view as well when Revelation 16:2 presents a vision of "harmful and painful sores" overcoming those who worship the beast.

Another well-known instance of boil-like disease occurs in Job, where the famous sufferer was covered "with loathsome sores from the sole of his foot to the crown of his head. And he took a piece of broken pottery with which to scrape himself while he sat in the ashes" (Job 2:7–8).

4. R. Laird Harris, Gleason L. Archer Jr., and Bruce K. Waltke, *Theological Wordbook of the Old Testament* (Chicago: Moody, 1980), 348.

5. Cited in Ralph W. Klein, *1 Samuel*, Word Biblical Commentary, vol. 10 (Waco, TX: Word, 1983), 50.

6. John I. Durham, *Exodus*, Word Biblical Commentary, vol. 3 (Waco, TX: Word, 1987), 119; R. Alan Cole, *Exodus: An Introduction and Commentary*, Tyndale Old Testament Commentaries (Leicester, UK: Inter-Varsity, 1973), 96.

Noting that these sores were only one of many physical symptoms that afflicted Job, Francis I. Andersen elaborates on this woeful condition:

> The brief data point to boils, ulcers, or one of the numerous diseases of the skin. . . . Some kind of acute dermatitis spreading everywhere and developing infections with darkened (Jb. 30:28) and peeling (30:30) skin and constantly erupting pustules (7:5b) would manifest the pruritis and purulence highlighted in 2:7. Other symptoms may be the results of complications in the wake of such a severe malady: anorexia, emaciation (7:16; 30:15f.), weeping (16:16a), sleeplessness (7:4), nightmares (7:14). These and other general sufferings, such as putrid breath (19:17; cf. 17:1), failing vision (16:16b), rotting teeth (19:20) and haggard looks (2:12) are less direct clues. They add up to a hideous picture of a man tortured by degrading disfigurement . . . and unendurable pain.[7]

Using language that parallels the passages in Job and Exodus, our final reference to boils is found among several verses in Deuteronomy 28, where God promises many curses if Israel is not "careful to do all his commandments and his statutes": "The LORD will strike you with wasting disease and with fever, inflammation and fiery heat. . . . The LORD will strike you with the boils of Egypt, and with tumors and scabs and itch, of which you cannot be healed. . . . The LORD will strike you on the knees and on the legs with grievous boils of which you cannot be healed, from the sole of your foot to the crown of your head" (Deut. 28:15, 22, 27, 35).

R. K. Harrison explains that the term "wasting disease"—also threatened in Leviticus 26:16—"could include such contagious and infectious conditions as dysentery, cholera, typhoid fever, typhus fever, malaria, tuberculosis and various types of cancer." The Leviticus passage adds the curse of "wasting disease and fever that consume the eyes and make the heart ache," which may refer to a type of gonorrheal blindness "marked by a disabling form of ophthalmia known as acute purulent conjunctivitis, which spreads rapidly from eye to eye and from person to person. It results in permanent blindness."[8] Meanwhile, Deuteronomy

---

7. Francis I. Andersen, *Job: An Introduction and Commentary*, Tyndale Old Testament Commentaries (Leicester, UK: Inter-Varsity, n.d.), 91–92.

8. R. K. Harrison, *Leviticus: An Introduction and Commentary*, Tyndale Old Testament Commentaries (Leicester, UK: Inter-Varsity, 1980), 232.

28:27 (above) uses the same Hebrew word for "boil" as Exodus 9 and Job 2; derived from a root meaning "hot or inflamed," it could here refer to smallpox, elephantiasis, or bubonic plague—while "scabs" may consist of a skin eruption, mange, or a literal covering of scabs.[9]

Despite the many references to bowels and boils, undoubtedly the most common disease in the Bible—and by far the most thoroughly examined one—is leprosy. Appearing in more than fifteen narrative passages, it is also the sole focus of all 116 verses in Leviticus 13 and 14. However, virtually every modern commentator agrees that what we now know as "leprosy," or "Hansen's disease," is not the ailment referred to by most uses of "leprosy" in both the Old and New Testaments.

The actual Hebrew word that appears throughout Leviticus 13 and 14 comes from a root meaning "to become diseased in the skin"; a generic rather than a specific description, it is most likely a general term for "all kinds of skin diseases."[10] We can say this unequivocally because in the first place, true leprosy did not reach the Middle East until New Testament times.[11] More important, the extensive Levitical regulations presuppose that those with a "leprous disease" can often be healed and restored (see, for instance, Lev. 14:3), whereas Hansen's disease was in ancient times an incurable condition. Furthermore, inanimate objects such as clothing and walls are sometimes said to be "leprous" (Lev. 13:47–49; 14:33–38)—and of course, actual leprosy can be contracted only by living organisms.

Indeed, it is unclear whether Hansen's disease is ever covered at all in the long list of ailments outlined in Leviticus 13 and 14. These passages require priests to examine and evaluate a nauseatingly specific array of external symptoms: eruptions or spots (Lev. 13:1); hairs that have turned white or yellow (Lev. 13:3, 30); white swelling (Lev. 13:10); raw flesh (or "ulcerating tissue"[12]) (Lev. 13:10); boils and "reddish-white" spots (Lev. 13:19); scars (Lev. 13:23); burned flesh (Lev. 13:24); the "itch" ("a leprous disease of the head or the beard") (Lev. 13:30–37); and some

9. J. A. Thompson, *Deuteronomy: An Introduction and Commentary*, Tyndale Old Testament Commentaries (Leicester, UK: Inter-Varsity, 1974), 274.

10. Gordon J. Wenham, *The Book of Leviticus*, New International Commentary on the Old Testament (Grand Rapids: Eerdmans, 1979), 201. See also *ESV Study Bible* (Wheaton, IL: Crossway, 2008), 231, 1959; Harrison, *Leviticus*, 136; and Selman, *2 Chronicles*, 471.

11. Wenham, *Leviticus*, 113.

12. Harrison, *Leviticus*, 141.

sort of greenish or reddish mold, fungus or mildew on clothing (Lev. 13:48–49) and on the walls of houses (Lev. 14:37). Modern-day theories on the conditions actually described here include severe eczema, burn-induced infection, ringworm, pustular dermatitis, fungal infection, "psoriasis, urticaria (hives), favus (which produces honeycomb-shaped crusts), and leukoderma (which produces white patches on the skin)."[13] In confirmation of this, several narrative passages compare the disease to "snow" (Ex. 4:6; Num. 12:10; 2 Kings 5:27). Despite some translations that indicate otherwise, these passages do not actually contain the Hebrew word for "white"; they may be referring not to color but to the scales or flakes associated with such maladies as psoriasis and eczema.[14]

These other passages find leprosy occurring in such individuals as Moses (Ex. 4), Miriam (Num. 12), and Naaman the Syrian (2 Kings), as well as Judah's King Uzziah (2 Chron. 26:19–21; 2 Kings 15:5–7), plus four unnamed Israelites who discovered that the Syrian army had abandoned its siege of their starving city (2 Kings 7:3–5). We get a few specifics on this ailment in the case of Moses' sister, Miriam, who was temporarily smitten with leprosy after challenging her brother's authority, for Aaron begs the Lord not to afflict his sister permanently, lest she be "as one dead, whose flesh is half eaten away when he comes out of his mother's womb" (Num. 12:1–12). Here, the reference is to a stillborn child whose dead flesh, having soaked at length in amniotic fluid, has begun to slough off and fall away.

Moving to Christ's lifetime, the *ESV Study Bible* again asserts that the Greek term *lepra* used in the New Testament "included a variety of serious skin diseases and was not limited to what is today called 'leprosy.'"[15] If in these New Testament instances it seems more likely that Hansen's disease was sometimes the case, this would have involved one of two ailments, "which can follow one another or co-exist in the same individual." The first causes horribly disfiguring nodes or tubercles, beginning on the face and then spreading to the limbs. "After a time these swellings soften, suppurate, . . . and slowly eat away the patient's

---

13. *ESV Study Bible*, 231. See also Dillard, *2 Chronicles*, 211; Trapnell, "Health, Disease and Healing," 459; and Wenham, *Leviticus*, 113.

14. Wenham, *Leviticus*, 113, 195–96.

15. *ESV Study Bible*, 1835.

mouth, nose, eyes, fingers, and limbs and damage his whole organism."[16] The second and perhaps better-known form of leprosy causes "loss of sensation, especially in the extremities," so that, among other things, sufferers can no longer feel what they are touching or tell when they have been injured; quite often, the illness results in loss of fingers, toes, and/or limbs.[17]

Yet these horrific symptoms did not prevent Christ from associating with and even touching several well-known New Testament lepers: Simon (at whose home he dined; see Matt. 26:6 and Mark 14:3); the importunate man who asked for healing "if you will" (Matt. 8:2–4; Mark 1:40–44; Luke 5:12–14); and the ten who were healed, of which only one turned back to thank his benefactor (Luke 17:11–19).

Hansen's disease or otherwise, Levitical regulations would have dictated that these figures were unclean and thus to be avoided by any law-abiding Jew; but as in the case of the hemorrhaging woman (pp. 188–89), the holy Christ transferred his own cleanness to the sufferers, rather than being tainted by these otherwise helplessly infectious and isolated victims.

16. W. Corswant, *A Dictionary of Life in Bible Times*, trans. Arthur Heathcote (New York: Oxford University Press, 1960), 172.

17. "Leprosy," in *The Columbia Encyclopedia*, 2nd ed., ed. William Bridgwater and Elizabeth J. Sherwood (Morningside Heights: Columbia University Press, 1950), 1122.

20

"Their Flesh Will Rot"

Vomit, Corpses, and Other Gross-Outs

VOMIT. AS WITH OTHER topics in this third section of the book—menstruation, semen, feces, urine—most of us have considerable familiarity with this common "fact of life," but we don't care to talk about it much. Fortunately, the Bible contains only a handful of passages on this revolting subject, though several of them are exceedingly unpleasant. In fact, every single instance uses the idea of vomit to make a stern warning or condemnation even more pungent and memorable.

Though most of the passages in question are literal, Scripture's earliest occurrences make use of vomiting in its figurative sense, with God warning Israel to obey him once the people settle in Canaan "lest the land vomit you out when you make it unclean, as it vomited out the nation that was before you" (Lev. 18:28; see also 18:25; 20:22).

Proverbs is more literal in its references, and more uncomfortable too. Chapter 23 counsels against eating too much food at the table of "a man who is stingy," for "you will vomit up the morsels that you have eaten" (Prov. 23:6–8). Chapter 25 offers a similar warning: "If you have found honey, eat only enough for you, lest you have your fill of it and vomit it" (Prov. 25:16).

Several prophetic passages connect vomiting with drunkenness, including Jeremiah 25:27, where God condemns sinful Israel to "Drink, be drunk and vomit, fall and rise no more." Or consider Jeremiah's even more graphic curse on the pagan nation of Moab: "Make him drunk, because he magnified himself against the LORD, so that Moab shall wallow in his vomit" (Jer. 48:26). The Hebrew word for "wallow" in this verse can also be translated "splash into," and is rendered "clap" or "strike" in other places; some commentators feel that its use here suggests someone slapping a hand to his stomach as he lurches violently forward to regurgitate: "The picture of a drunken man doubled over by vomiting is both disgusting and likely to provoke derision."[1]

Isaiah 19:14 offers the similar image of Egypt being made to "stagger in all its deeds, as a drunken man staggers in his vomit"; and Isaiah is even more explicit in chapter 28, though the condemnation here is directed at false Jewish priests and prophets, who "reel with wine and stagger with strong drink; . . . they stumble in giving judgment. For all tables are full of filthy vomit, with no space left" (Isa. 28:7–8). Both the *ESV Study Bible* and commentator Edward J. Young stress that this passage is probably literal and not intended as mere allegory. Young adds: "It is a sickening picture, and as though to give it a final emphasis Isaiah adds that there is no place remaining where cleanness may be found. The thought is expressed by two short words, 'without place.'"[2]

Proverbs 26:11, however, is surely the best-known Bible passage on regurgitation, probably because it is cited by Peter in the New Testament (2 Peter 2:22). The verse contains yet another memorable warning: "Like a dog that returns to his vomit is a fool who repeats his folly." "An intentionally repulsive simile," it juxtaposes "the fool's incorrigibility with the dog's repulsive nature to return to its vomit, to sniff at it, to lick it, and finally to eat it."[3]

That is not the only disgusting thing that gets eaten in the Bible. In its lengthy list of clean and unclean foods, for example, Leviticus gives permission for Israelites to eat, if they wish, certain types of bugs: "Among the winged insects that go on all fours you may eat those that have jointed legs above their feet, with which to hop on the ground. Of

---

1. J. A. Thompson, *The Book of Jeremiah*, New International Commentary on the Old Testament (Grand Rapids: Eerdmans, 1980), 708. See also R. K. Harrison, *Jeremiah and Lamentations: An Introduction and Commentary*, Tyndale Old Testament Commentaries (Leicester, UK: Inter-Varsity, 1973), 176–77.

2. Edward J. Young, *The Book of Isaiah: The English Text, with Introduction, Exposition, and Notes*, vol. 2, *Chapters 19–39* (Grand Rapids: Eerdmans, 1969), 273. See also *ESV Study Bible* (Wheaton, IL: Crossway, 2008), 1288.

3. Bruce K. Waltke, *The Book of Proverbs: Chapters 15–31*, New International Commentary on the Old Testament (Grand Rapids: Eerdmans, 2005), 354.

them you may eat: the locust of any kind, the bald locust of any kind, the cricket of any kind, and the grasshopper of any kind" (Lev. 11:21–22). Here is a regulation John the Baptist seems to have taken to heart many centuries later, for he famously went about eating "locusts and wild honey" (Matt. 3:4; Mark 1:6). It is worth noting that it was apparently not unusual to eat insects in that time and place; in fact, the desert locust "is a large grasshopper, still eaten today by poorer people in the Middle East and Africa."[4]

In addition, Exodus 16:20 describes leftover manna that "bred worms and stank." Presumably no one actually ate this, but that does not appear to have been the case with the shocking afterbirth passage in Deuteronomy 28. Here, God promised that disobedience on the part of Israel would eventually result in starvation so severe that "the most tender and refined woman among you, who would not venture to set the sole of her foot on the ground because she is so delicate and tender, will begrudge to the husband she embraces, to her son and to her daughter, her afterbirth that comes out from between her feet and her children whom she bears, because lacking everything she will eat them secretly" (Deut. 28:56–57). (See chap. 15 above for a detailed discussion of cannibalism in the Bible, especially as it involves children.)

Both insects and undesirable foodstuffs also come into play during several of the plagues God inflicted on Egypt in the period leading up to Israel's exodus. The second of these, in Exodus 8, involved a severe infestation of frogs, about which Moses warned Pharaoh in the early verses: "The Nile shall swarm with frogs that shall come up into your house and into your bedroom and on your bed and into the houses of your servants and your people, and into your ovens and your kneading bowls." This threat was soon fulfilled, after which "the frogs died out in the houses, the courtyards, and the fields. And they gathered them together in heaps, and the land stank" (Ex. 8:3–14).

"The man who first wrote and told this story had smelt dead frogs in tropical sunshine."[5] With slimy, dead amphibians in every nook and cranny—even in beds and kitchen equipment!—"the environmental effects would be disastrous. They are clearly a threat to the sanitary

4. *ESV Study Bible*, 1824.
5. R. Alan Cole, *Exodus: An Introduction and Commentary*, Tyndale Old Testament Commentaries (Leicester, UK: Inter-Varsity, 1973), 92.

preparation of food. And when they begin dying (vv. 13–14), their rotting bodies not only send up a horrible odor but also pose a public health catastrophe."[6] Indeed, the death of the frogs en masse seems to have been a response to Pharaoh's request that Moses "plead with the LORD to take away the frogs from me and from my people" (Ex. 8:8). The decomposing bodies, heaped in stinking piles throughout the land, perhaps recall the widespread stench of dead fish resulting from the previous plague of water turned to blood (Ex. 7:18–21); all this "must have prompted in Pharaoh a wish that he had been more specific about the means and timing of the frogs' removal."[7]

This second plague was followed by a third and fourth involving swarms of gnats and then flies. In the first of this pair, "the dust of the earth became gnats in all the land of Egypt," so that "there were gnats on man and beast" (Ex. 8:17). These may have been fleas or sand flies but were most likely mosquitoes, which "will breed in unbelievable numbers" and whose swarms can resemble "a black cloud."[8] Indeed, the reference to surface dirt here is "a symbol of both the endless number of the gnats and their universal extent."[9] Commentator Peter Enns observes that the gnat plague is one of only two (the other being boils in Ex. 9:8–12) that is never specifically said to end—so that both these afflictions may well have become a way of life in Egypt.[10]

Regarding the "swarms of flies" that later infested both the Egyptian people and their houses (Ex. 8:21–24), R. Alan Cole notes that "mixture" is a better word than "swarms," suggesting that this plague did not consist of only one species but rather "all sorts of flying creatures." He points out that the Septuagint—a late translation of the Old Testament produced in that region of the world—uses "dog fly," meaning the gadfly or March fly, which has a painful bite. Cole also hypothesizes that these swarms appeared partly in response to the heaps of decaying frogs. "Flies are a curse in every tropical country, especially after a flood, when filth and carcasses of drowned animals litter the land."[11]

6. Peter Enns, *Exodus*, The NIV Application Commentary (Grand Rapids: Zondervan, 2000), 205.

7. John I. Durham, *Exodus*, Word Biblical Commentary, vol. 3 (Waco, TX: Word, 1987), 105.

8. Cole, *Exodus*, 93.

9. Durham, *Exodus*, 106.

10. Enns, *Exodus*, 210.

11. Cole, *Exodus*, 93–94.

Ah, yes—decomposing carcasses. The final topic in this grisly chapter is the subject of more than a dozen Bible passages that depict the rotting corpses of soldiers left on the open battlefield. In most of these texts, the bodies are those of Israelites—and to make matters worse, they are often being eaten by scavengers from both land and sky. A typical passage is Deuteronomy 28:26, which promises such a fate if Israel disobeys God's commands: "Your dead body shall be food for all birds of the air and for the beasts of the earth, and there shall be no one to frighten them away" (see also Gen. 40:19; Ps. 79:2; Jer. 7:33; 19:7; 34:20). In the second volume of his study on Ezekiel, Daniel I. Block points out that "the practice of throwing bodies out into the open to be eaten by wild animals is well attested in ancient Near Eastern sources."[12] Indeed, commentator after commentator insists that this was an abomination to the people in that time period—"a curse," "loathsome," "reprehensible," "a thing of unspeakable horror," "a supreme disgrace," "more fearful even than death," "the final humiliation, as though one had departed unloved and of no account, as disposable as an animal."[13]

The value placed on proper burial can be seen, for example, in 2 Samuel 21, where seven sons of Israel's King Saul were hanged to avenge their father's treachery toward Gibeon. Rather than leaving these bodies exposed to the elements and to scavengers, Saul's concubine Rizpah "took sackcloth and spread it for herself on the rock, from the beginning of harvest until rain fell upon them from the heavens. And she did not allow the birds of the air to come upon them by day, or the beasts of the field by night"; after learning of this, King David had these remains buried, along with those of Saul and his son Jonathan, which also had never been formally interred (2 Sam. 21:1–14).

Several passages on scavengers and corpses offer variations on the basics laid out in Deuteronomy 28. Zechariah 14:12, for example, gives us an apocalyptic vision in which soldiers opposing God begin to decompose even before they are dead: "Their flesh will rot while they are still

12. Daniel I. Block, *The Book of Ezekiel: Chapters 25–48*, New International Commentary on the Old Testament (Grand Rapids: Eerdmans, 1998), 377.

13. The phrases, in the order presented, are taken from Thompson, *Jeremiah*, 404; Harrison, *Jeremiah*, 104, 147, 88; Young, *Isaiah*, 2:430; J. A. Thompson, *Deuteronomy: An Introduction and Commentary*, Tyndale Old Testament Commentaries (Leicester, UK: Inter-Varsity, 1974), 274; and Derek Kidner, *Psalms 73–150: An Introduction and Commentary*, Tyndale Old Testament Commentaries (Leicester, UK: Inter-Varsity, 1973), 286.

standing on their feet, their eyes will rot in their sockets, and their tongues will rot in their mouths." Commentator Thomas E. McComiskey points out that in the original text, most of the nouns in this verse are actually singular, focusing on one member of the attacking forces "in order to intensify our perception of what is transpiring"; but the final noun, "mouths," is plural even in the Hebrew, capping off this revolting passage with a grim reminder that every member of the invading army will be thus stricken.[14]

In other passages on decomposition, the prophet Jeremiah thrice refers to rotting human remnants as "dung" (Jer. 8:2; 9:22; 16:4), perhaps suggesting that they will eventually serve as a sort of fertilizer for the ground.[15] Indeed, if they are eaten by animals, the bodies will swiftly and quite literally be turned into excrement. Isaiah 34:3 pronounces this curse on Israel's enemies using language that is "concrete and vivid"[16]: "Their slain shall be cast out, and the stench of their corpses shall rise; the mountains shall flow with their blood."

This imagery of a blood-drenched landscape becomes even more pronounced in Ezekiel 32:5–6, where the following curse is levied on Egypt: "I will strew your flesh upon the mountains and fill the valleys with your carcass. I will drench the land even to the mountains with your flowing blood, and the ravines will be full of you." The Hebrew word for "carcass" in verse 5 can mean "to rot, decay," and may be used in this passage for "dead flesh eaten by worms." Verse 5 employs some obscure vocabulary that can mean "overflow" or "excrement," and in this way "the prophet has painted a vivid picture of the earth drinking the excrement, blood and other body fluids that were discharged when an animal is slain. One can scarcely imagine a more ignominious death."[17]

Jeremiah 8:1–2 portrays the deliberate disinterment of the bones of sinful kings, officials, priests, prophets, and other inhabitants of Jerusalem, which "shall be brought out of their tombs." It is an act R. K. Harrison calls "barbarous," "appalling," "gross humiliation and indignity,"[18]

---

14. Thomas Edward McComiskey, *Zechariah*, in *The Minor Prophets: An Exegetical and Expository Commentary*, vol. 3: *Zephaniah, Haggai, Zechariah, and Malachi*, ed. McComiskey (Grand Rapids: Baker, 1998), 1240.
15. Thompson, *Jeremiah*, 295.
16. Young, *Isaiah*, 2:430
17. Block, *Ezekiel 25–48*, 205.
18. Harrison, *Jeremiah*, 88.

yet the prophet drives his point home further by referring to the pagan deities these people had "sought and worshiped": The devotees' remains "shall be spread before the sun and the moon and all the host of heaven, which they have loved and served. . . . And they shall not be gathered or buried. They shall be as dung on the surface of the ground."

The image of bones strewn across the ground points to a particularly well known passage in this group—Ezekiel 37, where God brought the prophet to a valley full of bones, "very many on the surface of the valley, and behold, they were very dry." God then instructed Ezekiel to prophesy over the desolate remains, and on doing so the prophet witnessed what Block calls "a reversal of the decomposition process"[19]: "There was a sound, and behold, a rattling, and the bones came together, bone to its bone. And I looked, and behold, there were sinews on them, and flesh had come upon them, and skin had covered them." Ezekiel was then instructed to prophesy for the breath of life, and when he did, "the breath came into them, and they lived and stood on their feet, an exceedingly great army" (Ezek. 37:1–10).

Thus, slaughter, decay, and becoming prey for scavenging birds and rodents is not the final word regarding God's people. For his enemies, however, there is no such hope—as indicated by two graphic passages in Ezekiel and Revelation. In Ezekiel 39—a chapter addressing "Gog," a figure for those opposing Israel and Jehovah—Ezekiel receives the following command from God himself: "Speak to the birds of every sort and to all beasts of the field, 'Assemble and come, gather from all around to the sacrificial feast that I am preparing for you, a great sacrificial feast on the mountains of Israel, and you shall eat flesh and drink blood. You shall eat the flesh of the mighty, and drink the blood of the princes of the earth. . . . And you shall eat fat till you are filled, and drink blood till you are drunk, at the sacrificial feast that I am preparing for you'" (Ezek. 39:17–19).

The *ESV Study Bible* calls this a "grisly scene" representing "a wholesale inversion of what sacrifice intends." As Iain M. Duguid puts it, "Instead of animals being slain to feed the appetites of the human guests . . . , here the humans have been slain to feed the animals from all around." And John B. Taylor calls it "a graphic, though gruesome, picture; but the squeamish need to be reminded that atrocious acts have

19. Block, *Ezekiel 25–48*, 376.

to be expressed in corresponding imagery. . . . Judgment *is* a horrifying thing, and the more devastating its description is, the more men will fear it. Ezekiel was certainly never guilty of calling a spade anything but a spade."[20]

This horrific scene is deliberately echoed during the final wholesale destruction of God's enemies in Revelation: "Then I saw an angel standing in the sun, and with a loud voice he called to all the birds that fly directly overhead, 'Come, gather for the great supper of God, to eat the flesh of kings, the flesh of captains, the flesh of mighty men, the flesh of horses and their riders, the flesh of all men, both free and slave, both small and great.'" And once the leaders of this opposition have been cast alive into the lake of fire, then "the rest were slain by the sword" and "all the birds were gorged with their flesh" (Rev. 19:17–21). As Philip Edgcumbe Hughes puts it, "the scene envisaged is one of total carnage. . . . The horror of their self-invited doom is intensified by the spectacle of the birds gorging themselves on the flesh of their carcasses. The graphic imagery is a solemn reminder that 'it is a fearful thing to fall into the hands of the living God' (Heb. 10:31)."[21]

20. *ESV Study Bible*, 1563; Iain M. Duguid, *Ezekiel*, The NIV Application Commentary (Grand Rapids: Zondervan, 1999), 451; John B. Taylor, *Ezekiel: An Introduction and Commentary*, Tyndale Old Testament Commentaries (Leicester, UK: Inter-Varsity, 1969), 248.

21. Philip Edgcumbe Hughes, *The Book of the Revelation: A Commentary* (Leicester, UK: Inter-Varsity, 1990), 207–8.

21

"And the Dung Came Out"

Feces and Urine

AS IN MANY PREVIOUS CHAPTERS, we will begin our survey of Bible passages on excrement by looking at the Old Testament regulations; but unlike many of those detailed ordinances, here we find only two specific rules on this important but unpleasant subject.

The first law appears in five verses throughout the Pentateuch, all of which lay down instructions about what should be done with certain parts of animals once they had been butchered for use in Israel's system of sacrificial offerings. Most of the animal was to be burned on the altar inside the tabernacle or temple, with the priest commanded to observe the following exceptions: "The skin of the bull and all its flesh, with its head, its legs, its entrails, and its dung—all the rest of the bull—he shall carry outside the camp to a clean place, to the ash heap, and shall burn it up on a fire of wood" (Lev. 4:11–12; see also Ex. 29:14; Lev. 8:17; 16:27; Num. 19:5).

The Hebrew for "dung" in these five verses literally means "fecal matter." A rarer and slightly different word—one that is likely restricted to human waste—occurs in the following regulation from Deuteronomy: "You shall have a place outside the camp, and you shall go out to it. And you shall have a trowel with your tools, and when you sit down outside, you shall dig a hole with it and turn back and cover up your excrement." The passage then adds an explanation, one that may also shed light on the necessity for burning dung from sacrificial animals: "Because the

LORD your God walks in the midst of your camp, to deliver you and to give up your enemies before you, therefore your camp must be holy, so that he may not see anything indecent among you and turn away from you" (Deut. 23:12–14). Thus this stipulation to take great care in covering human excrement was "both a prescription of hygiene and also a cultic or religious requirement."[1] The "trowel" specified here is literally "peg"—as in "tent peg"—and the passage makes clear that this tool was to be part of the soldier's standard fighting equipment. Indeed, this and a few other key laws in Deuteronomy 23 seem specifically addressed to fighting men encamped against enemies (see v. 9); presumably, some similar treatment of waste was to be observed by civilians in Israel's traveling entourage, but there is, curiously, no passage in the Pentateuch addressing this issue for the population at large.

Despite the rather bold word "excrement" here—which means exactly that in Hebrew—note how the rest of the passage is somewhat indirect, assuming that the reader or listener already knows the purpose of "a place outside the camp"; and the phrase "when you sit down outside" is a clear but innocuous euphemism for defecation. This carefully tasteful approach is also found in a few other passages, most notably the well-known Hebrew idiom "covering his feet," accurately translated as "relieving himself" in Judges 3:24 and 1 Samuel 24:3. Since these are the Old Testament's only two uses of the phrase, it is possible that the latter—describing King Saul in a cave—is intended as a mildly insulting allusion to the first, in which the wicked pagan king Eglon is killed in ignominious fashion, so that "the dung came out" (see pp. 8, 132–33); the writer may wish to suggest that Saul's reign will soon come to a similarly dismal end.

The ESV also uses this modern English euphemism—"relieving himself"—in a somewhat humorous passage from 1 Kings, recounting the confrontation between the prophet Elijah and several hundred devotees of the pagan god Baal. The idea here was to see which deity—Israel's Jehovah or the Canaanite storm god—could miraculously set fire to a sacrificial bull atop a pile of cut wood. The Baalite prophets tried first, calling upon their god for several hours to no avail—at which point, "Elijah mocked them, saying, 'Cry aloud, for he is a god. Either he is

---

1. J. A. Thompson, *Deuteronomy: An Introduction and Commentary*, Tyndale Old Testament Commentaries (Leicester, UK: Inter-Varsity, 1974), 240–41.

musing, or he is relieving himself, or he is on a journey, or perhaps he is asleep and must be awakened'" (1 Kings 18:27). The Hebrew word used here for "relieving himself" literally means "moving away" and is usually translated "dross," meaning "waste products"; so it is no stretch to hear the great prophet ridiculing his opponents' hapless god for stepping out to the bathroom. Other translations have "using the toilet" (CEV) and "gone aside to answer the call of nature" (NLT).

In two Bible passages, however, the relation to excrement is tenuous at best. One is Philippians 3:8, where the apostle Paul uses strong language to label anything that impedes his relationship with Christ: "I count everything as loss because of the surpassing worth of knowing Christ Jesus my Lord. For his sake I have suffered the loss of all things and count them as rubbish, in order that I may gain Christ." The word "rubbish" here has sometimes been rendered "dung" (KJV, Lexham, New English Translation). This reading may be accurate, but the Greek term—*skubalon*, found only here in Scripture—often means simply "refuse" or "rubbish" in extrabiblical writers.[2] It is a "vulgar term" offering "a choice between human waste product and the unwanted food which is consigned to the rubbish heap. . . . A word like 'muck' conveys to the modern reader something of the distaste and disgrace of the original term."[3]

Equally uncertain is 2 Kings 6:25, which describes a siege of Samaria by the Syrian king Ben-hadad; this produced a famine so severe that "a donkey's head was sold for eighty shekels of silver, and the fourth part of a kab of dove's dung for five shekels of silver." Internet writer David Reagan says, "Most Bible scholars have done their best to make the dove's dung something else. However, there are other records of people collecting and eating dung in times of terrible famine." In its copious textual notes, however, the Internet resource *NET Bible* cites the work of scholars M. Cogan and H. Tadmor, who claim the term was "a popular name for the inedible husks of seeds"; thus, commentator Donald J. Wiseman uses "carob beans" here, while the NIV has "seed pods"—all of which seem more likely

2. William Hendriksen, *Exposition of Philippians*, New Testament Commentary (Grand Rapids: Baker, 1977), 164.

3. Ralph P. Martin, *The Epistle of Paul to the Philippians: An Introduction and Commentary*, Tyndale New Testament Commentaries (Leicester, UK: Inter-Varsity, 1989), 150.

than bird feces to be placed, along with a "donkey's head," in a category of semi-edibles.[4]

Thankfully, then, there is no Bible passage that clearly describes the eating of excrement—though two others come close.

In a later military campaign, Assyria—after a successful conquest of northern Jews in Samaria—came up against Jerusalem promising more of the same. Indeed, the Assyrian herald insisted on surrender lest, as he put it, those of the besieged city be forced "to eat their own dung and to drink their own urine" (2 Kings 18:27; see also Isa. 36:12). Since the Lord delivered Jerusalem from this godless threat, the Assyrian official's prediction was never fulfilled in this case. Nor did human excrement finally become associated with food in Ezekiel, where the great prophet was instructed to play-act various frightening scenarios depicting the imminent conquest of Jerusalem by the pagan nation of Babylon. Among these was the command to make "'a barley cake, baking it in their sight on human dung.' And the LORD said, 'Thus shall the people of Israel eat their bread unclean, among the nations where I will drive them'" (Ezek. 4:12–13).

Ezekiel responded to this mandate with horror, repulsed by the prospect of an act that would render him ceremonially unclean; insisting that he had carefully avoided this condition throughout life, the prophet then convinced God to allow cow's dung instead, "a perfectly normal form of firing" still used in some parts of the world today.[5] Nevertheless, God's initial command, drastic as it seems, is in perfect keeping with many other late-kingdom passages in which, for example, Isaiah was compelled to go naked—and Israel's spiritual infidelity was compared to a brazenly sluttish woman or a donkey in heat (see pp. 30, 59, 65–66). All of this is clearly designed to "shock the audience" into taking the threat of deportation seriously.[6]

With this shock effect in mind, it should not be surprising that most Old Testament passages on dung and urine use this imagery to convey

---

4. David Reagan, "Eating Dove's Dung," *Learn the Bible*, accessed August 30, 2010, http://www .learnthebible.org/eating-doves-dung.html; "2 Kings 6," footnote 40, *NET Bible*, accessed June 15, 2013, http://classic.net.bible.org/bible.php?book=2Ki&chapter=6#n36; Donald J. Wiseman, *1 and 2 Kings: An Introduction and Commentary*, Tyndale Old Testament Commentaries (Leicester, UK: Inter-Varsity, 1993), 210.

5. John B. Taylor, *Ezekiel: An Introduction and Commentary*, Tyndale Old Testament Commentaries (Leicester, UK: Inter-Varsity, 1969), 83.

6. Daniel I. Block, *The Book of Ezekiel: Chapters 1–24*, New International Commentary on the Old Testament (Grand Rapids: Eerdmans, 1997), 187.

a sense of condemnation and worthlessness—a curse, as it were—on those who sin against the Lord. Jeremiah, for example, contains four separate passages in which the bodies of slain sinners shall lie "like dung upon the open field," a sort of divinely ordained fertilizer for the "surface of the ground" that is mentioned so often in these texts (Jer. 9:22; see also Jer. 8:2; 16:4; 25:33; Ps. 83:10; Zeph. 1:17). 1 Kings combines two scatological references in a derisive passage about the lineage of the wicked King Jeroboam in Israel. Not only does the writer indicate that his descendants will be burned "as a man burns up dung until it is all gone," but also, when the Lord determines to do away with "every male" in Jeroboam's line, he uses for "male" a Hebrew idiom that is, literally, "one who urinates against a wall" (1 Kings 14:10). This baldly insulting phrase appears in similar fashion five other times, always indicating (if you'll pardon the pun) thorough elimination (see 1 Sam. 25:22, 34; 1 Kings 16:11; 21:21; 2 Kings 9:8). While most modern translations render this simply as "male," the blessedly literal KJV has: "him that pisseth against the wall."

The last use of this phrase for males inaugurates a lengthy section in which Ahab's house was likewise purged from Israel and Judah ("every male, bond or free," 2 Kings 9:8)—and one which brings together other excremental language as well. The corpse of Ahab's wicked wife, for instance, "shall be as dung on the face of the field" (2 Kings 9:37). And later on, Jehu—anointed here to wipe out Ahab's line—tricks all the prophets of Baal into a bogus pagan worship ceremony, then has them slain, at the same time demolishing their heathen temple: Jehu "made it a latrine to this day" (2 Kings 10:27). Literally "cloaca" or "cesspool," the Hebrew term here—used nowhere else in Scripture—is linguistically related to "dung"; and thus, a smelly outdoor toilet may well be exactly what Jehu made of this repulsive locale.[7] A similar instance occurs in Ezra 6:11, where King Darius declares that anyone disobeying a certain edict shall see his house "made a dunghill."

It should be admitted that translation difficulties make that latter reference uncertain—the phrase could mean "forfeit."[8] And similar difficulties occur in numerous references to "idols" throughout the Old

---

7. Wiseman, *1 and 2 Kings*, 228.
8. Derek Kidner, *Ezra and Nehemiah: An Introduction and Commentary*, Tyndale Old Testament Commentaries (Leicester, UK: Inter-Varsity, 1979), 58.

Testament, particularly in Ezekiel, where one Hebrew word for false gods—*gillul*—occurs nearly forty times (Ezek. 6:4–13; 14:3–7; 22:3–7; etc.). This term belongs to a large Hebrew word family that includes "dung" and often has also to do with turning or rolling; thus, some commentators feel that it is being used pejoratively and should be translated "dung pellets," indicating just how Ezekiel and other Old Testament writers feel about these worthless deities.[9]

Also uncertain is a passage in Nahum, where the Lord says to the oppressive city of Nineveh, "I will throw filth at you and treat you with contempt" (Nah. 3:6). Some writers feel that fecal matter is implied here. Brian Godawa, for example, sees this depiction of "pelting a body with excrement as a lucid metaphor of punishment for spiritual whoredom." On the other hand, Tremper Longman III points out that the actual word used for "filth" in this text is often associated with pagan idolatry, and thus it "may connote anything that God thinks is detestable."[10] A good deal clearer—and much more sickening—is Malachi 2:3, where God tells priests who have misled his people, "I will rebuke your offspring, and spread dung on your faces, the dung of your offerings, and you shall be taken away with it." Here the Hebrew word clearly refers to literal excrement, as it is the same one used in early regulations about burning actual dung from sacrificial animals (see above).

Yet even that is not the Bible's most revolting use of excremental language. No, this distinction is reserved rather for Isaiah 25:10–11, which directs this shocking statement against the enemies of God and his people: "Moab shall be trampled down in his place, as straw is trampled down in a dunghill. And he will spread out his hands in the midst of it as a swimmer spreads his hands out to swim, but the LORD will lay low his pompous pride together with the skill of his hands." Edward J. Young points out the similarity between the Hebrew words for "straw" (*mathben*) and "dunghill" (*madmenah*)—both of which bear an ironic resemblance to the Moabite city Madmenah (Isa. 10:31). And Alec Motyer

9. Daniel I. Block, *The Book of Ezekiel: Chapters 25–48*, New International Commentary on the Old Testament (Grand Rapids: Eerdmans, 1998), 500; R. Laird Harris, Gleason L. Archer Jr., and Bruce K. Waltke, *Theological Wordbook of the Old Testament* (Chicago: Moody, 1980), 163–64.

10. Brian Godawa, *Hollywood Worldviews: Watching Films with Wisdom and Discernment* (Downers Grove, IL: InterVarsity, 2002), 198; Tremper Longman III, *Nahum*, in *The Minor Prophets: An Exegetical and Expository Commentary*, vol. 2: *Obadiah, Jonah, Micah, Nahum, and Habakkuk*, ed. Thomas Edward McComiskey (Grand Rapids: Baker, 1993), 816.

observes that the passage is all the more horrific for the contrast it makes with one of the loveliest and most stirring Old Testament texts only a few verses earlier: Isaiah 25:6, describing "a feast of rich food, a feast of well-aged wine, of rich food full of marrow, of aged wine well refined." With this as a background, the later passage "disgusts us," writes Motyer, "but its implication is inescapable: the alternative to the banquet is the midden"—portrayed here as a soupy pool in which the wicked will sink despite "the skill of his hands" in attempting to keep himself afloat.[11] In his idiomatic modern translation of the Scriptures called *The Message*, Eugene H. Peterson renders this repugnant verse thus: "As for the Moabites, they'll be treated like refuse, waste shoveled into a cesspool. Thrash away as they will, like swimmers trying to stay afloat, they'll sink in the sewage. Their pride will pull them under."

11. Edward J. Young, *The Book of Isaiah: The English Text, with Introduction, Exposition, and Notes*, vol. 2, *Chapters 19–39* (Grand Rapids: Eerdmans, 1969), 200–201; Alec Motyer, *Isaiah: An Introduction and Commentary*, Tyndale Old Testament Commentaries (Leicester, UK: Inter-Varsity, 1999), 173.

Conclusion

"Think about These Things"

NEAR THE END of his letter to the church in Philippi, the apostle Paul offers this advice to his beloved fellow Christians: "Finally, brothers, whatever is true, whatever is honorable, whatever is just, whatever is pure, whatever is lovely, whatever is commendable, if there is any excellence, if there is anything worthy of praise, think about these things" (Phil. 4:8). One can surely insist that Holy Scripture falls into the category of things that are true, lovely, commendable, and excellent; and since Paul insisted elsewhere that *all* Scripture is "profitable for teaching" (2 Tim. 3:16), the terms "worthy" and "pure" must describe the Bible in its entirety, even the sometimes gross minutiae covered in this book. In the same verse Paul testifies that every word of Scripture is "breathed out by God"; thus, as Peter J. Leithart puts it in discussing the Bible's occasional "vulgarity and scatology," "We cannot find fault with the language without finding fault with God himself."[1]

So, then, what profit, what teaching, what conclusions are to be gained from a study like the one we have just completed?

In the first place, we learn that even though the Bible is perfectly willing to deal with such familiar matters as bloodshed, defecation, warfare, menstruation, vomit, and murder, it is not unhealthily obsessed with these types of issues. The Old and New Testaments contain roughly 31,000 verses; I have quoted just over 700 of those, some of which have nothing to do with sex and violence (like the first three cited in this conclusion). Even if we include many of the 900 other verses I refer-

---

1. Peter J. Leithart, *1 and 2 Kings*, Brazos Theological Commentary on the Bible (Grand Rapids: Brazos, 2006), 105.

enced but did not quote, that is still only three or four percent of the whole Bible—for *all* of the unsavory material in Scripture! It's a ratio that seems a good deal lower than that found in much modern music, TV, and cinema, especially considering that those cultural artifacts are not, like the Bible, attempting to regulate and sanctify vast areas of human activity.

Nor are the Scriptures unduly detailed in their handling of these matters. Most notably in the area of sexuality, the writers tend to prefer euphemism, indirection, and figures of speech over blunt or technical language. Despite more than 120 references to human sexual intercourse, for example, the Scriptures have only one specific word for this activity, compared to our "copulation," "coitus," "coition," and "consummation" (not to mention dozens of indecent slang terms).

Furthermore, this one Hebrew word appears in only four verses; other instances in both the Old and New Testament are all euphemistic— "know," "have," "lie with," etc. Similarly, we find only two lone verses with noneuphemistic terms identifying the penis and testicles—one for each. Once again, comparing this to modern English ... well, it's best not to think too much about the many crude terms our culture has for the male organ! As for the Old Testament, all the other references to male privates—dozens of them, actually—use such polite idioms as "feet," "thigh," "finger," and "hand." (See chaps. 2 and 6 for more information on this terminology.)

Along the same lines, the Bible has no specific term that refers only to menstruation; no word for vulva, vagina, anus, oral sex, defecation, lesbian—and no references at all, figurative or otherwise, to pus, snot, flatulence, or masturbation. In other words, its approach to indecent matters is not that of a twenty-first-century schoolboy, nor is it that of a nineteenth-century Victorian housewife.

The Bible is, in fact, refreshingly matter-of-fact in its approach, freely acknowledging what we all know: these things are an important part of life, and by no means to be ignored or overlooked. We want a religion that is true not just for some of life—for spirituality, worship, and service—but for all of our experience. The wide range of Scripture passages on sex, violence, and other uncomfortable material helps us to see that the Judeo-Christian tradition *is* true for all of life, that it does not prudishly overlook or sidestep certain issues; rather, it concerns itself—often quite closely—even with mundane bodily matters like menses, skin disease, and nocturnal emission.

At the same time, the Bible's treatment of violent activity such as torture, rape, decapitation, cannibalism, and child sacrifice presents a full-blown picture of human depravity that proves impossible to white-wash or ignore. Indeed, the no-holds-barred content in, for example, Judges and Ezekiel is among the most convincing evidence that this is no mere human document. What book written by men, and seeking to point the way to God and goodness, would contain so very few perfect people, so much bloodshed, so much adulterous betrayal and defiance of the very principles it seeks to espouse? The Old Testament's long history of sin and decadence—a constant downward spiral that ends with the word "curse" or "destruction"—provides ample background for Jesus' first-century claim, "No one is good except God alone" (Mark 10:18).

The Bible, in other words, wants to make sin seem as bad—as repulsive, disgusting, and abhorrent—as it really is. Sadly, there is often no other way to do this than by using repulsive, disgusting, and abhorrent language.

In some cases, this involves mockery and contempt—as when, for example, the powerful Moabite king Eglon was reduced to a pile of smelly feces (Judg. 3:15–25); when Elijah derided pagan prayers as unavailing because their god was busy "relieving himself" (1 Kings 18:27); when "every male" in the house of Jeroboam is referred to as "one who urinates against a wall" (see p. 211); or when Moab is depicted as drowning in a cesspool of manure (Isa. 25:10–11).

In other instances, the "badness" of sin is emphasized in order to bring home the gravity of admonitions against it; that is, to warn Israel in frighteningly graphic terms about the consequences of disobedience. Such consequences include the possible rape of Israelite women (Deut. 28:30; Ezek. 16:36–40); cannibalism carried out on Jewish children (Deut. 28:53–57); fallen Hebrew soldiers left to rot and be eaten by beasts (Deut. 28:26; Jer. 7:33); even the possibility of having to eat food cooked over human dung (Ezek. 4:12–13).

As we saw in chapter 21, the prophet Ezekiel was horrified when asked to perform this act as a public picture of Israel's doom. That may be our reaction as well when we read of such things; but rather than wishing away this shock effect, we might perhaps rather see it as essential to what God is trying to achieve or prevent in the lives of his people. In other words, the shock is a deliberate attempt to yank them back from the brink of self-destruction, calling them to recognize that, for example, they have eaten one another, like cannibals (Mic. 3:2–3); acted like a female donkey in heat (Jer. 2:24); and set themselves up for the kind of public exposure demonstrated when Isaiah himself went about "naked and barefoot for three years" (Isa. 20:3).

Perhaps most powerfully, they have indeed acted like the sluttish sisters portrayed so bluntly in Ezekiel 16 and 23—chapters that outline, in painfully explicit terms, adultery, prostitution, rape, and pagan lovers who "poured out their whoring lust" upon Israel (Ezek. 23:8); who "handled her virgin bosom" and "pressed" her "young breasts" (Ezek. 23:8, 21); whose "genitals were like those of donkeys and whose emission was like that of horses" (Ezek. 23:20, NIV).

For lovers of Scripture who wonder why the Lord and his spokesmen choose such blunt language, consider some reflections from Christian short-story master Flannery O'Connor, whose work also tends to inspire shock and horror:

> Suppose a Christian writer finds in life "distortions which are repugnant to him"—such as, for instance, the wholesale pagan worship and child sacrifice faced by so many Old Testament prophets; in these cases, the writer's problem will be to make these appear as distortions to an audience which is used to seeing them as natural; and he may well be forced to take ever more violent measures to get his vision across to this hostile audience. When you can assume that your audience holds the same beliefs you do, you can relax a little and use more normal means of talking to it; when you have to assume that it does not, then you have to make your vision apparent by shock—to the hard of hearing you shout, and for the almost-blind you draw large and startling figures.[2]

Perhaps, rather than being appalled by the "large and startling figures" God uses—by the blunt language and explicit imagery discussed throughout this book—we should rather see all this as yet another aspect of his grace, of his willingness to employ even the most extreme methods to reach and redeem his people: racy parables about whorish girls;

---

2. Flannery O'Connor, "The Fiction Writer and His Country," in *Mystery and Manners: Occasional Prose*, ed. Sally and Robert Fitzgerald (New York: Farrar, 1961), 33–34.

threats involving vomit, feces, and dismemberment; one prophet who goes about half-clothed and another who has to marry a whore. Is this type of content really more offensive than the sin and spiritual deadness that necessitate such radical terminology?

And as long as we're on the subject of sin: while finishing this book, I began taking notes for a very different volume, one on transparency in the body of Christ; more specifically, I am hoping to promote openness and vulnerability among believers about our weaknesses and ongoing struggles with sin. I have a vision for this because, as a church officer for nearly twenty years, I have seen again and again how individuals and families in God's kingdom are struggling and broken in their hearts and homes, often barely keeping it together; yet others in the body have absolutely no idea of those struggles—leaving us all to think, "Everybody else is fine except me!"

It did not take long for me to see a connection between my two books. The Bible has no trouble facing up to the ugliness of life, especially to the often abhorrent sins of God's people. But how many times have you heard a sermon on the raped and dismembered concubine in Judges 19? On the woman who ate her own child in 2 Kings 6? Or Onan's *coitus interruptus* in Genesis 38—followed swiftly by Judah having sex with his daughter-in-law because he thought she was a prostitute?

In his study of Ezekiel, Iain M. Duguid has pointed out that if modern-day sermons were labeled for content like contemporary movies, nearly all of them would receive a "G" rating,[3] which is certainly not true of the Bible! If we insist on sanitizing our church services and Sunday school classes, and we never talk about the graphic content that so clearly depicts the corruption and hopelessness in the heart of man, then we should not be surprised at how few of us are able to discuss the sin and depravity in our own lives.

Openness begins with Scripture.

And finally, some readers may feel that in outlining these materials with such detailed focus, I have only pandered to—and perhaps even encouraged—a culture that is already obsessed with sex, violence, and other gross-outs. In response, I would like to point out first that most of my chapters begin by outlining the laws and ordinances—often many, and often quite specific—against the sort of conduct presented in subsequent

3. Iain M. Duguid, *Ezekiel*, The NIV Application Commentary (Grand Rapids: Zondervan, 1999), 217.

pages. In this way, and also by carefully describing the historical situation behind most of these incidents, I have tried to respect and preserve the biblical *context* for explicit content. It is crucial to remember that the Bible never depicts sin in a positive light; and considering the way contemporary readers are daily assaulted by gratuitous sex and violence in popular culture, it is vital to recall that graphic material in Scripture is never presented merely to entertain or amuse (the latter word, after all, literally means "without thinking").

To fully address these aesthetic issues would, of course, require another and very different book from the one you are reading. Those interested in a deeper look at how to process and interact with secular culture might consider some of these fine works: Brian Godawa's *Hollywood Worldviews* (2002), Gene Veith's *State of the Arts* (1991), William Romanowski's *Eyes Wide Open* (2001), Ken Myers's *All God's Children and Blue Suede Shoes* (1989), and especially Leland Ryken's *The Liberated Imagination* (1989).

In any case, it certainly has not been my aim to "pander" to our culture's seemingly insatiable appetite for outlandish gore and sex. On the contrary, one does not seek to repair a depraved and lascivious society by becoming even more stuffy and standoffish; nor, as appears to be the case with some artists nowadays, by outdoing one another in obscene content. Rather, one restores sanity in these matters by dealing with them biblically.

In the case of sex, I am convinced that the best antidote for our culture's obsession is a truly biblical embracing of marital sexuality: a commitment to enjoy sex within God's parameters, yes, but to enjoy it fully and physically, with all the delirious abandonment modeled for us in Song of Solomon and Proverbs 5. If joyful married sex is God's intention from the beginning—to be naked and unashamed—then let us show the world how satisfying this is, and draw it back from the brink of romantic self-annihilation.

In the case of gore and violence, let's admit that these issues are real—they are constants in life, alternately repulsive and fascinating, neither to be prudishly imagined out of existence nor used as some sort of lewd entertainment by a culture that sometimes seems unable to find stimulation in any other way.

In my book, I have tried to show that this careful interface of frankness and restraint is exactly how the Bible approaches sex and violence. That probably ought to be our approach as well.

Select Bibliography

Akerley, Ben Edward. *The X-Rated Bible: An Irreverent Survey of Sex in the Scriptures*. Los Angeles: Feral, 1998.

Andersen, Francis I. *Job: An Introduction and Commentary*. Tyndale Old Testament Commentaries. Leicester, UK: Inter-Varsity, n.d.

Anderson, A. A. *2 Samuel*. Word Biblical Commentary, vol. 11. Waco, TX: Word, 1989.

Baker, David W. *Nahum, Habbakuk, Zephaniah: An Introduction and Commentary*. Tyndale Old Testament Commentaries. Leicester, UK: Inter-Varsity, 1988.

Baldwin, Joyce G. *1 and 2 Samuel: An Introduction and Commentary*. Tyndale Old Testament Commentaries. Leicester, UK: Inter-Varsity, 1988.

———. *Esther: An Introduction and Commentary*. Tyndale Old Testament Commentaries. Leicester, UK: Inter-Varsity, 1984.

Barrett, Michael P. V. *Love Divine and Unfailing: The Gospel according to Hosea*. The Gospel according to the Old Testament. Phillipsburg, NJ: P&R Publishing, 2008.

Bergsma, John Sietze, and Scott Walker Hahn. "Noah's Nakedness and Curse on Canaan (Genesis 9:20–27)." 2005. Available at http://www.godawa .com/chronicles_of_the_nephilim/Articles_By_Others/Bergsma - Noahs_Nakedness_And_Curse_On_Canaan.pdf?.pdf.

Bloch, Chana, and Ariel Bloch, trans. *The Song of Songs: The World's First Great Love Poem*. New York: Modern Library, 2006.

Block, Daniel I. *The Book of Ezekiel: Chapters 1–24*. The New International Commentary on the Old Testament. Grand Rapids: Eerdmans, 1997.

———. *The Book of Ezekiel: Chapters 25–48*. The New International Commentary on the Old Testament. Grand Rapids: Eerdmans, 1998.

———. *Judges, Ruth*. The New American Commentary. Nashville: Broadman, 1999.

Bruce, F. F. *The Book of the Acts*. The New International Commentary on the New Testament. Grand Rapids: Eerdmans, 1989.

Carr, G. Lloyd. *The Song of Solomon: An Introduction and Commentary*. Tyndale Old Testament Commentaries. Leicester, UK: Inter-Varsity, 1984.

Carson, D. A. *The Gospel according to John*. The Pillar New Testament Commentary. Leicester, UK: Apollos/Inter-Varsity, 1991.

———. *Matthew*. In Frank E. Gabelein, ed., *The Expositor's Bible Commentary*, vol. 8: *Matthew, Mark, Luke*. Grand Rapids: Zondervan-HarperCollins, 1984, 1–599.

Cole, R. Alan. *Exodus: An Introduction and Commentary*. Tyndale Old Testament Commentaries. Leicester, UK: Inter-Varsity, 1973.

———. *The Gospel according to Mark: An Introduction and Commentary*. Tyndale New Testament Commentaries. Leicester, UK: Inter-Varsity, 1999.

The Confession of Faith and Catechisms: The Westminster Confession of Faith and Catechisms as Adopted by the Orthodox Presbyterian Church, with Proof Texts. Willow Grove, PA: OPC Christian Education Committee, 2005.

Corswant, W. *A Dictionary of Life in Bible Times*. Translated by Arthur Heathcote. New York: Oxford University Press, 1960.

Cundall, Arthur E., and Leon Morris. *Judges & Ruth: An Introduction and Commentary*. Tyndale Old Testament Commentaries. Leicester, UK: Inter-Varsity, 1968.

Dillard, Raymond B. *2 Chronicles*. Word Biblical Commentary, vol. 15. Waco, TX: Word, 1987.

Douglas, J. D., ed. *The New Bible Dictionary*. 2nd edition. Leicester, UK: Inter-Varsity, 1982.

Duguid, Iain M. *Ezekiel*. The NIV Application Commentary. Grand Rapids: Zondervan, 1999.

———. *Numbers: God's Presence in the Wilderness*. Preaching the Word. Wheaton, IL: Crossway, 2006.

Durham, John I. *Exodus*. Word Biblical Commentary, vol. 3. Waco, TX: Word, 1987.

Edwards, James R. *The Gospel according to Mark*. The Pillar New Testament Commentary. Grand Rapids: Eerdmans, 2002.

Edwards, William D., Wesley J. Gabel, and Floyd E. Hosmer. "On the Physical Death of Jesus Christ." *Journal of the American Medical Association* 255, 11 (March 21, 1986), 1455–63.

Enns, Peter. *Exodus*. The NIV Application Commentary. Grand Rapids: Zondervan, 2000.

ESV Study Bible: English Standard Version. Wheaton, IL: Crossway, 2008.

Fee, Gordon D. *The First Epistle to the Corinthians.* The New International Commentary on the New Testament. Grand Rapids: Eerdmans, 1987.

Ferguson, Sinclair B. *Faithful God: An Exposition of the Book of Ruth.* N.p.: Bryntirion, 2005.

Fox, Michael V. *Character and Ideology in the Book of Esther.* Grand Rapids: Eerdmans, 2001.

France, R. T. *The Gospel according to Matthew: An Introduction and Commentary.* Tyndale New Testament Commentaries. Leicester, UK: Inter-Varsity, 1985.

Freedman, David Noel, ed. *Eerdmans Dictionary of the Bible.* Grand Rapids: Eerdmans, 2000.

Gaebelein, Frank E., ed. *The Expositor's Bible Commentary,* vol. 8: *Matthew, Mark, Luke.* Grand Rapids: Zondervan-HarperCollins, 1984.

Garland, David E. *1 Corinthians.* Baker Exegetical Commentary on the New Testament. Grand Rapids: Baker, 2003.

Godawa, Brian. *Hollywood Worldviews: Watching Films with Wisdom and Discernment.* Downers Grove, IL: InterVarsity, 2002.

Harris, R. Laird, Gleason L. Archer Jr., and Bruce K. Waltke. *Theological Wordbook of the Old Testament.* 2 vols. Chicago: Moody, 1980.

Harrison, R. K. *Jeremiah and Lamentations: An Introduction and Commentary.* Tyndale Old Testament Commentaries. Leicester, UK: Inter-Varsity, 1973.

———. *Leviticus: An Introduction and Commentary.* Tyndale Old Testament Commentaries. Leicester, UK: Inter-Varsity, 1980.

Hess, Richard S. *Joshua: An Introduction and Commentary.* Tyndale Old Testament Commentaries. Leicester, UK: Inter-Varsity, 1996.

Hubbard, David Allan. *Hosea: An Introduction and Commentary.* Tyndale Old Testament Commentaries. Leicester, UK: Inter-Varsity, 1989.

Hughes, Philip Edgcumbe. *The Book of the Revelation: A Commentary.* Leicester, UK: Inter-Varsity, 1990.

Jobes, Karen H. *Esther.* The NIV Application Commentary. Grand Rapids: Zondervan, 1999.

Katz, Bernard. "Biblical Euphemisms." www.freethoughtperspectives.net (n.d.). Accessed November 19, 2012. http://freethoughtperspective.net/?p=3028.

Kidner, Derek. *Ezra and Nehemiah: An Introduction and Commentary.* Tyndale Old Testament Commentaries. Leicester, UK: Inter-Varsity, 1979.

———. *Genesis: An Introduction and Commentary.* Tyndale Old Testament Commentaries. Leicester, UK: Inter-Varsity, 1967.

———. *Psalms 73–150: An Introduction and Commentary.* Tyndale Old Testament Commentaries. Leicester, UK: Inter-Varsity, 1973.

Klein, Ralph W. *1 Samuel.* Word Biblical Commentary, vol. 10. Waco, TX: Word, 1983.

Leithart, Peter J. *1 & 2 Kings.* Brazos Theological Commentary on the Bible. Grand Rapids: Brazos, 2006.

———. *A Son to Me: An Exposition of 1 & 2 Samuel.* Moscow, ID: Canon, 2003.

Liefeld, Walter L. *Luke.* In Frank E. Gaebelein, ed., *The Expositor's Bible Commentary,* vol. 8: *Matthew, Mark, Luke.* Grand Rapids: Zondervan-HarperCollins, 1984, 795–1059.

Loader, William. *Sexuality in the New Testament: Understanding the Key Texts.* Louisville, KY: Westminster John Knox, 2010.

Longenecker, Richard N. *Galatians.* Word Biblical Commentary, vol. 41. Nashville: Nelson, 1990.

Longman, Tremper, III. *Song of Songs.* New International Commentary on the Old Testament. Grand Rapids: Eerdmans, 2001.

Marshall, I. Howard. *The Acts of the Apostles: An Introduction and Commentary.* Tyndale New Testament Commentaries. Leicester, UK: Inter-Varsity, 1980.

Martin, Ralph P. *2 Corinthians.* Word Biblical Commentary, vol. 40. Nashville: Nelson, 1986.

McComiskey, Thomas Edward. *Hosea.* In Thomas Edward McComiskey, ed., *The Minor Prophets: An Exegetical and Expository Commentary,* vol. 1: *Hosea, Joel, and Amos.* Grand Rapids: Baker, 1992, 1–237.

———, ed. *The Minor Prophets: An Exegetical and Expository Commentary,* vol. 1: *Hosea, Joel, and Amos.* Grand Rapids: Baker, 1992.

———, ed. *The Minor Prophets: An Exegetical and Expository Commentary,* vol. 2: *Obadiah, Jonah, Micah, Nahum, and Habakkuk.* Grand Rapids: Baker, 1993.

———, ed. *The Minor Prophets: An Exegetical and Expository Commentary,* vol. 3: *Zephaniah, Haggai, Zechariah, and Malachi.* Grand Rapids: Baker, 1998.

———. *Zechariah.* In Thomas Edward McComiskey, ed., *The Minor Prophets: An Exegetical and Expository Commentary,* vol. 3: *Zephaniah, Haggai, Zechariah, and Malachi.* Grand Rapids: Baker, 1998, 1003–1244.

McConville, J. G. *Deuteronomy.* Apollos Old Testament Commentaries. Nottingham, UK: Apollos-InterVarsity, 2002.

Merriam-Webster's Collegiate Dictionary. 11th ed. Springfield, MA: Merriam-Webster, 2004.

Morris, Leon. *The Book of Revelation: An Introduction and Commentary.* Tyndale New Testament Commentaries. Leicester, UK: Inter-Varsity, 1999.

———. *The First Epistle of Paul to the Corinthians.* Tyndale New Testament Commentaries. Leicester, UK: Inter-Varsity, 1999.

———. *The Gospel according to John.* The New International Commentary on the New Testament. Grand Rapids: Eerdmans, 1971.

———. *The Gospel according to Matthew.* Pillar New Testament Commentary. Grand Rapids: Eerdmans, 1992.

Motyer, Alec. *Isaiah: An Introduction and Commentary.* Tyndale Old Testament Commentaries. Leicester, UK: Inter-Varsity, 1999.

New Geneva Study Bible: Bringing the Light of the Reformation to Scripture. Nashville: Nelson, 1995.

Peck, John. "Sex in Art—An Erotic Christian Imagination?" *Cornerstone* 30, 121 (2001): n.p.

Pope, Marvin H. *Song of Songs: A New Translation with Introduction and Commentary.* The Anchor Bible 7C. Garden City, NY: Doubleday, 1977.

Provan, Iain. *Ecclesiastes, Song of Songs.* The NIV Application Commentary. Grand Rapids: Zondervan, 2001.

Reisser, Horst. "*Porneuo.*" In *The New International Dictionary of New Testament Theology*, vol. 1, ed. Colin Brown, 497–501. Grand Rapids: Regency-Zondervan, 1986.

Robertson, O. Palmer. *The Genesis of Sex: Sexual Relationships in the First Book of the Bible.* Phillipsburg, NJ: P&R Publishing, 2002.

Ryken, Leland, James C. Wilhoit, and Tremper Longman III. *Dictionary of Biblical Imagery.* Leicester, UK: Inter-Varsity, 1998.

Selman, Martin J. *2 Chronicles: A Commentary.* Tyndale Old Testament Commentaries. Leicester, UK: Inter-Varsity, 1994.

Stein, Robert H. *Mark.* Baker Exegetical Commentary on the New Testament. Grand Rapids: Baker, 2008.

Stuart, Douglas. *Hosea-Jonah.* Word Biblical Commentary, vol. 31. Waco, TX: Word, 1987.

Taylor, John B. *Ezekiel: An Introduction and Commentary.* Tyndale Old Testament Commentaries. Leicester, UK: Inter-Varsity, 1969.

Thomas, Robert L., ed. *The New American Standard Exhaustive Concordance of the Whole Bible.* With Hebrew-Aramaic and Greek Dictionaries. Nashville: Holman, 1981.

Thompson, J. A. *The Book of Jeremiah.* The New International Commentary on the Old Testament. Grand Rapids: Eerdmans, 1980.

——. *Deuteronomy: An Introduction and Commentary.* Tyndale Old Testament Commentaries. Leicester, UK: Inter-Varsity, 1974.

Waltke, Bruce K. *The Book of Proverbs: Chapters 1-15.* The New International Commentary on the Old Testament. Grand Rapids: Eerdmans, 2004.

——. *The Book of Proverbs: Chapters 15-31.* The New International Commentary on the Old Testament. Grand Rapids: Eerdmans, 2005.

——. *A Commentary on Micah.* Grand Rapids: Eerdmans, 2007.

——. *Micah.* In Thomas Edward McComskey, ed., *The Minor Prophets: An Exegetical and Expository Commentary*, vol. 2: *Obadiah, Jonah, Micah, Nahum, and Habakkuk.* Grand Rapids: Baker, 1993, 591-764.

——, and Cathi J. Fredricks. *Genesis: A Commentary.* Grand Rapids: Zondervan, 2001.

Wenham, Gordon J. *The Book of Leviticus.* The New International Commentary on the Old Testament. Grand Rapids: Eerdmans, 1979.

——. *Genesis 16-50.* Word Biblical Commentary, vol. 2. Dallas: Word, 1994.

——. *Numbers: An Introduction and Commentary.* Tyndale Old Testament Commentaries. Leicester, UK: Inter-Varsity, 1981.

Wessell, Walter W. *Mark.* In Frank E. Gaebelein, ed., *The Expositor's Bible Commentary*, vol. 8: *Matthew, Mark, Luke.* Grand Rapids: Zondervan-HarperCollins, 1984, 601-793.

Wilcock, Michael. *The Message of Chronicles: One Church, One Faith, One Lord.* The Bible Speaks Today. Leicester, UK: Inter-Varsity: 1987.

——. *The Message of Judges: Grace Abounding.* The Bible Speaks Today. Leicester, UK: Inter-Varsity, 1992.

——. *The Message of Revelation: I Saw Heaven Opened.* The Bible Speaks Today. Leicester, UK: Inter-Varsity, 1975.

Wiseman, Donald J. *1 and 2 Kings: An Introduction and Commentary.* Tyndale Old Testament Commentaries. Leicester, UK: Inter-Varsity, 1993.

Wyatt, Robert J. "Immoral." In *The International Standard Bible Encyclopedia*, vol. 2, ed. Geoffrey W. Bromiley, 808-9. Grand Rapids: Eerdmans, 1982.

Young, Edward J. *The Book of Isaiah: The English Text, with Introduction, Exposition, and Notes*, vol. 1, *Chapters 1-18.* Grand Rapids: Eerdmans, 1965.

——. *The Book of Isaiah: The English Text, with Introduction, Exposition, and Notes*, vol. 2, *Chapters 19-39.* Grand Rapids: Eerdmans, 1969.

——. *The Book of Isaiah: The English Text, with Introduction, Exposition, and Notes*, vol. 3, *Chapters 40-66.* Grand Rapids: Eerdmans, 1972.

Index of Scripture

Genesis
1:28—46
2:24-25—46
2:25—27
4:1—44, 86
6-7—163, 167
6-8—79, 145
7:23—167-68
9:6—130
9:11—145
9:20-25—27, 78-81
9:21—49, 79
9:23—79
9:24-25—80
9:25—79
11:29—82
14:2—144
15:4—23
15:9-10—123
15:10—18
16:4—44
16:5—44
17—13
17:9-14
18:12—48
19—79
19:1-8—86
19:1-26—86-88
19:5—119
19:5-8—44
19:9-11—87
19:14-28—143-45
19:15-26—88
19:22—144
19:31-36—38, 45,
   79-80, 82-83
19:37-38—79

20:12—82
24:2—9, 24
24:9—9
24:16—44, 86
25:23—23
26:7-10—48
27:27—89
29—82
29:13—89
30:14-17—3-4
30:38-41—46
31:10-12—46
31:19—184-85
31:33-35—184-85
31:35—181
33:4—89
34—14, 36
34:1-27—115
34:2-7—45
34:3—117
34:7—115-16, 122
34:15—14
34:25—14
34:30—115
35:22—80, 82
36—168
38:6-9—219
38:9—80, 186
38:12-19—80
38:14-26—70-71
38:21—75
39:6-18—27
39:7-12—38
39:10-12—117-18
40:19—203
40:19-22—135-36
45:15—89

46:26—9, 24
47:29—9
49:3-4—80
49:4—82
49:5—14
49:25—17

Exodus
1:5—9, 24
1:15-22—155-56
2:1-6—155-56
4:6—196
4:24-26—9, 14
4:25—13, 38
4:27—89
7:17—169
7:17-21—101
7:18-21—201-2
8:3-14—201-2
8:8—202
8:16—169
8:17—202
8:21-24—202
9:8-12—202
9:10—193
12:22—96-97
12:29-30—167-68
16:20—201
17:4—133-35
17:6—169
18:7—89
19:13—133-35
20:3-4—64
20:13—130
20:14—33, 55, 60
20:17—56, 78
20:26—28-29

21:12-31—103-4
21:13—130
21:14—129
22:16—114
22:16-17—34
22:16-19—38
22:19—77
24:6-8—97
28:42-43—28-29
29:11—158
29:14—96, 207
29:17—123
29:20-21—97
32:1-6—64
34:12-16—41

Leviticus
1:6—123
1:6-9—96
1:12—123
1:15-17—96
1:17—123
3:3-4—96
3:9—96
3:14-15—96
4—127
4:11-12—207
4:5-7—97
4:8-9—96
7:3-4—96
8:17—207
8:20—123
9:12—158
10:1-2—145
11:21-22—200-201
13-14—195-96
13:1—195

227

13:3—195
13:10—195
13:18—193
13:19—195
13:23—195
13:24—195
13:30—195
13:30-37—195
13:47-49—195
13:48-49—195-96
14—127
14:2-14—97
14:3—195
14:19—158
14:33-38—195
14:37—196
15—181
15:2-3—11
15:2-12—187-88
15:3—187
15:16—185
15:16-17—185-86
15:18—45, 73-74, 185
15:19-24—182-83
15:24—183
15:25-27—188
16—127
16:27—207
18—28-29, 38, 118
18:6—82
18:6-18—81-82
18:8—45, 79-80, 84
18:9—45, 115
18:10—45
18:16—79-80
18:18—82
18:19—183
18:20—46, 55
18:21—156
18:22—79-80,
    85-86
18:23—44, 46, 77
18:25—199
18:28—199
19:19—46
19:28—104
19:29—72-73
20—29, 38, 118
20:2—134
20:2-5—156

20:10—55, 60, 114
20:11—45, 79-80
20:11-21—81-82
20:13—45, 79-80,
    85-86
20:15—46
20:15-16—77
20:17—79, 83
20:18—45, 181, 183
20:21—79-80
20:22—199
20:27—134
21:14-15—62
21:20—13
24:10-23—133-35
24:14—133-35
26:16—194
26:29—151

Numbers
5:11-31—55
5:20—46
5:21-22—10, 24
10:4—168
11:31-33—170
12:1-12—196
12:10—196
15:32-36—133-35
16:23-49—169-70
16:35—145
16:46—160
19:5—207
19:11—134
21:1-3—164
21:4-7—170
23:24—100
25:1-8—36, 125-26
25:4—136
25:7-8—167
25:9—170
31:7-17—170
31:17—44, 86
35:9-29—130

Deuteronomy
2:9—160
2:34—164
3:6—164
5:17—130
5:18—33, 55, 60

7:1—165
7:1-2—163-68
7:3—41
12:31—156
13—167, 175
13:9—133-35
13:10—133-35
13:12-16—145
13:16—172
14:1—104
14:21—153
17:2-7—167, 175
17:7—133-35
18:10—156, 158
19:4-10—130
19:11-12—129
20:10-15—165
20:13—176-77
20:16—163-68
20:16-17—165
20:19-20—160
21:22-23—135
21:23—136-37
22:5—85-86
22:13-21—34, 47
22:21—60
22:22-24—134
22:22-27—55
22:23-29—114
22:24—114, 184
22:28-29—34
22:29—184
22:30—38, 79-80
23:1—13, 15-16
23:9—208
23:10-11—185-86
23:12-14—207-8
23:17-18—74
23:18—59, 127
25:2-3—108
25:5-10—186
25:11—118
25:11-12—13
27:20—38, 79-80
27:20-23—38,
    45, 81-82
27:21—77
28:15-35—194-95
28:26—203, 217
28:27—194-95

28:30—113,
    118-19, 217
28:51-57—152-53
28:53-77—217
28:56-57—201
28:57—8, 20
29:23—144
32:26—124
32:30—168
32:42—100

Joshua
2:1-21—71
5:2—13
5:3—15
5:8—15
6—166
6-11—163-68
6:17-19—145
6:21—164
6:22-25—165
6:24—145
6:25—71
6:26—158-59
7:25—145
8:2—164
8:14-25—145
8:24-25—164
8:29—136
9:26-27—165
10-11—164-66
10:10—176
10:20—176
10:26—136
10:40—164
11:11—145
11:14-15—164-65
22:21—168
23:12—41

Judges
1-3—166
1:6-7—105
1:18-36—166-67
1:24-26—165
2:17—58
3:15-24—132-33, 217
3:24—8, 38, 208
3:29—171
3:31—130, 170-71

4:17-22—131-32
4:21—133
5:8—132
5:25-27—131-32
7:16-21—130
8:7—106
8:10—169-70
8:16—106
8:30—9, 24
8:33—59
9:22—130
9:46-49—146
9:50-54—130-31
11:30-40—160-62
11:33—171
12:6—171
14:19—171
15:4-5—130
15:6—146
15:8—171
15:15—130
15:16—171
16:1—70
16:4-21—36
16:21—105
16:27-30—171
19—219
19:1-3—61
19:2—59-60
19:14-29—119-22
19:16-24—87
19:25—44
19:29—123
19:30—122
20-21—171-72
20:6—121-22
20:40—172
21:10-11—172
21:25—172

Ruth
1:11—23
3—37
3:2—37
3:2-8—36-39
3:7—38
3:10-11—38-39

1 Samuel
1:13-14—49

2:22—38, 45
5-6—192-93
5:6-12—192
5:9—193
6:4-5—192-93
6:11—192-93
6:17—192-93
2:22—38, 45
2:22-25—36
4:17-18—36
10:1—89
11:2—105
11:7—123
13:19-22—132
14:11—22-23
15:1-9—173
15:33—123-24
17:35—121
17:38-39—89
17:50—116
17:50-51—89
17:51—124
18:1-4—88-90
18:20-27—15
19:1—88-90
19:8—176
19:24-29-30
20:30—88-89
20:41-42—88-90
21—173
21:9—89
21:13-14—187
22:18-19—173
23:5—176
24:3—8, 38, 208
25:22—211
25:34—211
27:9—172
31:9—124

2 Samuel
1:26—88-90
2:16—121
2:18-23—128
3:17-27—128
4:7-12—124
6:14-20—29
7:12—23
8:2—172-73
8:5-12—172

8:5-15—128-29
10:18—172
11:2-5—56-57
11:6-11—8
11:8-21—57
12:8—44, 80
12:11—45
12:24—44
12:26-28—166
12:31—105, 166
13:1-22—83, 115-17
13:6—116
13:12—114, 122, 184
13:14—38, 114,
        116, 184
13:15—117
13:17—117
13:22—114, 184
13:32—114
14:26—128
14:33—89
15:5—89
15:12—57
16:20-22—80, 83
16:22—57
18:5-15
19:39—89
20:1-12—129
20:9—89
20:10—192
20:29-30
21:1-14—203
21:6—136
22:18-19
23:8—171
24:9—98
24:15—170

1 Kings
1:1-4—44
1:4—86
2:13-25—80
3:16-28—69-70
8:63—98
12:4—106
12:4-10—10-11
12:14—105
12:18—133-35
14:10—211
14:24—74

15:12—74
15:27-29—174
15:29—174
16:3-4—174
16:9-11—174
16:11—211
16:18—146
16:34—158-59
18:23—123
18:26-28—104
18:27—208-9, 217
18:40—167
19:20—89
20:29-30—172
21:13—107, 133-35
21:19-25—126-27
21:21—211
22:34-38—126-27
22:38—70
22:46—74

2 Kings
1:2-12—146
3:20-24—98
3:25—160
3:25-26—166
3:27—159-60
5:11—159
5:27—196
6:25—209
6:25-29—152-53,
        219
7:3-5—196
8:7-15—176
8:12—156
9-10—174-75
9:6-9—174
9:8—211
9:14-27—174
9:24-26—127
9:30-37—127, 174
9:37—211
10:1-8—125, 174
10:11-14—174-75
10:18-27—167, 175
10:27—211
11:1-16—175
12:9—22-23
13:19—159
15:5-7—196

15:8–31—176
15:16—156
16:3—156-58
16:15—96
17—67
17:16—59
17:17—157
18:27—210
19:35—167-68, 170
19:37—176
21:6—156-58
23:7—74
23:10—59, 157-58
25:7—105

1 Chronicles
11:11—171
20:3—105
27:24—160

2 Chronicles
13:17—167-69, 176
15:11—98
16:10—107
21:14-19—190-91
24:20-26—175
24:21—107
25:12—176
25:25-27—175-76
26:19-21—196
28:6—167-68
29:32-34—97-98
32:26—160
33:24-25—176
35:7-9—98

Ezra
6:11—136-37, 211
9:3—104

Nehemiah
13:25—104

Esther
2:2-17—40-42
2:3—41
2:8—40
2:9—41
2:11—41-42
2:13—41

2:14—41-42
2:23—136
4:11—42
4:14—40
7:10—136
9:12-16—172
9:14—136

Job
1:21—29
2:7-8—193-94
2:12—194
4:10—105
6:6—187
7:4—194
7:5—194
7:14—194
7:16—194
9:3—168
13:27—107
16:16—194
17:1—194
19:17—194
19:20—194
24:7-10—29-30
24:15—60
29:17—105
30:15-16—194
30:28—194
30:30—194
33:11—107

Psalms
3:7—105
14:4—150
24:1—167
27:2—150
38:1—160
50:13—100
50:18—60
50:22—124
58:6—104-5
58:10—98
79:2—203
83:10—210-11
106:37-38—157-58

Proverbs
5:3—20
5:3-20—57

5:5—20
5:15-18—58
5:15-19—49
5:18-19—19, 220
7:6-19—57-58
7:10—59-60
7:11—20
7:12—75
7:13-18—118
7:17—4
7:22-23—118
9:17—58
12:4—39
23:6-8—199
25:16—199
26:11—200
30:14—150
30:20—60
30:33—98
31:10—39

Ecclesiastes
5:15—29
6:6—168

Song of Solomon
1:6—81
1:7—70
1:12—4
1:13—4, 17-18
2:5—4
2:17—18
4:1-7—23
4:3—4
4:5—18
4:6—18
4:9—50
4:12-13—21-22
4:14—4
4:16—21, 24-26
5:1—21, 25, 58
5:2—49
5:2-6—22-23
5:4-10-11, 23
5:9—11-12
5:14—11
6:5—50
6:11—81
7:1-6—23-25
7:2—23-25

7:3—18
7:7-8—18-19
7:13—4
8:5—4
8:8-10—19

Isaiah
6:2—8-9
7:20—9
9:20-21—150
10:31—212
13:16—113, 118, 156
19:14—200
20:2—30
20:3—218
20:4—30
23:16—75
23:17-18—59
25:6—212-13
25:10-11—212-13, 217
28:7-8—200
34:3—204
34:3-7—100
36:12—210
47:2-3—30
47:3—31, 118
49:1—23
49:26—49, 100, 151
53:4-6—141
57:3-10—58
57:5—157-58
57:8—10
58:7—29-30
60:10—160
60:16—17
62:4-5—48
63:3—98
64:6—183-84
66:10-11—17

Jeremiah
2:2—48
2:20—59, 75
2:24—59, 218
3:1-13—58-59
3:2—113
3:3—75
3:8-9—60
4:30—75

5:7—60
6:24—119
7:31—157-58
7:33—203
8:1-2—204-5
8:2—204, 210-11
9:22—204, 210-11
13:22—8
13:22-26—30-31, 119
13:27—58
16:4—204, 210-11
19:5—157-58
19:7—203
19:9—151
20:2—107
25:27—199
25:33—210-11
29:26—107
32:35—157
34:20—203
37:15—107
38:6—107
44:19—5
46:10—100
48:26—199-200

Lamentations
1:8—30-31
1:17—181
2:20—151-52
4:10—151-52
4:14—98
5:11—119
5:12—107

Ezekiel
4:12-13—210, 217
5:9-10—151-52
6:4-13—211-12
7:19-20—181
8:7—22-23
14:3-7—211-12
16—xi-xii, xiv-xv, 12, 59, 65-67, 72-73, 218
16:1-8—65
16:4—24
16:6—72-73, 98
16:7-8—20-21

16:7-9—47
16:8-14—64
16:9—37
16:13-25—65-66
16:16—72-73
16:20-21—157-58
16:23—75
16:25—8, 20, 46, 75
16:26—12
16:26-29—66
16:32-26—60
16:32-34—73
16:36—21
16:36-40—119
16:39-40—133-35
16:40—124, 133-35
18:6—183-84
20:31—157-58
22:3-7—211-12
22:10—38, 184
22:10-11—46
23—xi, xiv-xv, 12, 59, 65-67, 218
23:1-5
23:3—19-20
23:5-8—66
23:8—19-20, 186, 218
23:17-21—66
23:20—12-13, 16, 186-87, 218
23:20-21—21
23:21—19-20, 218
23:25—124
23:29-30—31
23:34—124
23:37—60
23:37-39—157-58
23:40—75
23:44—44
32:5-6—204
32:6—100-101
37:1-10—205
38:21-22—144
39:17-19—100, 205-6

Daniel
2:5—124
2:32—11

3:8-27—146, 150
3:29—124
6:12-13—150
10:6—38, 39

Hosea
1-3—59, 61-65
1:2—61, 63-65
1:3-8—61
1:8—62
2:2—20, 60
2:3—32
2:7—64
2:10—31-32
2:15—64
2:16-20—48
3:1—4-5, 60, 62-63
3:1-3—61-62, 65
3:2—62
3:3—60
4:13-14—60
4:14—74-75
8:9—73
9:1—37-38, 75
9:9—122
10:9—122
10:14—156
13:8—124
13:16—156

Joel
3:3—70

Amos
1:13—156
2:7—83
2:16—28

Micah
1:7—59, 74
1:8—29-30
1:11—30
3:2-3—150-51, 218
5:2—168
6:7—168
7:5—44

Nahum
3:4-5—31
3:4-6—30

3:5—118
3:6—212
3:10—156

Habakkuk
2:16—30

Zephaniah
1:17—210-11

Zechariah
12:5-6—168
14:2—113
14:12—22-23, 119, 203-4

Malachi
2:3—212
3:5—60

Matthew
1:3—71
1:5—71
1:6—71
1:19—34-35
2:16—155
3:4—201
3:12—111-12
5:27—55
5:27-28—92
5:28—56, 78
5:31-32—92
5:32—35, 56
8:2-4—196-97
8:12—112
9:20-22—188-89
10:17—108
12:39—58
13:42—111-12
13:42-50—147
13:50—112
14:3-12—84
14:4—43
14:6-12—125
15:1-20—189
19:3-9—92
19:4-5—56, 92
19:9—35, 56
19:10—56
19:12—92

19:18—55
21:31-32—71
21:35—133-35
22:13—112
24:36-51—124
24:51—112
25:30—112
25:41—111, 147
26:6—196-97
26:48-49—89
27:5—135
27:26—108-10
27:29—110
27:31—137-41
27:46—141
27:55—28

Mark
1:6—201
1:40-44—196-97
5:25-34—188-89
6:17-29—84, 125
6:18—43
7:6-23—189
9:43-48—111-12,
   147
10:11-12—56
10:18—217
10:19—55
13:9—108
14:3—196-97
14:51-52—28
15:15—108-10
15:20—137
15:24—28, 137-41
15:34—141

Luke
3:17—147
3:19-20—84
5:12-14—196-97
7:9—125
7:45—89
8:43-48—188-89
11:27—17
13:1—98-99
13:28—112

15:30—71
16:18—56
16:19-31—112
17:11-19—196-97
18:20—55
22:41-44—99
22:42-44—141
23:16—108-10
23:33—137-41

John
2:15—105-6
3:29—47
4:18—35, 43
6:51-56—149
12:32—136-37
19:1—108-10
19:2—110
19:17—138
19:18—137-41
19:23-24—28
19:32-33—140
19:34—99
21:7—28

Acts
1:18—135, 192
7:54-59—133-35
14:19—133-35
16:22—108
19:16—28
22:19-20—108
22:24—188
26:11—108

Romans
1:26-27—85, 91-92
5:8—64
9:10—90
13:9—55
16:16—89

1 Corinthians
5:1—35, 43
5:1-2—84-85
6:7-8—52
6:9—85, 90-92

6:12—52
6:15-18—71-72
6:15-20—51
6:18—35
7:1-5—50-52
7:2—35
7:7—51
7:9—35
7:32-38—51
12:22-24—7-8

2 Corinthians
11:24—108

Galatians
3:13—135-37
5:12—15

Ephesians
1:11—167
5:25-32—48

Philippians
3:8—209
4:8—215

Colossians
1:21—64
2:11-12—15

1 Thessalonians
4:2-7—35

2 Thessalonians
1:9—141

1 Timothy
1:10—90, 92

2 Timothy
3:16—215

Hebrews
9:13-14—189
10:31—206
11:31—71
11:35-37—106-7

11:36—188
11:37—133-35
12:16—35
13:4—35, 55-56, 90

James
2:11—55
2:15—28
2:25—71
4:4—58

1 Peter
2:24—141
5:14—89

2 Peter
2:22—200

Jude
7—35, 87

Revelation
8:7-9—147
9:3-10—110-11
9:15-18—167-68
11:5—147
14:9-11—111
14:19-20—101-2
16:2—193
16:6—100
16:8-11—111
16:15—91
17:1-5—72
17:6—100
17:16—147
18:8—147
19—72
19:2—127
19:7-9—48
19:9—127
19:13—98
19:17—127
19:17-21—206
20:7-10—111, 147
20:13-15—167-68
20:14-15—147-48
21:8—148

Index of Subjects and Names

Aaron, 97, 126, 145, 169, 193, 196
Abednego, 146, 150
Abihu, 145
Abijah, 168
Abimelech (son of Gideon), 130–31, 146
Abiram, 159, 169–70
Abishag, 44
Abishai, 128–29
Abner, 128
Abraham, 9, 13, 44, 82, 86, 123, 143
Absalom, 57, 80, 83, 115–17, 128–29
abscesses, 193
Achan, 145
Adoni-bezek, 105
adultery, vii, xv, 4, 10, 12, 20, 30–33, 46,
    55–67, 69, 71–73, 78, 90, 92, 114,
    118–19, 121, 124, 134, 186, 217–18
    See also prostitution; whore
afterbirth, 8, 152, 201
Agag, 124
Ahab, 126–27, 174–75, 211
Ahasuerus, 40–41, 136
Ahaz, 156–57
Ahaziah (king of Israel), 146
Ahaziah (king of Judah), 174
Ahimelech (priest at Nob), 173
Akerley, Ben Edward, 29, 88, 221
aloes, 4, 57–58
Alter, Robert, 25
Amasa, 129, 192
Amaziah (king of Judah), 175–76
Ammon (son of Lot), 79

Amnon, 83, 115–17, 122
Amon, 176
anal sex. See homosexuality; sodomy
Andersen, Francis I., 194, 221
Anderson, A. A., 29, 117, 128, 221
anus, 133, 193, 216
aphrodisiacs, 3–5, 58
Archer, Gleason L., 46, 60, 169,
    181, 193, 212, 223
Asa, 74, 98, 107
Asahel, 128
assassination, 174–76
assault, 31, 103–9, 114, 117–18, 137, 151, 188
    See also flogging; torture
Athaliah, 175
attacks. See assault; flogging; torture
axe. See weapons

Baal, 104, 157, 167, 175, 208, 211
Baasha, 174
Baker, David W., 31
Baldwin, Joyce G., 29, 42, 83, 89,
    116, 128, 169, 173, 192, 221
ban, the (Old Testament), 163–68,
    172–73, 177, 213
Barrett, Michael P. V., 62–65, 221
bathing, 22, 37, 47, 56, 70, 78, 104
Bathsheba, 8, 44, 56–57, 71, 90
Bauckham, Richard J., 87
Beasley-Murray, George R., 47
beatings. See assault; flogging; torture
Ben-hadad, 153, 176, 209

Bergsma, John Sietze, 79–80, 221
bestiality, 33, 46, 77–78, 81, 92
Bloch, Chana and Ariel, 4, 25, 221
Block, Daniel I., 12, 20–21, 37–39, 47,
    61, 67, 72–73, 98, 106, 121, 123,
    131, 133, 144, 152, 157, 162, 172,
    184, 186–87, 203–5, 210, 212, 221
blood, vii, viii, 11, 14, 34, 47, 65, 70, 72,
    93, 95–102, 104, 108–10, 119, 123,
    126–30, 137, 140–41, 147–49, 151,
    158, 174, 181–83, 187–88, 202, 204–5
  drinking of, 100, 126, 149, 205
Boaz, 37–39, 71
boils, 153, 193–95, 202
bones, 109, 123, 138, 150, 204–5
bowels, 133, 135, 191–92, 195
  See also disembowelment; entrails
breasts, xi, 4, 17–21, 23–24, 47,
    49, 57, 60, 66, 124, 218
  See also nipples
brimstone. See sulfur
Brooks, Beatrice, 75
Brownmiller, Susan, 113
Bruce, F. F., 108
Brueggemann, Walter, 56–57
bubonic plague, 192, 195
Burney, C. F., 171
buttocks, 30

Calvin, John, 62
camels, 173, 184, 210
Canaan (son of Ham), 79–80
cancer, 194
cannibalism, 149–53, 201, 217–18
  See also blood: drinking of
capital punishment, 55, 77, 81, 86,
    103–4, 114, 129–30, 134, 167, 175
  See also crucifixion; decapita-
    tion; hanging; stoning
Carr, G. Lloyd, 4–5, 10, 19,
    21–25, 49–50, 70, 222
Carson, D. A., 99, 106, 108–9,
    112, 137, 140, 188, 222

ceremonial regulations. See uncleanness
Chemosh, 159
children. See killing children
child sacrifice, 156–62
cholera, 194
Christ. See Jesus Christ
cinnamon, 4, 57–58
circumcision, 9, 13–15, 36
clothing, 28–29, 33, 57, 65,
    70, 98, 117–18, 173
  See also cross-dressing; priestly garments
coitus interruptus, xii, 186, 219
Cole, R. Alan, 101, 134, 141, 193, 201–2, 222
concubines, 40–42, 57, 61, 80,
    82–83, 87, 119–23, 203, 219
  See also harem
conjunctivitis, 194
corpses, 122, 124, 127, 129, 133, 135,
    140, 171, 202–4, 206, 211
  See also decomposition
Corswant, W., 135, 197, 222
covering the feet (euphemism for
    defecation), 8, 133, 208
cross-dressing, 86
crown of thorns, 110
crucifixion, 28, 99, 108–10, 136–41
  See also hanging
cult prostitution. See fertility rites
Cundall, Arthur E., 37, 38, 106, 120–22,
    131–33, 161, 170–71, 222

Darius, 136, 211
Dathan, 169–70
David, 8, 29, 44, 56–57, 71, 78, 80, 88–90,
    98, 105, 117, 124, 128, 172, 203
Davis, Dale Ralph, 57
death. See assassination; capital pun-
    ishment; death by fire; decom-
    position; killing children; mass
    killings; murder; violent death
death by fire, 111, 143–48, 157–58
death penalty. See capital punishment
decapitation, 124–26, 174, 217

decomposition, 135, 194, 202–5, 211, 217
defecation. *See* dung; excrement; feces
Delilah, 36, 171
dermatitis, 194, 196
Dillard, Raymond B., 158,
    168–69, 191, 196, 222
Dinah, 14, 36, 115–17, 122
discharges, 11, 21, 181–82, 185, 187–89
    See also menstruation; semen
diseases, xiv, 111, 118, 170, 181,
    187–89, 191–97, 217
    See also leprosy; plagues
disembowelment, 129, 135, 192
    See also entrails
dismemberment, 123–25, 219
    See also decapitation
Doeg, 173
donkeys, xi, 12, 59, 66, 120–21, 128,
    164, 171, 173, 186, 209, 218
Douglas Stuart, 31–32, 74
Duguid, Iain M., xi–xii, 10, 21, 66–67,
    100, 101, 124, 205–6, 219, 222
dung, 127, 132–33, 204–5, 207–13
    See also feces
Durham, John I., 14, 193, 202, 222
dysentery, 170, 192–94

eating. *See* food, disgusting types
eczema, 196
Edwards, James R., 109–10, 141
Edwards, William D., 99, 109, 137–38
Eglon, xii, 132–33, 208, 217
Ehud, 132–33
ejaculation. *See* semen
Elah, 174
elephantiasis, 195
Elijah, 126–27, 146, 167, 191, 208, 217
Enns, Peter, 14, 101, 202, 222
entrails, 96, 109, 135, 207
Esther, 36, 39–42, 122, 136, 172
euphemisms, xiii, 7–11, 14, 20–22,
    25, 31, 38, 43–46, 48, 51, 84,
    90, 181, 184, 208, 216

excrement, 132–33, 204, 207–13, 217
    See also dung; feces; toilet; urine
execution. *See* assassination; capital
    punishment; hanging; mur-
    der; stoning; violent death
extispicy, 96
extramarital sex. *See* adul-
    tery; premarital sex
Ezekiel, 30, 210
Ezra, 104

feces, 8, 96, 133, 193, 199, 207–8,
    210, 212, 215–17, 219
    See also dung
Fee, Gordon D., 7, 8, 51–52, 84, 223
feet, 8–9, 14, 20, 22–23, 30, 37–39, 57,
    97–98, 107, 124, 127, 131, 135,
    138–39, 152, 200–201, 204–5, 216
Feinberg, C. L., 189
Ferguson, Sinclair B., 39, 223
fertility rites, 37, 69, 73–75
fever, 194
fire, 88, 96, 111, 144–48, 157, 167, 206–8
    See also death by fire
flatulence, 216
flogging, 106, 108–10, 122,
    136–37, 139, 188
flood (Genesis 6–8), 78, 145, 163
food, disgusting types, 200–201, 210, 217
    See also cannibalism; scav-
    enging animals
fornication, 24, 33, 35–36, 59, 64
    See also adultery; premarital sex
Fox, Michael V., 40, 49
France, R. T., 125, 155, 168, 188, 223
Fredricks, Cathi J., 9, 80–81, 144, 185, 226
frogs, 201–2
fungus, 196

Gabel, Wesley J., 99, 109,
    137–38, 139–40, 222
Gaertner, Dennis, 135
Gagnon, Robert A. J., 85

gang rape, 86, 119–20
Garland, David E., 7–8, 50–52,
    85, 90–91, 223
Geldenhuys, Norval, 141
gender roles, xiii
genitalia, female, 5, 7–8, 11,
    20–26, 31, 58, 188, 216
genitalia, male, 4, 7–13, 15–16,
    22, 38, 187, 216, 218
Gershom, 9, 14
Gideon, 106, 130, 146, 170
Godawa, Brian, xii, 11, 16, 23,
    79, 119, 212, 220, 223
Goliath, 116, 124, 173
Gomer, 32, 61–65
gonorrhea, 187–88, 194
gouging out eyes, 105
guts. See entrails

Hahn, Scott Walker, 79–80, 221
Ham, 27, 78–81
Haman, 42, 136
Hanani, 107
hanging, 124, 135–38, 143, 203
    See also crucifixion
harem, 40–42, 122
    See also concubines
Harrison, R. K., 31, 59, 74, 77,
    81–82, 107, 182, 187–88,
    194–95, 200, 203–4, 223
Harris, R. Laird, 46, 60, 169,
    181, 193, 212, 223
Hart, H. St. J., 110
Hazael, 176
heathen. See paganism
hell, xii, 111–12, 141, 147–48
hematidrosis, 99, 109
hemorrhage, 188, 197
hemorrhoids, 192–93
Henry, Matthew, 162
Herodias, 84, 125
Herod Philip, 84
Herod the Great, 155

Herod the tetrarch, 43, 84, 125
Hess, Richard S., 15, 223
Hezekiah, 97
Hiel, 158–59
Hodge, Charles, 91
homosexuality, vii, xiii, 35, 74,
    77, 79–81, 85–92, 121
Hophni, 36
Hosea, 61–65
Hoshea, 176
Hosmer, Floyd E., 99, 109, 137–40, 222
Hubbard, David Allan, 5, 32,
    62–63, 74–75, 83, 223
Hughes, Philip Edgcumbe, 206, 223

impalement, 136
    See also hanging
incest, vii, 33, 35, 57, 77, 79–85,
    88, 92, 115, 117
infection, 188, 196
insects, 110, 139, 200–202
    as food, 200
    See also locusts
intercourse. See sexual intercourse
Isaac, 9, 48
Isaiah, 30, 107
Ish-bosheth, 124, 128

Jacob, 3, 9, 14, 82, 184
Jael, 131, 133
Jehoiada (chief priest), 175
Jehoram (king of Israel), 153
Jehoshaphat, 74
Jehu, 125, 127, 167, 174–76, 211
Jephthah, 158, 160–62, 171
Jeremiah, 63, 107
Jeroboam I, 174, 211, 217
Jesus Christ, 15, 28, 35, 37, 42–43, 47,
    55–56, 64, 71, 78, 85, 92, 95,
    98–99, 105, 108–12, 124, 133,
    135–41, 147, 149, 155, 188–89,
    196–97, 209, 217, 219
    and crown of thorns, 110

and homosexuality, 92
crucifixion of. *See* crucifixion
flogging of, 108–10, 122
Jezebel, 126–27, 174–75, 211
Joab, 128–29, 192
Joash, 175
Job, 193–94
Jobes, Karen H., 40–42, 223
John the Baptist, 43, 47, 84, 125, 201
Jonathan, 88–90, 203
Joseph (father of Jesus), 34–35
Joseph (son of Jacob), 9, 27, 117
Joshua, 136, 164
Josiah, 74, 98, 157, 176
Judah (son of Jacob), 70–71, 75, 80
Judas, 135, 192

Keil, C. F., 62
Kidner, Derek, 44, 136, 186, 203, 211, 223
killing. *See* assassination; killing children; mass killings;
murder; violent death
killing children, 134, 151–53, 155–62,
166, 171, 174–75, 217–18
See also cannibalism
King James Version, iv, 13, 44, 105, 183
Klein, Ralph W., 15, 89, 193, 224
know (verb for sexual intercourse), 43–44, 86, 119–20
Knust, Jennifer Wright, 88–89
Korah, 145, 169–70

Laban, 184
latrine, 175, 211
Laurin, R. B., 52–53
Leah, 3, 82, 184
Leithart, Peter J., 11, 57, 89–90, 117,
127, 153, 157, 160, 176, 215, 224
leprosy, 97, 189, 195–97
lesbianism, 91
Levite and concubine (Judges 19), 119–23
Loader, William, 47, 56, 85, 92, 224
locusts, 110–11, 201

Longenecker, Richard N., 16, 224
Longman, Tremper, III, 11,
23–25, 31, 212, 224–25
Lot, 45, 79–80, 82–83, 86–88,
120, 122, 143–45
Luther, Martin, 50

malaria, 194
Manasseh (king of Judah), 156–57
mandrakes, 3–4
mange, 195
marital sexuality, 43, 47–53, 220
Mark, 28
Marshall, I. Howard, 135
Martin, Ralph P., 108, 209
mass killings, xiii, 146, 163–76
masturbation, 186, 216
McComiskey, Thomas Edward, 31,
63–64, 151, 204, 212, 224
McConville, J. G., 34, 165, 185–86, 224
Menahem, 156, 176
menstruation, 11, 34, 45–46, 56,
181–85, 187–88, 199, 215–17
Mesha, 158–60
Meshach, 146, 150
Micah, 30
Michal, 15, 29
mildew, 196
Millard, A. R., 144–45
Miriam, 196
Mishnah, 25, 134
Moab (son of Lot), 79
Moffatt, James, 38
mold, 196
money-changers, 106
Mordecai, 40, 42
Morris, Leon, 37–38, 51–52, 84, 99,
106, 110–12, 120–22, 131–33,
135, 137, 139–40, 155, 161,
170–71, 222, 224
Moses, 9, 14, 82, 126, 156, 162, 164,
166, 168–69, 193, 196, 201–2

Motyer, Alec, 8–9, 100, 158, 183, 212–13, 225
murder, xii, 78, 103, 113, 116, 121–22, 129–30, 153, 166, 177, 215
  See also assassination; killing children; mass killings; violent death
Murray, John, 91
myrrh, 4, 18, 22, 57–58

Naaman, 196
Naboth, 107, 126–27
Nadab (son of Aaron), 145
Nahor, 82
naked(ness). *See* nudity
Naomi, 36, 38–39
navel, 23–25
Nebuchadnezzar, 124, 146, 150
Nehemiah, 104
nipples, xi, 19–20, 66
Noah, 27, 78–81, 130
nocturnal emission, 185, 217
  See also semen
nudity, 5, 10, 27–32, 38, 45–47, 65–66, 78–82, 84, 89, 91, 118–19, 137, 183, 210, 218, 220

O'Connor, Flannery, 218
Onan, xii, 80, 186, 219
onanism. *See* masturbation
ophthalmia, 194
oral sex, 24–25, 216

paganism, 5, 29–31, 36, 41–42, 59, 64, 66, 69, 72–74, 86, 96, 104–5, 122, 124, 126–27, 134, 136, 145–46, 151, 157–60, 166–68, 170, 172–73, 175–76, 184, 192, 199, 205, 208, 210–12, 217–18
  See also fertility rites
pagan worship. *See* paganism
Passover, 96–98
Paul, xii, 7, 15, 35, 43, 50–52, 55, 71, 84–85, 90–91, 107–8, 134, 209, 215

Peck, John, 48, 225
Pekah, 168, 176
Pekahiah, 176
penis. *See* genitalia; male
Perez, 71
Peterson, Eugene H., 213
Pharaoh, 97, 100–101, 136, 155, 168, 193, 201–2
Philip. *See* Herod Philip
Phinehas (1 Samuel 2), 36
Phinehas (Numbers 25), 36, 126
Pilate. *See* Pontius Pilate
plagues, 97, 101, 168, 170, 191–93, 201–2
  See also diseases
Pontius Pilate, 99, 110
Pope, Marvin H., 4, 18–19, 22–24, 50, 53, 225
pornography, 33, 35, 78
Potiphar's wife, 27, 117–18
premarital sex, xiii, 33–42, 182
priestly garments, 28–29
promiscuity. *See* adultery; fornication; premarital sex; prostitution; whore
prostitution, xv, 30–32, 35, 38–39, 44, 51, 57, 59–63, 65, 67, 69–75, 82, 85, 96, 126–27, 147, 166, 218–19
  See also adultery; fertility rites; whore
Provan, Iain, 4, 17–19, 21, 23–24, 41, 70, 225
psoriasis, 196

Rachel, 3, 82, 184
Rahab (woman of Jericho), 71, 165
Rao, Valerie J., 143
rape, xv, 11, 14, 27, 31, 33–34, 36, 58, 87, 92, 113–23, 156, 184, 217–19
Rebekah, 48, 90
regurgitation. *See* vomit
Rehoboam, 10, 74, 106, 134
Reisser, Horst, 36, 225
Reuben, 3, 80, 82
ringworm, 196

ritual sex. *See* fertility rites
Ruth, 36–39
Ryken, Leland, 11, 23, 220, 225

sacrifices (Old Testament), 95–98,
99, 100, 123, 127, 145, 158,
160, 162, 172, 205, 207
See also child sacrifice
Samson, 36, 70, 105, 130, 146, 171
Samuel, 124
Sarah, 48, 82
Saul (Old Testament king), 15, 30,
88–89, 123–24, 136, 173, 203, 208
saws, 105
scabs, 194–95
scavenging animals, 203–6
Schnackenburg, Rudolf, 47
Selman, Martin J., 157, 169,
176, 192, 195, 225
Selvaggio, Anthony, 49
semen, 11–13, 45, 66, 80, 181,
183, 185–88, 199, 218
Sennacherib, 168, 170, 176
Septuagint, 16, 35, 90, 187, 202
seraphim, 8
sexual intercourse, xii, 21–22, 25, 28, 31,
34–36, 38, 41, 43–52, 58, 66, 73–75,
79–80, 82, 84, 86–87, 90, 96, 114–
15, 119, 126, 182–83, 185–86, 216, 219
during menses, 182–83
See also fertility rites; *know*;
prostitution; whore
sexually transmitted dis-
eases, 187–88, 194
Shadrach, 146, 150
Shallum, 176
Shamgar, 130, 170
Shechem (Hivite prince), 14,
36, 115–17, 122
Shemaiah, 107
Silas, 107–8
Simon of Cyrene, 138
Simon the leper, 197

Sisera, 131
skin diseases. *See* boils; dermatitis;
eczema; inflammation; leprosy;
mange; scabs; sores; ulcers
slut, 59–60, 65, 72, 186, 210, 218
See also adultery; prostitution; whore
smallpox, 195
Sodom and Gomorrah, 79,
82, 86–88, 143–45
See also homosexuality; Lot; sodomy
sodomy, 33, 81, 87, 90
See also homosexuality
Solomon, 69
sores, 111, 193
Spencer, Richard A., 107
Spurgeon, C. H., xi, 67
Stein, Robert H., 109, 137, 141, 188, 225
Stephen, 134
stocks, 107
stoning, 106, 133–35, 143, 145, 175
sulfur, 88, 111, 144, 147
sweating blood. *See* hematidrosis
sword. *See* weapons

Tamar (daughter-in-law of Judah),
70–71, 75, 82, 186
Tamar (daughter of David), 83, 115–17, 122
Taylor, John B., 67, 157–58,
205–6, 210, 225
teeth, 104–5, 110, 150, 194
temple prostitutes. *See* fertility rites
testicles, 10, 13, 216
thigh, 8–10, 24, 55, 129, 132, 171, 216
Thomas, Robert L., 12, 181
Thompson, J. A., 31, 59, 153, 165–66,
176–77, 195, 200, 203–4, 208, 225
toilet, 175, 209, 211
See also excrement
torture, 103, 105–7, 110–12, 115,
140–41, 147–48, 194, 217
See also crucifixion; flogging; stocks
transvestite. *See* cross-dressing
Trapnell, D. H., 192, 196

Trench, R. C., 112
tuberculosis, 194
tumors, 192–94
typhoid fever, 194
typhus fever, 194

ulcers, 194
uncleanness, 11, 45–46, 56, 73, 77, 134–35, 181–89, 197, 199–200, 210
Uriah (husband of Bathsheba), 8, 56–57, 90
urine, 59, 199, 210–11, 217
    See also excrement
Uzziah, 196

vagina. *See* genitalia, female
Vashti, 40
Via, Dan O., 85
violent death, 103–4, 126–41, 150
    See also assassination; decapitation; mass killings; murder
virginity, 21, 34, 40–41, 44, 47, 60, 62, 64, 66, 86–88, 114–15, 120, 122, 160–61, 172, 218
vomit, 199, 200, 215, 219
voyeurism, 78–79, 81

Waltke, Bruce K., 4, 9, 19–20, 46, 49, 58, 60, 74–75, 80–81, 118, 144, 151, 169, 181, 185, 193, 200, 212–23, 226
weapons, 88–89, 100, 103, 105–6, 108, 125, 128–33, 145, 164, 170–73, 176, 206

Webb, Barry G., 29–30
Wenham, Gordon J., 3, 9–10, 45, 48, 78–79, 86, 88, 115, 118, 144, 170, 182–83, 185, 187, 195–96, 226
Wessell, Walter W., 109, 138–40, 226
Westminster Confession of Faith, 33, 189, 222
Westminster Larger Catechism, 33
whip, 105–6, 108, 137, 188
    See also flogging
whore, xi, xiv, 31, 35, 58–63, 65–66, 71–73, 85, 125, 127, 186, 212, 218–19
    See also adultery; prostitution; slut
Wilcock, Michael, 102, 120–21, 131, 157, 226
Wilhoit, James C., 11, 23, 225
Wilson, Nancy, 19
Wiseman, Donald J., 104, 106, 157, 159–60, 169–70, 174, 209–11, 226
Wyatt, Robert J., 35, 226

Xerxes I. *See* Ahasuerus

Young, Edward J., 9, 30, 40, 62, 151, 184, 200, 203–4, 212–13, 226

Zechariah (king of Israel), 176
Zechariah (son of Jehoiada), 107, 175
Zedekiah, 105
Zerah, 71
Zimri (king of Israel), 146, 174
zoophilia. *See* bestiality